# GEORGE ELIOT

# GEORGE ELIOT

*HER LIFE AND BOOKS*

BY

GERALD BULLETT

NEW HAVEN

YALE UNIVERSITY PRESS

1948

# ACKNOWLEDGMENTS

SINCE their publication in 1885–87, the chief debt of any biographer of George Eliot has been to the three volumes in which John Walter Cross contrived that the life should, as he puts it, "write itself in extracts from her letters and journals." Because throughout the present essay I have made a point of letting the witness, whether George Eliot or another, speak in his or her own words, rather than run the risk of misrepresentation by paraphrase, my citations from Cross's book are necessarily numerous. But Cross's editing was ultra-discreet, designed as much to obscure some facts as to disclose others; and, largely through the kindness of two American scholars, Dr. Gordon S. Haight of Yale and Professor Anna T. Kitchel of Vassar, I have had access to material not available to previous biographers. To Dr. Haight, who is preparing a comprehensive edition of the letters from which Cross made his selection, and to his publishers, the Yale University Press, I am indebted for permission, generously given, to quote from sources first brought to light in his *George Eliot and John Chapman* (1940); and to Professor Kitchel I am grateful for information derived from her pioneer work *George Lewes and George Eliot* (The John Day Company, 1933). My thanks are due also to Messrs. C. A. Watts & Co. for a long quotation from Herbert Spencer's *Autobiography*, to the National Portrait Gallery for portraits of George Eliot and Herbert Spencer, to the British Museum for permission to reproduce a drawing of George Henry Lewes, and to the London Library for continuing in difficult times to be what it has always been. A few minor debts are recorded in footnotes.

Finally, I owe grateful thanks to two old friends: Richard Church for inciting me to attempt this work, and Harry Roberts for constant and active encouragement.

G. B.

# CONTENTS

## Part I
## HER LIFE

## Part II
## HER BOOKS

## Appendices

# ILLUSTRATIONS

*Part 1*

HER LIFE

## Chapter One

## THE FIRST THIRTY YEARS

### I

IN THE Pantheon of nineteenth-century English novelists there has been for the past few decades one conspicuously empty place. Scott, Jane Austen, Dickens, Thackeray, the Brontës, George Meredith, Thomas Hardy, these have remained unchallenged; and recently, in the interval between our two world wars, a newcomer, Trollope, has been admitted to their company. But the once formidable figure of George Eliot has fallen from its pedestal, to be swept away in fragments by the discreet janitor. A year or two ago (there have been signs of renewed interest since) little remained of her but an admiring reference to *Middlemarch* in a Shaw preface, and the memory, in middle-aged and elderly readers, of having read *Adam Bede* in their childhood. The present essay attempts nothing so ambitious as to claim for her the preeminence she once enjoyed, but is offered in the belief that the time has come when her life and work can at least be usefully reconsidered. If she achieved greatness, in what does her greatness consist? If she missed greatness, how, with her massive talent, did she come to miss it? The phrase "life and work" in this context is very nearly a tautology; for if we want the "real" George Eliot it is in her writings that we shall find her. Nor shall we find her by concentrating attention on her earlier and better-known fictions. To do that would be largely to obscure the fact that she was, for good and for ill, the most intellectual novelist of her time. If we read her novels in the order in which they were written, we shall find that nearly all the qualities that distinguish the later works are implicit in the earlier ones: to see them emerge, sometimes to the enrichment and sometimes to the detriment of her art, is a spectacle of great critical interest.

Any novel that aspires to the condition of art is born of a marriage of high imaginative concentration with a controlling intelligence. It is the product of creative dreaming and intelligent planning; and, granted the capacity for these activities, the artistic success or failure of the process to which the novelist lends himself depends on the relationship or balance between the two. Imagination, at any given point, must in the interests of the whole be kept within bounds; but the control must be exercised with infinite tact, and with a discretion so delicate, so sensitive to the prompting of intuition, as to know when it should efface itself and let the moment's impulse have its way. George Eliot, during her twenty years of novel writing, put more and more of her mind into her books, and while never losing her grip on human values became more and more enamored of "ideas"; but at times, whether from heedlessness or because her rush of thoughts would not be curbed, the powerful intellectuality which is an important constituent of her virtue as a writer gets out of hand and distracts her from her proper, imaginative business. In her very last novel, for instance, imagination and intention are definitely in conflict; the arid theme she proposed to herself is exhibited side by side with an intensely imagined human story as moving and significant as the other is vapid and verbose. She began writing fiction at the age of thirty-seven, in a year when Dickens and Thackeray were at the height of their fame and Trollope was at work on the book that was to bring him instant popularity, *Barchester Towers*. If one wished to indulge in special pleading one might plausibly argue that it was an excess in George Eliot of intellectual energy, rather than a deficiency of imaginative power, that prevented her from becoming the greatest novelist of her time. To say that she was a little too intense is only half the truth. She had wit. She had humor. Her work is rich in racy characterization. But she was serious in grain and her humor, though exquisite on occasion, was very far from being all-pervading. Where herself and her work were concerned it was almost totally lacking.

The causes of what she was in maturity lie no doubt in her earliest years. We cannot hope to find those causes: nor could we if the available facts were far more numerous. She was born, Mary Ann Evans, at Arbury Farm in Warwickshire, at five o'clock in the morning of November 22, 1819. The event is recorded in her father's diary with a precision that was characteristic of him. Robert Evans, son of a builder and carpenter, was then in his forty-seventh year. Some twenty years earlier he had leased a farm at Kirk Hallam, in Derbyshire, from Francis Newdigate, and on Newdigate's succeeding to the Arbury estate had moved with him into Warwickshire to become his agent. Mary Ann, later to be known as Marian, was the third and last child of Robert's second marriage. She had a brother and a sister a few years older than herself, and a half brother and a half sister born of the first marriage.

She was born into an England seething with economic

misery and political unrest. The Napoleonic wars were just ended. The battle of Waterloo was still a recent event, and the French Revolution only a little less recent. It was a time of sick reaction from the excitement of national endeavor and high hopes. The spirit of reform was growing more active, and the inertia which under the flag of "practical politics" opposes all political change was itself changing into an alarmed hostility. In the garish light of what had happened in France, religious observances were seen as a patriotic duty: the landed gentry on the one hand, and the large employers of labor on the other, lost no time in enlisting God on the side of firm government, government whose first care it was to keep the lower orders busy and quiet. The slave trade had been abolished by law in 1807, a measure bitterly opposed by those who held, with James Boswell, that "to abolish a status which in all ages God has sanctioned and man has continued would not only be robbery to an innumerable class of our fellow-subjects, but it would be an extreme cruelty to the African Savages, a portion of whom it saves from massacre, or intolerable bondage in their own country, and introduces into a much happier state of life." To abolish that trade, he concluded in all seriousness, would be to "shut the gates of mercy on mankind." The gates of mercy were duly shut; but though the trade in slaves became thereby illegal nearly thirty years were to pass before "African Savages" throughout the British Empire had to suffer the extreme cruelty of final emancipation. Meanwhile, in the year of George Eliot's birth, the condition of many workers in England was not very different from slavery. It was the era of cottage industry, when in these midland shires nearly every humble household had its hand loom and earned an arduous livelihood by piecework. The rural scene blended squalor and beauty in perhaps equal proportions. The curse of Adam was heavy upon it. The landscape was flat, with no rivers, no lakes, no hills or valleys. The only water to be seen was the brown water of the canals. At points the earth was blackened with coal-pits, and the rattle of the hand loom was heard in hamlet and village. But there was solace and charm, for those who could feel it, in the lush green fields, the trees, the wide sky. There were rural traditions that were older than politics: courage and gaiety and the primal human sanctities, as well as drudgery and drunkenness. For good or ill it was the very heart of England, indeed of two Englands, the England of large mansions standing in well-wooded parks, and the England of green fields and of villages dingy with coal dust or noisy with looms. Institutional religion was flourishing. Side by side with a reinvigorated Anglicanism, preëminently the religion of the ruling classes, evangelical Dissent, the extreme of Protestantism, was now a rising force in the life of the common people.

Such things would have no direct effect on the character of a newborn child; but they made a permanent mark on her father, and it is a safe guess that Robert Evans, whose virtues are exhibited in her portrayal of Adam Bede and Caleb Garth, was the dominant influence in Marian's young life. To a large extent he made her what she was. He was already, when she first knew him, firmly set in his ways and opinions; a man of abundant good nature and iron integrity, thorough and conscientious almost to a fault, and much given, one imagines, to sententious moralizing; imperfectly educated in an academic sense, but shrewd and sagacious, with skill in his hands and the coun-

tryman's knowledge in his eyes; an affectionate father and
the docile husband of his second wife, who being of substantial yeoman stock was thought to be a cut above him
socially; a man who by industry and force of character
had raised himself, as his daughter tells us, from being an
artisan to be one "whose extensive knowledge in very
varied practical departments made his services valued
through several counties. He had large knowledge of
buildings, of mines, of plantations, of various branches of
valuation and measurement—of all that is essential to the
management of large estates. He was held by those com-
petent to judge as *unique* amongst land agents for his man-
ifold knowledge and experience." He could estimate with
remarkable accuracy the quantity of timber in a standing
tree. He could carry unaided a ladder which daunted two
of his own workmen. And there is a story told of him
that one day, when he was traveling in Kent on the top
of a coach and a woman appealed to him for protection
from a burly sailor who was making himself offensive
to her, he seized the offender by the collar, forced him
down under the seat, and held him there for the rest
of the stage.

Whether history or fiction, the legend is suggestive of
the general esteem in which Robert Evans was held.
Equally suggestive of his hold on her admiration is the
warmth with which Marian writes of him ten years after
his death: there is true filial complacency in her "unique."
Clearly he was the law and the prophets to her, and more
than half her world, notwithstanding that her mother was
a vigorous, warmhearted, affectionate, and perhaps somewhat managing woman, having, it is said, a dash of Mrs.
Poyser in her. When the French Revolution began Robert

Evans was sixteen; when this youngest of his children was born, he was already going gray; and in the interval he had seen a great tide of liberal enthusiasm rise, break, and recede. Ecstatic hopes of a millennium of justice and concord, of which the Revolution was to have been the prelude, gave place to fear and distrust of anything that seemed to threaten the established order, or disorder, and he had developed, like the later Wordsworth, an excessive reverence for "government" as such, and would use the word (if the essay *Looking Backward* is, as seems probable, thinly disguised autobiography) "in a tone that charged it with awe, and made part of my effective religion, in contrast with the word *rebel*, which seemed to carry the stamp of evil in its syllables, and, lit by the fact that Satan was the first rebel, made an argument dispensing with more detailed inquiry."

Four months after Marian's birth the family moved into another house, at Griff, described as a charming, red-brick, ivy-covered house on the Arbury estate, with attractive farm buildings, an old-fashioned garden, and near by a pond and a canal to fish in. Robert and Frances Lucy, the children of their father's first marriage, did not for long form part of Marian's immediate environment. Robert becoming agent for the Kirk Hallam property, he set up house there with his sister, and the infant Marian grew up at Griff with her sister Christiana and her brother Isaac. Isaac was the nearer to her in age, and the two became inseparable companions. Like Maggie with Tom in *The Mill on the Floss*, she was always at her brother's heels. While there is obviously something of her author in Maggie, and the natural descriptions have the warmth and intimacy of things remembered from childhood, to identify the characters with persons who actually lived would be not merely misleading but inept, and it is not necessary to suppose that Isaac Evans is fully or intimately portrayed in that unlikable boy Tom Tulliver. He was, however, as Tom was, the first of his little sister's possessions and the one possessed most jealously. John Walter Cross tells us that "in her moral development she showed, from the earliest years, the trait that was most marked in her all through life—namely, the absolute need of some one person who should be all in all to her, and to whom she should be all in all." Isaac, since she could not look for exclusive possession of her parents, was chosen by destiny to minister to this need of her, without, we may be sure, entirely satisfying it.

There are, then, factual correspondences between her childhood and that of Maggie Tulliver; but fiction, though it may deal with the same incidents, is not history, and it is rather to the directly autobiographical sonnet sequence called *Brother and Sister,* than to *The Mill on the Floss,* that we must look for the facts. Even there we shall find them not nakedly presented, but varnished with an idealizing gloss, mixed with the sentiments not of a child but of a middle-aged woman wistfully recalling her childhood. Isaac was the elder by three years, and she remembers how, "puppy-like," she followed him about, and how, when they wandered in the fields together, noticing birds and small beasts,

> If he said "Hush!" I tried to hold my breath,
> Wherever he said "Come!" I stepped in faith.

Long years, she says, have left their writing on her brow:

> But yet the freshness and the dew-fed beam
> Of those young mornings are about me now . . .

The firmaments of daisies since to me
Have had those mornings in their opening eyes,
The bunched cowslip's pale transparency
Carries that sunshine of sweet memories,
And wild-rose branches take their finest scent
From those blest hours of infantine content

Those hours—and here she surely touches on a universal truth of childhood—"were seed to all my after good." The imperceptible movement of time, the past continuing into the present, this is the animating idea of these sonnets, implicit throughout, and finding clear expression in what is perhaps the best of them:

Our brown canal was endless to my thought;
And on its banks I sat in dreamy peace,
Unknowing how the good I loved was wrought,
Untroubled by the fear that it would cease.
Slowly the barges floated into view
Rounding a grassy hill to me sublime
With some Unknown beyond it, whither flew
The parting cuckoo toward a fresh spring time.
The wide-arched bridge, the scented elder-flowers,
The wondrous watery rings that died too soon,
The echoes of the quarry, the still hours
With white robe sweeping-on the shadeless noon,
Were but my growing self, are part of me,
My present Past, my root of piety.

## II

Byron died when she was four years old, and Goethe when she was thirteen. In her childhood the steam locomotive was in its early experimental stage, poachers—if they escaped the mantraps and spring guns set for their destruction—were transported for seven years, children were still being hanged for stealing,[1] the factory system was not yet established, and Sir Robert Peel's policemen, with their top hats and truncheons, were a new institution.

Such things would not impinge deeply upon the consciousness of a child, and in rural Warwickshire, before the coming of the telegraph wires and the penny post, life moved at a slow pace. Little Marian Evans enjoyed an outwardly tranquil childhood, in a world as fascinating to a young apprehension as it was small. Outwardly tranquil, in an atmosphere of warm family affection, but not always inwardly so, for like Maggie Tulliver she was a sensitive, passionate, possessive little creature, with an immense appetite for life and knowledge. In infancy she and Isaac, three years her senior, attended a local dame's school, while Christiana, the elder sister, was sent further afield, to a school in a neighboring village. Marian was not precocious in learning, where school subjects were concerned. She was exceptionally impressionable, temperamental, easily moved to tears or laughter, and too introspective to strike an observer as especially quick in the uptake. Hers was a deep and slowly developing nature; she retained, as her books were to prove, much that those around her did not credit her with noticing; and she is said to have been early possessed of the notion, not uncommon

1. In 1810 Lord Ellenborough, then Chief Justice, had moved the rejection of a bill designed to abolish the death penalty for "stealing in a shop to the value of 5s." "My Lords," he said, "if we suffer this bill to pass, we shall not know whether we are on our heads or our feet." He spoke "to an approving Senate, and in the name of a unanimous Bench." Walter de la Mare, from whose *Desert Islands* I steal this note, remarks: "Malefactors of fourteen are not publicly hanged nowadays. Yet there are things we take for granted that may seem equally atrocious a century hence."

in children and as often self-delusive as prophetic, that she would some day make a mark in the world. There was the inevitable conflict within her between self-assurance and a secret diffidence. Her father made much of her; she never forgot the pleasure and importance of standing between his knees as he drove about in his dogcart; and being the petted youngest of the family she was no doubt encouraged to ask questions and air her opinions up to a point, to be duly curbed and corrected, beyond that point, by her sensible and much-loved mother.

Her greatest periodical excitement in these earliest days was the passing of the stage coach on its way between Birmingham and Stamford. Two coaches went by the house every day, two bright events breaking the serene monotony of life at Griff. When she was five, and her brother eight, she was sent to join her sister as a boarder at Attleborough, where she remained for three or four years, and her brother Isaac was sent to continue his schooling at Coventry. At her next school, at Nuneaton, she was taught by a Miss Lewis, who exercised a great influence over her and became in later years an intimate friend; and at the age of thirteen she was sent to yet another school, this time the Misses Franklins' at Coventry. Miss Lewis was an ardent, evangelical churchwoman; the Franklin sisters were the equally ardent daughters of a Baptist minister; and these ardencies were matched by Marian's own, her large, receptive, admiring nature eagerly responding to both varieties of the current Christianity. And though, as she shall see, she rejected in maturity the creed so zealously embraced in girlhood, she remained to the end a religious woman.

When she was fifteen her mother died. In the spring of

the following year Christiana became the wife of Edward
Clarke, a Warwickshire surgeon; and from that day the
whole burden of running the Griff household devolved
upon Marian's shoulders. Such a responsibility, at such an
age, can only have tended to intensify the child's innate
seriousness. But unquestionably the seriousness was there
already: destiny and personal character played into each
other's hands. She had been recognized at school, by
teachers and classmates alike, as a remarkable young person, old for her years, warmly affectionate, with an "original" personality and an exceptionally powerful mind.
And she responded to the challenge of this sudden new
responsibility in just the way that might have been predicted of her. Like her father, the example and oracle of
her childhood, she was dominated by a stern sense of duty
and soon became a most efficient housewife.

But she was not the kind of person to take a narrow
view of what constituted a young woman's duty. Hers
was now twofold. There was her duty to the father and
the brother who depended solely on her for their domestic comfort, and there was her duty to herself. For to
know oneself possessed of exceptional potentialities is
itself a responsibility not to be shirked. She had no notion
yet of becoming a writer, but she had already a voracious
intellectual appetite which would not be gainsaid. And
so, though she did with exemplary thoroughness all that
had to be done, including such works of charity as visiting the poor and organizing clothing clubs, she also saw
to it that the needs of her mind were not overlooked. One
visiting tutor from Coventry gave her regular lessons in
Italian and German, and another, from the same neighboring town, continued her instruction in music. Even so,
she had time to get through a great deal of miscellaneous

reading. It was not quite what one would choose for a warm-blooded and brilliantly gifted young girl, this being shut up in a remote farmhouse with no light relief, no social gaiety, no chance of exchanging ideas with her intellectual kindred; and she cannot always have felt satisfied with her lot. But the enforced solitude brought its own compensations and opportunities. This was the growing time of the mind, a time unenlivened, and a mind undistracted, by the normal pleasures of youth.

Nature and circumstance had conspired to make her a prig. Within a few years of assuming the maternal office, we find her writing to her former schoolmistress, Miss Lewis, in a ponderous, humorless, moralizing style which would be positively repellent if it were not comic, and if we did not, as we must, make allowance for the manners and conventions of the period. The self-complacent rotundity of eighteenth-century prose still cast its shadow over a carefully educated young lady when she took up her pen to engage in epistolary correspondence with an esteemed preceptress, especially if the young lady in question was conscious of her own intellectual parts and of having been a favorite pupil. It would be unfair to accuse her of affectation or suppose her insincere. Her sincerity is patent: it is even oppressive, accustomed as we are to the self-protective evasions of humor. For humor, which is the salt of discourse, can itself serve the purposes of insincerity and become a mode of "evasive action." More than one great writer has lacked it (Milton and Wordsworth, for example), and to lack it at a certain youthful stage of development is normal, if not positively a sign of grace. But with all allowances made these letters remain astonishing.

In the middle of her nineteenth year Marian paid a first

visit to London, with her brother Isaac. She was "not at all delighted," she tells Miss Lewis, "with the stir of the great Babel." From Isaac's own testimony we learn that what most deeply impressed her was hearing the great bell of St. Paul's. Having renounced the pleasures of the world, she would not go to the theater with Isaac but spent all her evenings alone reading. At her earnest request he bought her a copy of Josephus' *History of the Jews*, and for himself a pair of sporting prints from the same shop. Brother and sister had taken divergent ways: they had nothing in common now but family affection. In the letter to Miss Lewis already quoted she says:

When I hear of the marrying and giving in marriage that is constantly being transacted, I can only sigh for those who are multiplying earthly ties which, though powerful enough to detach their hearts and thoughts from heaven, are so brittle as to be liable to be snapped asunder at every breeze. You will think that I need nothing but a tub for my habitation to make me a perfect female Diogenes; and I plead guilty to occasional misanthropical thoughts, but not to the indulgence of them. Still I must believe that those are happiest who are not fermenting themselves by engaging in projects for earthly bliss, who are considering this life merely a pilgrimage, a scene calling for diligence and watchfulness, not for repose and amusement. . . . Oh that we could live only for eternity! that we could realise its nearness!

And, speaking of Wilberforce:

Oh that I might be made as useful in my lowly and obscure station as he was in the exalted one assigned to him! I feel myself to be a mere cumberer of the ground. May the Lord give me such insight into what is truly good, that I may not rest contented with making Christianity a mere addendum to my pursuits, or with tacking it as a fringe to my garments! May I seek to be sanctified wholly!

To which pious wish she guilelessly adds:

My nineteenth birthday will soon be here—an awakening signal.

Music and literature, more especially fiction, invite Marian's censure, though she had studied the one and was destined to excel in the other. She hesitates to pronounce on the "propriety or lawfulness" of musical performances (an oratorio being in question) on the ground that she had no soul for music.

I am a tasteless person, but it would not cost me any regrets if the only music heard in our land were that of strict worship, nor can I think a pleasure that involves the devotion of all the time and powers of an immortal being to the equipment of an expertness in so useless (at least in ninety-nine cases out of a hundred) an accomplishment, can be quite pure or elevating in its tendency.

As to literature, she graciously concedes that some acquaintance with certain specified "standard works whose contents are matter of constant reference" may perhaps be desirable, but she believes "that the same causes which exist in my own breast to render novels and romances pernicious have their counterpart in that of every fellow-creature."

But, confidently though she expounded her callow opinions, she was the reverse of satisfied with herself and at least intermittently alive to the dangers of egoism and conceit. Four months after her nineteenth birthday, in a letter to the wife of her father's younger brother, she speaks of her "lack of humility and Christian simplicity," which makes her, she says, willing to obtain credit for greater knowledge and deeper feeling than she really possesses. She amplifies her confession.

Instead of putting my light under a bushel, I am in danger of ostentatiously displaying a false one. You have much too high an opinion, my dear aunt, of my spiritual condition, and of my personal and circumstantial advantages. . . . I feel that my besetting sin is the one of all others most destroying, as it is the fruitful parent of them all,—ambition, a desire insatiable for the esteem of my fellow-creatures. This seems the centre whence all my actions proceed.[2]

Is it this appetite for esteem, or merely a wholesome desire to share good things with a friend, that makes her display her pious erudition to Miss Lewis? "I do not wonder you are pleased with Pascal; his thoughts may be returned to the palate again and again with increasing rather than diminished relish. I have highly enjoyed Hannah

2. This, presumably, is one of the "nombreuses professions d'humilité" of which M. Bourl'honne, in his *George Eliot: essai de biographie intellectuelle et morale* (Paris, 1933) speaks with some severity. His view is that "la jeune fille" was eaten up with an egoistic desire for saintliness, and that her letters at this time betray a total lack of true spirituality: "elle confondit la connaissance du mal avec la vertu, une intuition psychologique avec un acte de contrition. L'ambition d'excellence morale resta vivace dans son âme, invisible et d'autant plus malfaisante qu'elle se trouvait maintenant recouverte du manteau opaque de la fausse humilité." But to deplore one's lack of humility is not quite the same thing as claiming to possess it, and humility is not necessarily "false" because intermittent and therefore ineffective. True it is that she was too much preoccupied with herself, and conceivably (though here we are guessing) she took an unholy pride in her capacity to recognize and confess her faults. Nevertheless, even in youth she was as far from the false humility of the hypocrite as from the unself-regarding grace that comes only with spiritual maturity.

More's letters: the contemplation of so blessed a character as hers is very salutary." In a later year there is a note in commendation of the Epistle to the Colossians, which she has been reading in conjunction with a book by Isaac Taylor, "one of the most eloquent, acute, and pious of writers. Five numbers only have yet appeared. Have you seen them? If not, I should like to send you an abstract of his argument. I have gulped it (pardon my coarseness) in a most reptile-like fashion." But even during the first three years of this correspondence with Miss Lewis we can discern, behind the stilted complacencies of the prose, some evidence of changing taste and the growth of a powerful and well-stored mind. Marian herself, within sight of her twentieth birthday, remarks that her mind presents an assemblage of disjointed specimens, comparing it with a geological stratum that shows "here a jaw and rib of some ponderous quadruped, there a delicate alto-relievo of some fern-like plant, tiny shells, and mysterious nondescripts encrusted and united with some unvaried and uninteresting but useful stone." Her mental conglomeration, she says, contains "scraps of poetry picked up from Shakespeare, Cowper, Wordsworth, and Milton; newspaper topics; morsels of Addison and Bacon; latin verbs, geometry, entomology, and chemistry; Reviews and metaphysics—all arrested and petrified and smothered by the fast-thickening everyday accession of actual events, relative anxieties, and household cares and vexations." The change in tone is very gradual. The juvenile formality does not easily relax. But literature does break in. Wordsworth, as well as Hannah More, delights her; and the few stanzas of Shelley's "Cloud" "contain more poetic metal than is beat out in all Mr. B.'s pages."

Music, too, resumes its hold on her. Only two years after her disdainful remarks about oratorio she was moved to hysterical sobbing at the Birmingham Festival.

Other and more radical changes were on the way, two in particular: a change of scene which brought her within reach of new and exciting friends, and, rather by coincidence than as a consequence of that, a change in her view of religion. These marked the beginning of a new chapter in her development, the specious maturity of her teens and early twenties giving place to a mellower, more tolerant, and more open-minded attitude to herself and the world. Throughout her life she cherished glowing memories of her childhood, but looking back from the vantage ground of her middle twenties she refuses to believe that our youngest days are our happiest. "Childhood," she writes to Sara Hennell,

is only the beautiful and happy time in contemplation and retrospect: to the child it is full of deep sorrows, the meaning of which is unknown. Witness colic and whooping-cough and dread of ghosts, to say nothing of hell and Satan, and an offended Deity in the sky, who was angry when I wanted too much plum-cake. Then the sorrows of older persons, which children see but cannot understand, are worse than all.

All this, she adds with a smile, "all this to prove that we are happier than when we were seven years old, and that we shall be happier when we are forty than we are now, which I call a comfortable doctrine, and one worth trying to believe!"

That reference to "an offended Deity" tells its own story, implies the new point of view. And we are glad of the smile: it has been a long time coming.

### III

In 1841 Isaac Evans married a wife and took over his father's house and business at Griff. Father and daughter went to live in a house in Foleshill Road, Coventry. It was a semidetached house whose upper windows commanded a wide view of the surrounding country; but at ground level the outlook was restricted by mills and chimneys. The change from rural to urban life brought its own compensations. Only a year before, Charles Bray, still a young man not yet thirty, had bought a small property known as Rosehill on the outskirts of the town. It consisted of a pleasant house and garden, with a large tree-shaded lawn. Chief among the trees was a fine old acacia, the sloping turf about whose roots (he tells us) made a delightful seat in summertime. The Brays used to spread a large bearskin on the grass and entertain their friends there in woodland seclusion, far enough from the town for country quiet, yet near enough to hear the bells and chimes of St. Michael's Church, and on weekdays the distant hum of the world going about its business. Among the most welcome of these friends was Marian Evans.

At Rosehill there was a free and easy mental atmosphere which, harmonizing with the absence of all pretension and conventionality, gave—in Bray's own words [3]—"a peculiar charm to this modest residence." The phrase "when the bearskin is under the acacia" became a playful symbol for the flow of talk unrestrained, the free interchange of ideas. Everyone who came to Coventry with a queer mission, or a crotchet, was sent up to Rosehill. Bray himself had a plentiful supply of crotchets; but with all his in-

3. Charles Bray, *Phases of Opinion and Experience.*

genuous self-assurance he was an amiable and sensible person, a man of benign humor and energetic mind. Many of his favorite notions, which seemed eccentric then, are taken for granted today; he was zealous for economic justice as well as for the advancement of science and the spread of sound philosophy, and the complacency with which he writes of himself in old age is not unmixed with humor. George Combe the phrenologist was one of his admired visitors, but it did not surprise him when Mrs. Combe dropped asleep in the middle of her husband's wise discourse, "her head inclined towards him in a reverent attitude of attention." The publishers of his *Philosophy of Necessity*, the object of which was to show "that Law reigned equally in Mind and Matter" and that "there could be no mental, moral, and social science if it did not," assured him that it was *the* book upon the subject, which he took to mean "the best book because there was no other, like the boy who was top but one in his class of two." His doctrine had affinities (unknown to him at the time) both with Positivism and with Spinoza's pantheism; and among other and more questionable propositions he held that repentance for past misdeeds is proper and useful only in so far as it induces us to alter our conduct in the future, and that revenge, remorse, and retributive punishments "are the sources of half the crime and misery in the world." Here he is in advance of his own time, and of ours too. His claim to have "laid down the base" of George Eliot's life philosophy must be disallowed, but one can readily see that as a talking companion he must have been a godsend to her. She certainly shared some of his opinions, and as certainly rejected others.

There was some resemblance, too, between his upbringing and hers. He was bred as a country boy, and was frequently boarded out at various farmhouses in the neighborhood of Coventry, where his father was a prosperous ribbon manufacturer. There in early childhood he ran wild among plowmen and farmers' boys. When one of his playmates mentioned ships at sea he scornfully exclaimed: "Ships at sea! Why, a ship's on the common, a-ettin the graass!" When nine years old he was sent to a boarding school, where, though he learned nothing but reading, writing, and arithmetic, which was all that was taught there, he soon became a "daily assistant," wearing a brass plate round his neck bearing that designation. This triumph did not prevent his rebelling against authority, getting into scrapes, and ultimately running away from school. Later on he became "converted" and embraced Evangelical Dissent with an extravagant fervor not unlike that of Marian Evans herself. In strict accordance with the logic of that faith, he avoided general society, accepting the injunction to "touch not the unclean thing" as applicable to all convivialities. This attitude of mind naturally engendered an enormous self-sufficiency and religious pride. But doubts, though he struggled to ignore them, would obtrude themselves. Try as he might, he could never quite abandon the exercise of private judgment, and this led "to what many will regard as my fall, and which I look upon as my emancipation." The resemblance between his and Marian's mental history is evident enough. At only one point is it significantly different. His final "emancipation," his espousal of freedom of thought, was achieved only with much conflict, terror, and agony of mind. In Marian, so far as our evidence goes, there was no such thing. She seems to have moved logically forward, with some intellectual excitement perhaps but with no distress of spirit, from one set of opinions to quite another.

One stage of Bray's progress from evangelicalism to the "philosophy of necessity" had been marked by his confident attempt to convert a Unitarian minister, whom at the time he regarded as "worse than an infidel," modest, intelligent, and well-informed though he evidently was. This laudable enterprise obliged him to study the apologetics of his subject far more closely and critically than he had done hitherto, with the result that his own faith was undermined, while the position of his opponent was left unshaken. Later history provided an amusing parallel to this unexpected sequence of events. In 1836 he married Caroline Hennell, a girl of one-and-twenty who had been saturated in Unitarian doctrine and tradition from her earliest years. Bray, four years her senior, had by now far outstripped the Unitarians in "infidelity"; but though he had changed his opinions he had the same blithe confidence in his power to enlighten others, and he thought he had only to lay his new religious views before his wife for her to accept them at once. He therefore provided himself with Mirabeau's *System of Nature*, Volney's *Ruins of Empire*, and, as he charmingly says, "other light reading of that sort to enliven the honeymoon." The young woman resisted his arguments: he only succeeded in making her very uncomfortable. Ultimately the questions at issue were referred to her elder brother, Charles Hennell, who, himself a convinced Unitarian believer, at length consented, under pressure from Bray, to reëxamine the arguments and evidences for Christianity. This he did, we must suppose, with a view to confuting his brother-in-law's skepticism and fortifying his sister's faith; but the effect of his studies was quite otherwise, for they led to his writing and publishing (in 1838) an *Inquiry Concerning the Origin of Christianity*, a work described by Bray as "one of the first attempts to regard Christianity from a purely historical point of view, and to analyse the life and work of its Founder in a reverent, truthful, and appreciative spirit, while separating from it all that was obviously legendary or mythical." It is significant that Marian Evans was acquainted with this book, and admired it, *before* she met the Brays.

George Eliot, wrote Bray in old age, "always held with me that one of the greatest duties of life was unembittered resignation to the inevitable." This not very novel maxim followed, we are given to understand, from his favorite "doctrine of consequences," a doctrine consistent with the phrenological theories that were then exciting his enthusiasm. "At that time," he says,

we were both very much interested in Phrenology, and in 1844 she had a cast taken of her head by Deville, in the Strand, which is still in my possession. We afterwards took lessons of Mr. Donovan, on Organology, when he was staying at Coventry and converting all the leading men of the city to the truth of the science by the correctness of his diagnosis of character. Miss Evans's head is a very large one, 22¼ inches round; George Combe, on first seeing the cast, took it for a man's. The temperament, nervous lymphatic, that is, active without endurance. . . . In her brain-development the Intellect greatly predominated; it is very large, more in length than in its peripheral surface. In the Feelings, the Animal and Moral regions are about equal; the moral being quite sufficient to keep the animal in order and in due subservience, but would not be spontaneously active. The social feelings were very active, particularly the adhesiveness. She was of a most affectionate disposition, always requiring some one to lean upon, preferring what has hitherto been considered the stronger sex, to the other and more impressible. She was not fitted to stand alone.

But we can learn more of her from Charles Bray than the circumference of her head. By eavesdropping on her thoughts, in so far as her letters speak them, we have gathered an impression of her inward life, of what she was and what she seemed to herself to be: Bray's account of her, brief though it is, will help us to see her objectively, in the round, as her contemporaries saw her. Although he had known her as a child at her father's house at Griff, he tells us,

our real acquaintance began in 1841, when after she came with her father to reside near Coventry, my sister, who lived next door to her, brought her to call upon us one morning, thinking, amongst other natural reasons for introducing her, that the influence of this superior young lady of Evangelical principles might be beneficial to our heretical minds. She was then about one-and-twenty, and I can well recollect her appearance and modest demeanour as she sat down on a low ottoman by the window, and I had a sort of surprised feeling when she first spoke, at the measured, highly cultivated mode of expression, so different from the usual tones of young persons from the country. We became friends at once.

During the next few years he was to see a great deal of her. They had long frequent walks together. He was impressed as much by her gentleness and charm as by her erudition. She knew everything, he says, but had little self-assertion, her aim being always "to show her friends off to the best advantage—not herself. She would polish up their witti-cisms, and give them the *full* credit of them. But there were two sides; hers was the temperament of genius which has always its sunny and shady side. She was frequently very depressed—and often very provoking." They had "violent quarrels." But "the next day, or whenever we met, they were quite forgotten, and no allusion made to them."

We know from her own testimony that Marian much enjoyed talking and arguing with Bray. It is not recorded whether she ever laughed at him. "We soon found," says Bray, "that her mind was already turning towards greater freedom of thought in religious opinion, that she had even bought for herself Hennell's *Inquiry*, and there was much mutual interest between the author and herself in their frequent meetings at our house." For all her "adhesive-ness" she was not the kind of young woman to abandon her cherished opinions lightly, without severe thought. She already knew something of Christian origins, much of her leisure time at Griff having been devoted to the com-pilation of a chart of ecclesiastical history. Moreover, it is believed that the works of Isaac Taylor had set her mind running on lines of which that pious author would hardly have approved. But though the change in her religious opinions was almost certainly the effect of a gradual proc-ess, the effect itself, when it emerged, may well have ap-peared with dramatic suddenness, and it is probable that Charles Hennell's book was one of the contributory causes. In November she writes to Miss Lewis:

My whole soul has been engrossed in the most interesting of all inquiries for the last few days, and to what result my thoughts may lead I know not—possibly to one that will startle you, but my only desire is to know the truth, my only fear to cling to error. I venture to say our love will not decompose under the influence of separation, unless you excommunicate me for differing from you in opinion.

Apparently unwilling or afraid to be more specific, she adds wistfully, as if hoping to be absolved before confession: "Think—is there any *conceivable* alteration in me that would prevent your coming to me at Christmas?"

Whether Miss Lewis came to her at Christmas is not known. The letters to that lady end, for a while, at this point. Perhaps the change in Marian Evans *was* too much for her, at any rate for a time. That it was an important one is obvious enough, and she herself felt it to be pure gain. But there is some danger of regarding it as more important, more radical, than in fact it was. It was a change of specific opinions rather than of mind, and certainly it was not a change of heart. She rejected theological Christianity. She did not reject religion. She had always had a lively ethical sense, and a social conscience. "The prevalence of misery and want in this boasted nation of prosperity and glory is appalling," she writes at this time, "and really seems to call us away from mental luxury." In after years she was to declare, with manifest sincerity, that writing was part of her religion and "the only effect I ardently long to produce by my writings is that those who read them should be better able to imagine and feel the pains and the joys of those who differ from themselves in everything but the broad fact of being struggling, erring, human creatures." Explicitly again and again, and implicitly in all her work, she insists that the greatest benefit we owe to the artist is "the extension of our sympathies." A warmly affectionate girl with a generous capacity for admiration, she admired where she loved and imitated where she admired. She had taken over the doctrines of evangelical Christianity from friends who had been eminently good and kind to her, and now, finding herself among other friends equally good who entertained quite other opinions, she was free, or rather she was forced, to exercise her own considerable powers of independent judgment.

She was now able to look back with amused contrition to the time, only a year or two back, when she used to "go about like an owl" and sought to deny her brother Isaac "what I now see to have been quite lawful amusements." Even before her change of opinions she had been shocked by what seemed to be a divorce between religion and ethics in the minds of some of the cottagers she visited, citing to her friend Mrs. Sibree the case of a woman who, when convicted of deliberate lying, complacently remarked that she "did not feel she had grieved the Spirit much." Mrs. Sibree was distressed by Marian's apostasy and in doubt whether to accept her offer to teach her daughter German, saying affectionately: "I cannot help fearing you might influence Mary, though you might not intend to do so." She added, however, that her husband saw no such danger; and the lessons were duly given. This same Mary has left a warm tribute to her dear Miss Evans, who was consistently kind to her and scrupulous to preach nothing more questionable than tolerance, which was, she said, "the great lesson of life."

Nor did Marian content her conscience with mere maxims. She was unobtrusively active in works of charity, eager to do a kindness where she could, and a friend to everyone, irrespective of social class: "the servants," she said, "come to me in all their troubles." Ready though she was to discuss and defend her new point of view, she had no ambition to make proselytes. To Mrs. Sibree she remarked that it would be extreme arrogance in so young a person as herself to "suppose she had obtained *yet* any just ideas of truth." Here was a change indeed! On the other hand she was fully capable of holding her own in argument with those to whom truth had been supernaturally revealed. One of these, a Baptist minister well read in divinity, after a friendly tussle with her said with beautiful innocence: "That young lady must have had the devil at her elbow to suggest her doubts, for there was not a book that I recommended to her in support of Christian evidences that she had not read."

Meanwhile "that young lady" was enjoying the delights and shouldering the responsibilities of her liberation. For a liberation it was. She had not exchanged one sectarianism for another, had acquired no vested interest in a dogmatic negativism. The bias of her mind was still toward affirmation, and the impulse of her heart toward what Schweitzer has called "reverence for life," notwithstanding that this attitude could no longer find adequate expression in the old formulas. She still valued "the poetry of Christianity." She had then and always a profound respect for "that which is essentially human in all forms of belief," and later, in her work, wished to "exhibit it under all forms with loving truthfulness." Herein lies her true greatness, that with all her intellectual acuteness she remained free from intellectual snobbery and abounding in human sympathy. Conscious of possessing unusual mental power, she was yet essentially humble, simple, brotherly, in her attitude to human things. In middle life we find her saying to

Charles Bray: "I have had heart-cutting experience that *opinions* are a poor cement between human souls." And something deeper than opinions sustained her at this earlier stage. In a letter to Mrs. Pears, written from Griff in March, 1842, she speaks of the

deep, blue, glorious heavens, bending as they do over all, presenting the same arch, emblem of a truer omnipresence wherever we may be chased, and all the sweet peace-breathing sights and sounds of this lovely earth. These, and the thoughts of the good and great, are an inexhaustible world of delight; and the felt desire to be one in will and design with the great mind that has laid open to us these treasures is the sun that warms and fructifies it.

But what was she doing back at Griff, the guest of brother Isaac and his wife, when her home for the past twelve months had been Coventry? This was no mere routine family visit. Something painful and unprecedented had happened: she had quarreled with her father. By challenging his authority she had asserted her moral independence, and the closest relationship of her life was disrupted. The collision of wills held dramatic implications which must have been clear to them both. Marian was still a warmly affectionate daughter, as she had always been, but no longer a child whose obedience could be taken for granted. Robert Evans was now close on seventy. He had always been powerfully attached to his own opinions, and the longer he lived with them the more manifestly right they seemed. We do not know to what extent Marian confided to him her changing views on Christianity: most probably she did not expand on such subjects except in letters to friends. But he had to know, sooner or later, the simple fact that she no longer accepted the religion of her

fathers, and of her father; because to her mind a logical
consequence of that rejection was that she must abstain
from going to church. It is likely that she saw this absti-
nence less as a release than as a duty: she felt it dishonest to
avow implicitly, by attending church, what she was at
pains to disavow in conversation with her intimates. This
is to take religion seriously, to treat it as religion and not
as a mere social convenience: an attitude which the world
at large, to say nothing of the flesh and the devil, is apt
to regard as lacking in humor. It is true that a livelier
sense of humor at this crisis of her growth might have
persuaded Marian Evans that it did not in the least matter
whether she went to church or not; but "humor"—in this
escapist sense—might equally well have suggested that
nothing matters except one's personal comfort, all so-
called moral problems being the province of the prig.

Lacking that technique of evasion, Marian decided
against churchgoing and announced the decision to her
father. It is not recorded that he troubled himself overmuch about her change of opinions, the details of which
would in any case have been beyond him; but as a true-
blue conservative, and a man moreover who had raised
himself by his own talent and industry and to whom social
respectability was therefore all in all, he was outraged by
her refusal to go to church. Failure to believe in what the
church taught was eccentric and no doubt a great pity;
but failure to conform outwardly was to become a by-
word and a hissing. The course and tone of the dispute is
a matter for conjecture: all we know is that Robert issued
his ultimatum and that Marian rejected it. He decided to
put the Coventry house into an agent's hands and to go
and live with his married daughter. Marian's idea, on hear-

ing this, was to find lodgings for herself at Leamington and earn a livelihood by teaching.

Neither plan was put into effect, for at the end of this same month, February, 1842, Robert canceled his instructions to the house agent, and Marian, as we have seen, went to stay at Griff. Some three weeks later, by which time they had punished themselves and each other enough, Marian returned to Coventry at her father's request. He, whether he said so or not, must have sorely missed her: without her management, to say nothing of her companionship, the house must have seemed painfully empty and comfortless. And she, torn to pieces by the conflicting demands of her conscience, by the duty of cherishing an aged father and the no less imperative duty of truthfulness in matters religious above all things, longed to be home again, freed from her anxieties about him. Home had always meant a great deal to her. "I must have a *home*," she writes to Mrs. Pears from Griff, "not a visiting place. I wish you would learn something from my father, and send me word how he seems disposed."

It was through the intervention of her brother, the Brays, and Rebecca Franklin, her former schoolmistress, that the reconciliation was arrived at. Her father was very glad to have her back, and she fell again into the habit of going to church with him each Sunday. Whether or not the churchgoing was provided for in the peace treaty is not recorded: one would prefer to think that it was not, that both disputants gave way, and that Marian's subsequent conformity was a silent and unobtrusive act of grace and affection. And though she yielded her point and never ceased to regret a collision which with a little management might (she afterward thought) have been prevented, she can hardly have avoided knowing that by accepting nominal defeat she had won a real victory.

### IV

During the summer of this year, 1842, Sara Hennell, the sister of Charles Hennell and of Mrs. Bray, came on a visit to the Brays at Rosehill and so enlarged the intimate circle of Marian's friends. These friendships took deep root and never withered, and for the next few years, until events separated them geographically, the Brays and the Hennells formed her social and intellectual world. She was stimulated but in no sense dominated by their points of view. Mrs. Bray ("Cara") was an affectionate companion to her, and with Charles Bray she loved to argue; but it was to Sara that she most resorted for intellectual sympathy. She had many a musical evening with the Brays (she herself was a good amateur pianist and singer), and at their house, or in their company, met a number of well-known people, such as Robert Owen ("I think if his system prosper it will be in spite of its founder"), Harriet Martineau, and Ralph Waldo Emerson who said of Marian: "That young lady has a calm, serious soul." She took holidays with these friends in Wales, the Lake District, and Scotland. In November, 1843, says Bray, "we went to London to be present at Charles Hennell's marriage with Miss [Elizabeth Rebecca, nicknamed Rufa] Brabant. . . . Miss Evans went with us, and was one of the bridesmaids, and she afterwards paid a visit to Dr. Brabant at Devizes, in order to cheer him upon the loss of his only daughter."

In this endeavor Marian seems to have been almost too

successful. Her zeal, the zeal of an intellectual young woman eager to devote herself to the service of an elderly scholar, knew no discretion. With a man of sense, with anyone but a pompous egoist hungry for flattery, this would not have mattered; but Dr. Brabant at sixty-two was as foolish and self-centered as Marian at twenty-two was callow and innocently ardent. It was decided between them that she was to be his second daughter. She was given access to his library. They read, walked, and talked together. They read Greek together; she read German aloud to him; he called her *Deutera;* she was in ecstasies over his goodness, learning, and charm. But there were other ladies of the household, a sister-in-law and a wife, who preferred their Dr. Brabant to be daughterless. Marian suffered the mortification of being virtually expelled. Rufa, years later, told John Chapman that her father had "acted ungenerously and worse towards Miss Evans; for though he was the chief cause of all that passed, he acted towards her as though the fault lay with her alone." [4] Chapman adds that Dr. Brabant's "unmanliness in the affair" was condemned more by Rufa (Mrs. Charles Hennell) than it was by Marian herself when she (Marian) told him the story in 1850.

Dr. Brabant was a personal friend of David Friedrich Strauss, and Rufa Brabant, under her father's direction, had begun translating Strauss's *Das Leben Jesu.* But after her marriage she abandoned the work, and Marian was persuaded by Charles Hennell to take it on. This monstrous task occupied much of her leisure for two years. It was perhaps good discipline for one who was to become a

4. Gordon S. Haight, *George Eliot and John Chapman, with Chapman's Diaries* (Yale University Press, 1940).

writer; and up to a point it was congenial work; but Strauss' mind repelled as much as it attracted her, and she wearied of what she sometimes felt to be thankless drudgery. When within sight of its end she writes to Sara Hennell that more than anything else "I should like to be idle with you for a little while." But alas, she says, "leathery brain must work at leathery Strauss for a short time before my butterfly days come. Oh how I shall spread my wings then!" She had already, since her conversion from Christianity, come to the conclusion that mere identity of opinion signifies little in comparison with "truth of feeling," which she calls the only universal bond of union; and this, evidently, was a bond she did not enjoy with Strauss. She did not fall into the converse error of allowing feeling to dictate her opinions on matters of fact. She was no mere wishful thinker. "Assuredly this earth is not the home of the spirit—it will rest only in the bosom of the Infinite." In this pronouncement she echoes the mystics of all times and climes; but she instantly sees the fallacy of the traditional argument that the existence of unsatisfied desires in this mortal life logically implies their particular satisfaction hereafter. The infinite, whatever that may be, is rather the end than the "true object" of our desires. She was, however, aware, as so many of her fellow rationalists were not, of the tension in human life between time and eternity; and she repudiated as the "quackery of infidelity" the notion that a new set of opinions, however enlightened, was all that mankind needed for its salvation. She confesses herself at times to be "Strauss-sick" and that "dissecting the beautiful story of the crucifixion" makes her ill. She does not regret having undertaken the work, but she is inclined to vow that she will never translate again.

Her own way of regarding the Gospel legends is shown in a letter to Sara written after the publication of her work. "I have been thinking," she writes,

of that most beautiful passage in Luke's Gospel—the appearance of Jesus to the disciples at Emmaus. How universal in its significance! The soul that has hopelessly followed its Jesus—its impersonation of the highest and best—all in despondency; its thoughts all refuted, its dreams all dissipated! Then comes another Jesus—another, but the same—the same highest and best, only chastened—crucified instead of triumphant—and the soul learns that this is the true way to conquest and glory. And then there is the burning of the heart, which assures us that "this was the Lord"—that this is the inspiration from above, the true comforter that leads unto truth. But I am not become a Methodist, dear Sara; on the contrary, if I am pious one day, you may be sure I was very wicked the day before, and shall be so again the next.

The note of playfulness in the last sentence is characteristic of her at this period. The completion of her work on Strauss [5] was like a release from prison, and her letters begin to show a hitherto hardly suspected capacity for gaiety and humor. "My affections are always the warmest when my friends are within an attainable distance. I think I can manage to keep respectably warm towards you for three weeks without seeing you, but I cannot promise more." And to the same correspondent, Mrs. Bray, three weeks later: "I cannot deny that I am very happy without you, but perhaps I shall be happier with you, so do not

5. For Strauss, see Appendix I.

fail to try the experiment. . . . Everybody I see is very kind to me, and therefore I think them all very charming; and having everything I want, I feel very humble and self-denying." She stipulates that Mrs. Bray is to "come in a very mischievous, unconscientious, theatre-loving humour"—a far cry from the time, not so many years before, when she had spent her evenings in London reading Josephus while her unregenerate brother went to the theater. These particular letters were written from Hackney, where she was staying with Rufa and Sara. Mrs. Bray joined them in London, and they stayed there till June 5 (1846). Strauss in English appeared ten days later.

In the following month Marian and her father went to Dover for a fortnight. A troubled and anxious fortnight, because it was then, at Dover, that her father's health began to show signs of finally breaking up. He had long been ailing; his needs had for long claimed much of her time; and henceforth he was more than ever dependent on her services. He had an insatiable appetite, it seems, for being read to; and time and again, weary but ungrudging, she put her own affairs aside. He lived for another three years, sometimes seeming a little better, sometimes not so well: a heartbreaking alternation of hopes and fears. On April 14: "Dear father gets on very slowly, if at all." A week later: "Dear father is so decidedly progressing towards recovery that I am full of quiet joy." But, in the following month, to Charles Bray:

Father has done wonders in the way of walking and eating—for him—but he makes not the slightest attempt to amuse himself, so that I scarcely feel easy in following my own bent even for an hour. I have told you everything now, except that I look amiable in spite of a strong tendency to look black, and speak gently, though with a strong propensity to be snappish. Pity me, ye happier spirits that look amiable and speak gently, because ye *are* amiable and gentle.

There is far less time now for letter writing, for "Father's tongue has just given utterance to a thought which has been very visibly radiating from his eager eyes for some minutes—'I thought you were going on with the book.'" She has moments of deep despondency, when her life seems to her a "perpetual nightmare" haunted by things to be done which she never has time or energy to do; yet in the last year of her father's life we find her translating Spinoza.

No one, I think, has called George Eliot a good letter writer. The tone is too apt to be stilted, the total effect too much that of a formal composition. But these faults diminish as she matures, and there are passages to be found in the letters written before she was thirty that for "truth of feeling" (to borrow her own phrase) are hardly surpassed by her later self. Prosy these letters may be, but they do reveal her, and without gloss. She is unshakably sincere. And she is as keenly alive to her failings as any reader can be. She tells her half sister Fanny (Mrs. Houghton) that she has been holding a court of conscience and calling to mind the sins of her tongue, her criticisms of the faults of others.

When shall I attain to the true spirit of love which Paul has taught for all the ages? . . . I need the Jesuits' discipline of silence, and though my "evil speaking" issues from the intellectual point of view rather than the moral, though there may be gall in the thought while there is honey in the feeling, yet the evil speaking is wrong. We may satirize character and qualities in the abstract without injury to our moral nature, but persons hardly ever. Poor hints and sketches of souls as we are—with some slight transient vision of the perfect and the true—we had need help each other to gaze at the blessed heavens instead of peering into each other's eyes to find out the motes there.

And again, this time to Sara Hennell: "Miserable dust of the earth we are, but it is worth while to be so, for the sake of the living soul—the breath of God within us. You see I can do nothing but scribble my own prosy stuff—such chopped straw as my soul is foddered on."

Though there is no direct evidence of his influence, except that she unquestionably admired him, now and again her "chopped straw" seems to have fallen from Emerson's nosebag. But:

No mind that has any *real* life is a mere echo of another. If the perfect unison comes occasionally, as in music, it enhances the harmonies. It is like a diffusion or expansion of one's own life, to be assured that its vibrations are repeated in another, and words are the media of those vibrations. Is not the universe itself a perpetual utterance of the one Being?

v

Obviously, the death of her father, on the last day of May, 1849, marks the end of a chapter in Marian Evans' life. She is not, by a long way, George Eliot yet; nor can any such metamorphosis be foretold of her. That there are the makings of a writer in her can be conceded: she is cultured, bookish, critical, highly articulate, and possessed by an insatiable curiosity about ideas. A writer, yes; but hardly a writer of fiction. She is now six months short of thirty. The conflict in her between theorist and creative artist was never to be finally resolved; but up till now, 1849, it has not visibly begun. Already, some three years earlier, Mrs. Bray has remarked in a letter to Sara Hennell that Marian "looks very brilliant just now. We fancy she must be writing her novel." But the allusion remains unexplained and can perhaps be dismissed as playful, for there is no supporting evidence that a novel was in prospect at the time, and another nine years are to pass before we shall hear of her first fictional attempts.

Destiny, however, has its own ways of going to work; and it is easy for us, being wise after the event, to see her early life as a fit preparation for what was to come. She was the youngest child in a good and affectionate but busy household. The comparative isolation and monotony of rural life gave her time to grow. With a capacity for love larger than brother Isaac, her everyday companion, could cope with (and we need not blame him, for if we may judge from Maggie Tulliver her demands were excessive), she was conscious of loneliness, of being more important to herself than to others, and, as all imaginative children are, of a disparity between the outer world and the inner. Driven in upon herself she became, it would seem, an "oldfashioned" child, wise beyond her years and very ready to air her opinions. At the school of the Misses Franklin, whose evangelicalism provided an outlet for her pent-up emotions, she was encouraged to display herself at prayer meetings, to visit the poor of the parish, and to set herself, by conspicuous piety, a little above her schoolfellows, among whom, so far as is known, she formed no intimate friendships. That in spite of all this she was respected at school, and that she emerged from the prig factory not irretrievably ruined in character, says much for her innate good sense; for though good sense was in abeyance for a while it did, as we have seen, resume control in due time. There followed the long loneliness at Griff, the household cares, the daily round, the omnivorous reading, the lack of anyone (but Miss Lewis) to exchange ideas with; and then the change, the release, the plunge into new friendships at Coventry, and all the unparalleled excitement of contact with congenial minds.

It must be emphasized again that coexisting with her consciousness of being an unusually gifted person there was a deep-seated diffidence, an extravagant self-mistrust. More intensely than most, she needed love, moral support, the assurance of being thought well of. She needed affection and encouragement and we must be grateful to the Brays and the Hennells that they gave her both in good measure. They were and had been good friends to her, but at the purely intellectual level she was more than a match for them. She outgrew them. To what extent they were aware of her true quality, her latent powers, we do not know; but certainly their contribution to her development was made and completed during the period that ended with her father's death. Intellectually she could henceforward walk alone; but morally she was dependent to the very end; she had always to have "someone to lean on."

Never more so, naturally, than in this moment of bereavement and desolation. On the morning when her father is known to be dying she writes to the Brays: "What shall I be without my father? It will seem as if a part of my moral nature was gone." The Brays came at once to the rescue. By good luck they had already planned a trip to the Continent; it was arranged that Marian should go with them; and on June 11, only a week or so after the funeral, they set off, going by way of Paris, Lyons, Avignon, Marseilles, Nice, Genoa, Milan, Como, Lago Maggiore, Martigny, and Chamonix, to arrive at Geneva late in July. The Brays, before returning home, settled her in a comfortable *pension*, and there at Geneva she stayed for the next eight months, "quietly and peacefully happy." Here, again, circumstances may be said to have played into the hands of destiny; for these eight months of outward idleness, in a brilliant foreign scene and among stimulating new acquaintances unlike any she had known before, gave her just what she needed of rest and refreshment, and put her past life, as perhaps nothing else could have done, into perspective. That life at Coventry was over, never to be resumed. Not merely was her father gone, with all that he stood for in terms of love and duty, but also the Brays and Hennells, dear friends now as always, had been painlessly removed from their position of influence.

This interval at Geneva marks as it were a stage, a halting place, a pause between one life and the next. She was still utterly unaware of her true vocation, but the egg of her genius was slowly incubating, and for the first time her letters begin to reveal the potential novelist. She gives brief, lively sketches of her fellow guests at the pension. One of the first to make friends with her was an elderly English lady, a Mrs. Locke. "She began to say very kind things to me in rather a waspish tone yesterday morning at breakfast. I liked her better at dinner and tea, and to-day we are quite confidential. I only hope she will stay—she is just the sort of person I shall like to have to speak to—not at all 'congenial,' but with a character of her own."

Teatime, in general, bores Marian, however. "The American lady embroiders slippers—the mamma looks on and does nothing. The Marquis and his friends play at whist; the old ladies sew; and Madame says things so true that they are insufferable." She at once softens this last asperity by adding: "She has been very kind and motherly to me. I like her better every time I see her." Kindness, then and always, she valued above everything, and was entirely free from that snobbery of cleverness which thinks it a sign of grace to be bored by the conversation of simple people.

The dear little old maid, Mlle. Faizan, is quite a good friend to me—extremely prosy, and full of tiny details; but really people of that calibre are a comfort to one occasionally, when one has not strength enough for more stimulating things. She is a sample of those happy souls who ask for nothing but the work of the hour, however trivial—who are contented to live without knowing whether they effect anything, but do really effect much good, simply by their calm and even *maintien*. I laugh to hear her say in a tone of remonstrance—"Mme. de Ludwigsdorff dit qu'elle s'ennuie quand les soirées sont longues: moi, je ne conçois pas comment on peut s'ennuyer quand on a de l'ouvrage ou des jeux ou de la conversation." When people who are dressing elegantly and driving about to make calls every day of their life have been telling me of their troubles, their utter hopelessness of ever finding a vein worth working in their future life, my thoughts have turned towards many whose sufferings are of a more tangible character, and I have really felt all the old commonplaces about the equality of human destinies. . . .

Though she likes her "town life" in Geneva "vastly" and finds "an indescribable charm in this form of human nest-

GEORGE ELIOT AT GENEVA (1849)
BY FRANÇOIS D'ALBERT DURADE

making," sometimes she is homesick for England and old friends, and always, conscious or subconscious, there is a craving in her heart for a love that shall be complete and all-sufficing.

She is now thirty, an accomplished young woman, liked and admired by her friends. She is capable of giving—and of demanding—a passionate personal devotion. That, indeed, is the deepest need of her nature, and until it is fulfilled her creativeness lies dormant and there can be no George Eliot.

## Chapter Two

## A JOURNALIST IN LONDON

### I

SHE had never been a beautiful girl. She was not a
beautiful woman. A scrutiny of the existing portraits
may suggest that this is an understatement; for there
is indeed something formidable and ungainly, if not gro-
tesque, in the heavy face that confronts us in her later
years. It is a safe guess that during adolescence, if not before and after, she was wincingly conscious of her plain-
ness, and that her excessive seriousness of mind, her
precocious intellectuality, not to mention her (at first
unbridled) spiritual ambition, was a species of "compensa-
tion" in the psychologist's sense. She had, we cannot doubt,
the normal girl's instinctive desire to attract, to be desired;
and her incorrigible diffidence, her secret self-depreciation
which existed side by side with a consciousness of unusual
talents, may well have been due in part to the bitter knowledge that nature had not been kind to her. At least once in
her letters, in a passage palpably sincere, she refers in passing to her ugliness: not playfully, inviting contradiction,
but as one taking account of an evident fact. And there is
an episode narrated by John Chapman in his private diary
which, as we shall see, bears painful witness to her unhappiness in that fact. In her novels, too, she cannot quite
hide her resentment of man's susceptibility to the charms
of mere prettiness in a woman. With her warmly sympathetic nature and her eager interest in people she had

no difficulty in finding friends; affection she gave and received in abundance; but she had more than affection to give, and that more, it seemed, was not demanded of her.

But, though she was not personally alluring, her beauty of character was reflected, as it could not fail to be, in certain features, and her total effect—this is where some later portraits so sadly malign her—must have been attractive. Witnesses both early and late testify to the beauty of eyes and voice and to the transfiguring radiance of her smile. Herbert Spencer, who met her shortly after she had embarked on a journalistic career in London and was soon on terms of intimate friendship with her, described her in a letter as "the most admirable woman, mentally, I ever met," adding: "I am very frequently at Chapman's where she was lodged, and the greatness of her intellect, conjoined with her womanly qualities and manner, generally keep me by her side most of the evening." In his autobiography [1] he gives a detailed sketch of her person and character at this time (1852) which is worth quoting at some length:

In physique there was, perhaps, a trace of that masculinity characterizing her intellect; for though of but ordinary feminine height she was strongly built. The head, too, was larger than is usual in women. . . . Striking by its power when in repose, her face was remarkably transfigured by a smile; but with her smile there was habitually mingled an expression of sympathy, either for the person smiled at or the person smiled with. Her voice was a contralto of rather low pitch and I believe naturally strong. On this last point I ought to have a more definite impression, for in those days we occasionally sang together; but the habit of subduing her voice was so con-

1. Herbert Spencer, *An Autobiography* (London, Watts & Co., 1904).

stant, that I suspect its real power was rarely if ever heard. Its tones were always gentle, and, like the smile, sympathetic. . . . Conscientious and just in all relations and consequently indignant against wrong, she was nevertheless so tolerant of human weaknesses as to be quickly forgiving; and, indeed, was prone to deprecate harsh judgments. This last trait was I doubt not in part caused by constant study of her own defects. She complained of being troubled by double consciousness—a current of self-criticism being an habitual accompaniment of anything she was saying or doing; and this naturally tended towards self-depreciation and self-distrust. . . . Her philosophical powers were remarkable. I have known but few men with whom I could discuss a question in philosophy with more satisfaction. Capacity for abstract thinking is rarely found along with capacity for concrete representation, even in men; and among women, such a union of the two as existed in her has, I should think, never been paralleled. In early days she was, I believe, sometimes vivacious; but she was not so when I first knew her, nor afterwards. Probably this was the reason why the wit and the humour which from time to time gave signs of their presence were not frequently displayed. Calmness was an habitual trait. There was never any indication of mental excitement, still less of mental strain; but the impression constantly produced was that of latent power—the ideas which came from her being manifestly the products of a large intelligence. And yet this large intelligence working easily, of which she must have been conscious, was not accompanied by any marked self-confidence. Difference of opinion she frequently expressed in a half apologetic manner.

## II

She arrived back from Geneva on March 23, 1850, having been escorted as far as Paris by Monsieur D'Albert, the kindly and cultivated man (he later became Conser-

vateur of the Athénée, the National Gallery of Geneva)
in whose house she had lived for the greater part of her
time abroad and who, with his wife, had showered affection upon her at a time when she most needed it—though
indeed, being what she was, there was never a time when
she did not need it. On reaching England she went straight
to the Brays at Rosehill, where, with intervals at Griff and
elsewhere, she was to live for the next nine months.

Among the Brays' visitors was John Chapman, prospective new editor of the *Westminster Review*, an organ of
philosophical liberalism which was in a state of rapid decline and into which it was hoped he would inject new
life. He brought with him, to Rosehill, Robert William
Mackay, whose chief work, *The Progress of the Intellect*,
had just been published. Marian's review of this book appeared in the *Westminster* in January of the following
year. It was her first essay in criticism, but it is more than
that, for it reflects the bias of her own mind and expounds
ideas which were to be dominant assumptions throughout
her fiction. "It is Mr. Mackay's faith," she writes—and
evidently it was also George Eliot's—

that divine revelation is not contained exclusively or pre-
eminently in the facts and inspirations of any one age or
nation, but is coextensive with the history of human development, and is perpetually unfolding itself to our widened experience and investigation, as firmament upon firmament becomes visible to us in proportion to the power and range of
our exploring instruments. The master-key to this revelation

and to the underlying philosophy of George Eliot's novels

is the recognition of the presence of undeviating law in the
material and moral world—of that invariability of sequence
which is acknowledged to be the basis of physical science,

but which is still perversely ignored in our social organization, our ethics, and our religion. It is this invariability of
sequence which can alone give value to experience, and
renders education, in the true sense, possible. The divine yea
and nay, the seal of prohibition and of sanction, are effectually
impressed on human deeds and aspirations, not by means of
Greek and Hebrew, but by that inexorable law of consequences, whose evidence is confirmed instead of weakened as
the ages advance; and human duty is comprised in the earnest
study of this law and patient obedience to its teaching. . . .
A correct generalization gives significance to the smallest detail, just as the great inductions of geology demonstrate in
every pebble the working of laws by which the earth has become adapted for the habitation of man. In this view religion
and philosophy are not merely conciliated, they are identical;
or rather, religion is the crown and consummation of philosophy—the delicate corolla which can only spread out its
petals in all their symmetry and brilliance to the sun, when
root and branch exhibit the conditions of a healthy and
vigorous life.

This "inexorable law of consequences"—that whatsoever
a man sows, that shall he also reap—is the thesis which
again and again, with an almost tiresome iteration, her
novels illustrate. That they do much more is not in question. But they do that.

Acutely intelligent, deeply and widely read in several
literatures, she had all the literary skill and judgment that
Chapman lacked, as well as the habit of untiring industry;
and when he became prospective owner of the *Westminster* she was glad to become prospective assistant editor. She was to be paid, it seems, only for her original
contributions. Happily she was not entirely dependent on
what she earned, for she had inherited from her father an

income of £80 to £100 a year—in those days a substantial sum. Chapman had a flair for bold schemes, but in this new venture he would have been lost without Miss Evans to correct his errors of taste and judgment. She was to be in effect editor, subeditor, proofreader, and general factotum. She had joined the Chapman household in January, 1851: he completed his purchase of the periodical in October. Much of the esteem which the *Westminster* was now to enjoy, as the "leading expositor of the philosophic and scientific thought of the age," must have been due to her loyal and drudging efforts. The contributors included such eminent writers as Herbert Spencer, George Henry Lewes, James and Harriet Martineau as well as others, prominent in their time, whose names mean almost nothing to us today; and a former proprietor, John Stuart Mill, son of the original founder, still shed the light of his prestige on the undertaking. It was a brilliant covey of Necessitarians and Positivists, and the Chapmans' house was their nesting-ground.

Chapman was a man of parts, an odd mixture of adventurer and idealist, quack, philosopher, and philanderer. For some years now he had been an active, enterprising publisher of tendencious literature, one of his unrealized schemes, in which he succeeded in interesting Ralph Waldo Emerson, being the establishment of a journal common to Old and New England, to be published simultaneously in London and Boston, in which the most advanced thought of the English-speaking world should find expression. Emerson, who occupied rooms in the Chapmans' house for some three months during a visit to England, wrote of him as "a phoenix of a publisher, a man of integrity and of talent in his trade." There was truth in this estimate, though it was not the whole truth. Chapman had practiced many trades, and publishing was not to be his last. And if he was capable of a disingenuousness bordering on trickery, he was capable too of a disinterested promotion of the ideas he believed in. He was facile, emotional, eminently likable, and in the last resort as eminently unreliable. Short, however, of that last resort, he was by all accounts a good friend and a most engaging companion. Born in 1821, the son of a Nottinghamshire druggist, he was apprenticed in boyhood to a watchmaker, but finding the situation not to his taste he ran away and took refuge with his brother, who was studying medicine in Edinburgh. The brother purchased for him a stock of "watches, chronometers, sextants, etc.," and armed with these he went to Adelaide and set up in business. Returning thence some years later he is said, on doubtful authority, to have studied medicine at Bart's, and again, under Gay-Lussac, at Paris: on the strength of which studies, or for less cogent reasons, he describes himself in the marriage register as a surgeon. Soon after the wedding he and his wife went to London and eventually settled at 142 Strand, a house which combined the functions of book publishing, private residence, literary salon, and selective boardinghouse, the business being accommodated on the ground floor. His publications, before he acquired the *Westminster Review* and the services of Miss Evans, had included Emerson's *Poems* and her own translation of *Das Leben Jesu*, both in 1846.

Chapman was now in his thirtieth year, Marian some nineteen months older. Facially, and in some other respects, he bore a striking resemblance to Byron. With his energetic mind and eager friendliness he was just the sort of man to attract a serious young woman who had begun to suspect that life might hold more for her than literary and philosophical studies. With no means of knowing her side of the story, one hesitates to assert that she fell deeply (if briefly) in love with Chapman; but his recently discovered diaries establish an overwhelming probability that she did. 142 Strand was an unusual household. It consisted at this time of Chapman, his wife Susanna, his two young children, and Elisabeth Tilley, an attractive but not very sensible young woman with whom Chapman was amorously involved. Nominally the children's governess, in spite of her own defective education, she was in fact his mistress. Chapman's was an expansive, an overflowing nature. He was fond of women and he was extremely fond of John Chapman. He had, it would seem, a genius for precipitating romantic situations and then not quite knowing what to do about it. He was no "heartless" philanderer. On the contrary he had too much heart: it beat impetuously and bled freely. He was always aware of the unimpeachable kindness of his intentions toward women, and always distressed—distressed, puzzled, and disappointed —when it was demonstrated to him, yet once again, that a policy of unlimited kindness all round does not, where women are concerned, give undiluted general satisfaction. How—one can imagine his asking—how can the darlings fail to be happy in an arrangement that gives *me* so much pleasure, or would do if it weren't for these tears and tantrums?

It is possible that Susanna and Elisabeth, sharing that capacious heart of his, had in fact been tolerably contented until Marian turned up: whether or not that was so, it is evident that they made common cause against her.

For, whether as disturber of the peace or as author of a new concord hostile to herself, Marian soon found herself the subject of bitter contention. Chapman needed Marian's help in his business; Marian was indispensable to him; and Marian needed to be needed. In her, moreover, he found an intellectual companionship such as neither Elisabeth nor Susanna could give him, neither Elisabeth with her mindless beauty, nor Susanna who, without personal attractiveness to recommend her, made foolish pretensions to literary judgment and was in the habit of airing, poor woman, the crudest opinions on matters in which she had no competence. In pursuit of this intellectual companionship he went with her to choose a piano for her use, sat in her room while she played Mozart to him, persuaded her to give him lessons in German, and allowed himself to be discovered holding her hand. Elisabeth decided that she, too, must learn German; and Susanna agreed to the purchase of a piano for the drawing room.

But peace did not return. There followed a dreary sequence of accusations, dark looks, sulky silences, arguments, protestations. Elisabeth started it. She, knowing her Chapman, had been jealous from the very first. He did so wish she would be "a little more charitable and generous"! Susanna, knowing him still better, was more tolerant, more patient, and would perhaps have been willing to shut her eyes to what she could not prevent without precipitating disaster. But Elisabeth worked on her, and soon both women were in full cry against the interloper. They succeeded in driving her away, back to Coventry. Chapman saw her off at the railway station. "She was very sad," he confides to his diary,[2] "and hence made me feel so. She

2. Gordon S. Haight, *George Eliot and John Chapman, with Chapman's Diaries.*

pressed me for some intimation of the state of my feelings. I told her that I felt great affection for her, but that I loved E and S also, though each in a different way. At this avowal she burst into tears." It was probably the thought of Elisabeth, with her pretty face and soft physical charms, that provoked these tears. For Susanna's position was impregnable, and Marian's relations with Chapman had been perfectly "innocent," for her part, however sentimental. Nevertheless he knew, had made it his business to know, that her heart as well as her mind was at his disposal. What hopes she entertained of him is a matter for conjecture, but that she was deeply hurt and mortified by their extinction is evident. It was all very sad for the long-suffering polygamist, and inconvenient too, for who now would prepare the analytical catalogue of his publications by which he set so much store? Who so well qualified, so willing, so utterly dependable, as Marian Evans?

Two months after her departure from the Strand he visits her at Coventry, as guest of the Brays, to discuss the whole situation, and in particular the analytical catalogue and the prospectus of the new *Westminster Review*. There had been some correspondence between them in the interval, and he had been thoughtful enough to send her certain letters in which Susanna, writing to him from Truro where she was staying for a time, referred to her in terms of great bitterness. In reply she had at first declined to undertake the compilation of the catalogue, and then, the same day, had agreed to do it only with "the utmost repugnance" and on the understanding that she would accept no remuneration for it. Arriving at Coventry on May 27 (1851) he "found Miss Evans shy, calm, and affectionate." Next day they went to Leamington together, stopping on the way to look at Kenilworth Castle, and—"As we rested on the grass, I remarked on the wonderful and mysterious embodiment of all the elements, characteristics, and beauties of nature which man and woman jointly present. I dwelt also on the incomprehensible mystery and witchery of beauty. My words jarred upon her and put an end to her enjoyment. Was it from a consciousness of her own want of beauty? She wept bitterly." [3]

### III

Since they were evidently not to be lovers, there were now, in theory, three courses open to these two. They could take a final farewell of each other and go their separate ways. They could continue to work together, editorially, across the distance between London and Coventry. Or they could contrive Marian's return to London on the understanding that there was to be no more nonsense. The first would have meant jeopardizing the *Review;* the second was scarcely practicable; and the third, for a variety of reasons, was more easily said than done. Chapman gave much anxious thought to the problem. He knew that both Susanna and Elisabeth would resist any attempt to reinstate Marian at 142 Strand, and he suspected that they would be equally opposed to her living elsewhere in London; yet she could not effectually help him with the *Review* from a distance.

What she could do, however, she did. During this visit of his to Coventry, which lasted ten days, she worked zealously on the prospectus; and after his return to Lon-

3. *Ibid.*

don he continued to consult her by post. From her letters we can guess how invaluable her coöperation must have been to him. In the realms of strategy, tactics, literature, and philosophy, she is equally at home: her grasp of practical detail is as evident as her general culture. Elisabeth greeted his return with rapture, but very soon made it clear that she would not tolerate Marian's return to London. This was checkmate, for Elisabeth, he had decided, was his "first love" and would also, he believed, be his last. However, after a further exchange of letters and some more visits to Coventry, the women in possession allowed themselves to be persuaded. What is perhaps more astonishing is that Marian, too, was persuadable. She returned to the bosom of the Chapman household at the end of September, 1851, and for the next two years lived there in peace and propriety.

Whether or not there were further disagreements among the women we do not know. The records are silent on the point. But certainly they enjoyed an active social life. Boarders came and went, and Chapman had the knack of gathering interesting celebrities about him. It was good for trade (which, alas, did not flourish however), and moreover he liked it for its own sake. He was a genuinely convivial creature and genuinely interested in ideas. He was also a man of spirit and resource. When he came into conflict with a monopolistic organization known as the Booksellers' Association he fought them on their own ground and won a victory which, while it did his business no good, redounded much to his credit. Marian's letters at this time to Sara Hennell and others bear witness both to the richness of her social life and to her interest in the *Review*.

Harriet Martineau called on Monday morning with Mr. Atkinson. Very kind and cordial. I honour her for her powers and industry, and should be glad to think highly of her. I have no doubt that she is fascinating when there is time for talk. We have had two agreeable soirees. Last Monday I was talking and listening for two hours to Pierre Leroux—a dreamy genius. He has found the true *pont* which is to unite the love of oneself with the love of one's neighbour. He is in utter poverty, going to lecture—autrement il faut mourrir.

That was in February. Ten days later: "We went to quite a gay party at Mrs. Mackay's on Saturday. Good Mr. Mackay has been taking trouble to get me to Hastings for my health—calling on Miss Fellowes, daughter of the *Religion of the Universe*, and inducing her to write me a note of invitation." In April, "Grote is very friendly, and has propitiated J. S. Mill, who will write for us when we want him. We had quite a brilliant soiree yesterday evening. I had a pleasant talk with [W. R.] Greg and Forster. Greg was 'much pleased to have made my acquaintance.' Forster, on the whole, appeared to think that people should be glad to make *his* acquaintance."

She describes, too, a meeting of writers held in support of Chapman's campaign against the Booksellers' Association. "Dickens in the chair—a position he fills remarkably well, preserving a courteous neutrality of eyebrows, and speaking with clearness and decision. His appearance is certainly disappointing—no benevolence in the face, and, I think, little in the head—the anterior lobe not by any means remarkable." (Evidently she had not forgotten George Combe's phrenology.)

Babbage moved the first resolution—a bad speaker, but a great authority. Charles Knight is a beautiful, elderly man, with a modest but firm enunciation; and he made a wise and telling speech which silenced one or two vulgar, ignorant booksellers who had got into the meeting by mistake. . . . The most telling speech of the evening was Professor Tom Taylor's—as witty and brilliant as one of George Dawson's. . . . Dr. Lankester, Professor Newman, Robert Bell, and others, spoke well. Owen has a tremendous head, and looked, as he was, the greatest celebrity of the meeting. George Cruikshank, too, made a capital speech in an admirable moral spirit. He is the most homely, genuine-looking man, not unlike the pictures of Captain Cuttle.

Mazzini, James Anthony Froude, the Martineaus (James and Harriet), Theodore Parker, Thomas Henry Huxley ("an agreeable evening on Wednesday, a Mr. Huxley being the centre of interest"), a "note from Florence Nightingale," "Bryant the poet last evening—a pleasant, quiet, elderly man," Mr. Lewes, Mr. Spencer, Mr. Chapman, herself "bothered to death with article-reading and scrap-work of all sorts" or "correcting proofs from morning till night," these are the interests and incidents of her new life in London. At times she suffers from rheumatism, or head-aches which disable her for days. At other times her troubles, she says, are

purely psychical—self-dissatisfaction, and despair of achieving anything worth the doing. . . . When we are young we think our troubles a mighty business—that the world is spread out expressly as a stage for the particular drama of our lives, and that we have a right to rant and foam at the mouth if we are crossed. I have done enough of that in my time. But we begin at last to understand that these things are important only to our own consciousness, which is but as a globule of dew on a rose-leaf, that at mid-day there will be no trace of. This is no high-flown sentimentality, but a simple reflection.

She has her lighter moments too. Mr. Greg, speaking of a book review, said that there was not much in it—"dreadfully true," remarks Marian, "since there was only all his book." She quotes appreciatively a bon mot she has heard —"C'est un homme admirable: il se tait en sept langues"— and writes warmly of Herbert Spencer. "My brightest spot, next to my love of *old* friends, is the deliciously calm *new* friendship that Herbert Spencer gives me. We see each other every day, and have a delightful camaraderie in everything. But for him my life would be desolate enough." The emphasis on calmness is perhaps an oblique tribute to Chapman's powers of disturbance. With Spencer she was deliciously calm and safe. Perhaps a little too much so.

Spencer was already well acquainted with Chapman when in October, 1851, at 142 Strand, he first met Marian Evans. It was at the first evening party after her return from Coventry, and he at once fell heavily into friendship with her, as we have seen. Born like herself in a midland shire, son of a schoolmaster and a Wesleyan mother, author of the recently published *Social Statics* (1850), apostle of "evolutionary progress," accredited philosopher of the rising scientific movement, and aiming at nothing less than a synthesis of all knowledge, Herbert Spencer had almost everything to commend him to Marian's liking, including a warm appreciation of herself. He was good-looking, courteous, kindly, and within a few months of her own age. They met and moved together on the highest levels, and their friendship ripened so quickly that it was small wonder if matchmaking observers began saying they were made for each other. She shared his appetite for abstract discussion. He shared her delight in music and the arts. They represented the two most brilliant intellects in the England of their day. Incidentally, it was Spencer who first suggested to her that she should try her hand at novel writing. He thought he saw in her many if not all of the necessary qualifications: quick observation, great power of analysis, unusual and rapid intuition into others' states of mind, deep and broad sympathies, wit and humor and wide culture. But she would not listen to his advice. She did not believe she could do it. It is tempting to conjecture whether, if she had married Spencer, she would have ultimately allowed herself to be persuaded, as she was by Lewes, to make the attempt.

For the question of their marrying did arise, if not between themselves certainly in the minds and talk of others. "There were reports that I was in love with her, and that we were about to be married," he says. "But neither of these reports was true." He was not in love with her. The sagacious fellow had his emotions under perfect control. Only a year ago he had written to a friend that marrying under existing circumstances was out of the question for him, "and as for twisting circumstances into better shape, I think it is too much trouble. As I think you have heard me say—I don't mean to get on. I don't think getting on is worth the bother. On the whole I am quite decided not to be a drudge; and as I see no probability of being able to marry without being a drudge, why I have pretty well given up the idea." That is Herbert Spencer at the age of thirty-one: evidently not the kind of man to have his head turned, and his program modified, by "the most admirable woman, mentally," he had ever met. The clue to his decision is perhaps in that fatal qualification "mentally," for he will not have us suppose him unappreciative of physical beauty. In later life he declares beauty to have been a *sine qua non* for him—"as was once unhappily proved when the intellectual traits and the emotional traits were of the highest."

Is this last a reference to Marian Evans? We do not know, but it seems likely, and if so it would suggest that the possibility of marrying her did occur to him, only to be rejected. If it occurred to him it is more than likely that it occurred to her, and that she would not have been unwilling. "We have agreed that we are not in love with each other," she writes to the Brays, "and that there is no reason why we should not have as much of each other's society as we like. He is a good, delightful creature, and I always feel better for being with him." [4] If to her intellectual and moral qualifications had been added the physical allure of a Helen, she might conceivably have kindled a spark of humanity in this admirable thinking-machine; and in view of her experience with Chapman she must surely have known that and wished herself different; but "one who devotes himself to grave literature must be content to remain celibate," he remarks in his autobiography, "unless, indeed, he obtains a wife having adequate means for both, and is content to put himself in the implied position. Even then, family cares and troubles are likely to prove fatal to his undertakings." How true! And how tragic if Herbert Spencer's ponderous undertakings had been hindered!

The disaster, if ever it threatened, was averted. They had long walks and talks together; and, having the priv-

4. Quoted also in *George Eliot and John Chapman* by G. S. Haight, from whom I borrow the words omitted by Cross in his edition of the letters: "that we are not in love with each other." An example of Cross's "discretion."

ilege of free admission for two, he took her to the theaters and the Royal Italian Opera. They enjoyed a delightful companionship, and discussed, no doubt, everything under the sun. We do not know whether marriage between them was ever mooted; but that they did not exchange views on marriage in general is out of the question. The point is important, because Spencer had definite opinions on the subject, as on everything else, and whether she fully shared them or not they may well have made a deep enough impression on her to influence her, in a greater or less degree, and in part to determine the one revolutionary act of her life, her unlegalized union with George Henry Lewes. Writing to a friend, some seven years before, Spencer had said:

I do not conceive the most perfect happiness attainable in marriage while the legal bond continues; for as we can never rid ourselves of the consciousness of it, it must always influence our conduct. But the next best thing to destroying it is to banish it from our minds, and let husband and wife strive to act towards each other as they would were there no such tie.

There is much more to a similar effect. One does not contend that George Eliot entertained a doctrinaire objection to legal marriage such as would have prevented her marrying Lewes had he been free; but merely that the opinions of Spencer, whom she so much admired and liked, must at least have had weight with her, and may well have played a part in reconciling her to a course of conduct repugnant to her innate moral conservatism.

Readers with a taste for conjecture may like to imagine what might or might not have happened if Spencer and

Marian Evans had married each other. Spencer was a man who seemed not to understand the difference between living reasonably and living by reason. With all his subtlety of intellect he was simple minded enough to make a god of rationality. His eccentricities turned him into a legendary character, and many anecdotes are told of him, some of them certainly apocryphal. Whether the story is true that when traveling long distances by train he engaged a first-class carriage and suspended himself in a hammock slung from its ceiling, in order to reduce the effects of friction, we do not positively know; but that it would have been characteristic of him is fully attested. Toward the end of his long life he made his home with two maiden ladies; and their testimony [5] leaves us in no doubt that he was a kindly and benevolent old gentleman, as well as an oddity. He used to arrive from his club at about nine in the evening, they tell us, and sit with them for an hour or so; and if the conversation proved too trying for him he would plug his ears with a pair of ear stoppers made to his own specification. Logical behavior is always in danger of becoming ridiculous, but this was one of the truths he cheerfully disregarded. He insisted on his bed being made in a certain fashion of his own, with a hard bolster placed under the mattress to raise a hump on which the small of his back could rest, and with the bedclothes pleated down the middle so that they should fall in loose folds on either side of him. When out driving on one occasion he suddenly ordered the coachman to stop, in order that he might feel his own pulse and make sure that it was safe to proceed. He announced his intention (never fulfilled) of writing a cookery book, but this

5. *Home Life with Herbert Spencer* (Two, London, 1906).

HERBERT SPENCER IN 1872
BY J. B. BURGESS

remark may well have been playful, for, like Milton's "unwieldy elephant" which,

> To make them mirth used all his might and wreathed
> His lithe proboscis,

he had his own notion of humor. He spent a good deal of time inventing a mousetrap. He ordered that the daily *Times*, when he had finished with it, should be passed on to the servants. He was often, but not always, observant: when it was pointed out to him that his horse was harnessed with a barbarous nineteenth-century device called a bearing rein, he there and then made the coachman get down and remove it. He detested cruelty and had a disinterested passion for justice. He professed himself astonished by "the irrationality of human beings" but had the wit to add: "And I show my irrationality by ever expecting them to be rational." His eccentricities were not the fruit of old age, though no doubt they grew more numerous with time: they were the logical outcome of his ardent individualism.

It can hardly be supposed that marriage with a strong-minded woman would not have knocked some of the nonsense out of Spencer, but it seems extremely unlikely that Marian would have found in him "someone to lean upon." She was as emotionally clinging as she was intellectually independent. Her talent needed all the cosseting it could get and her egoism, which she was always deploring, required that she should be in the middle of the picture. Spencer had nothing, one imagines, of Lewes' unexpected talent for self-effacing devotion; and the odds are that if she had married him she would never have become a novelist.

IV

It will be convenient, at this point, before coming to the matter of George Henry Lewes, to look a little more closely at what she was and did during the years immediately preceding and following her union with him. Her inner, emotional life, her hopes and fears, her griefs and ecstasies, we can know only by conjecture, in the light of what has already been told here. That Chapman continued for some time to represent an emotional problem for her is highly probable, and that she brought common sense and dignity to its solution is evident. Once or twice after her return to the Strand she intended to leave but did not do so. With so much hard work to get through she can have had little time to spare for unhappiness. In addition to her editorial tasks, advising, revising, planning, reading, proof correcting, she began during 1853 to translate Ludwig Feuerbach's *Das Wesen des Christenthums*, which Chapman was to publish,[6] and there is talk at this time of her writing a book on *The Idea of a Future Life*, a project which seems to have been stillborn.

Among her fellow boarders at 142 Strand was a young man, William Hale White, who was ultimately to become well known in the reading world as Mark Rutherford. He recorded his personal impressions of her many years later. "She had a dark room at the end of a long dark passage," he tells us,

and in that room I have read proofs to her. My own room, the quietest I have known in London, or out of it, was over hers, and looked across the river to the Norwood hills. Mrs. Chapman kept an American boarding-house, and her family, Chap-

6. For Feuerbach, see Appendix II.

man's staff, and the visitors had meals together. I remember vividly the day on which I came to No. 142 and had lunch there. Miss Evans sat opposite me. I was a mere youth, a stranger, awkward and shy. She was then almost unknown to the world, but I had sense enough to discern she was a remarkable creature. I was grateful to her because she replied even with eagerness to a trifling remark I happened to make, and gave it some importance. That was always her way. If there was any sincerity (an indispensable qualification) in the person with whom she came into contact, she strove to elicit his best, and generally disclosed to him something in himself of which he was not aware. I have never seen anybody whose search for the meaning and worth of persons and things was so unresting as hers.

The style of her conversation, Mark Rutherford continues, was perfect. "It was quite natural, but never slipshod, and the force and sharpness of her thought were never lost in worn phrases." He adds an illuminating note on her looks.

She was attractive personally. Her hair was particularly beautiful, and in her grey eyes there was a curiously shifting light, generally soft and tender, but convertible into the keenest flash. The likeness by Sir Frederick Burton is good, but it gives permanence to that which was not permanent in her face. It lacks the generality combined with particularity which we find in portraits by the greatest masters.

One evening she played Beethoven to him alone. It was an experience he never forgot.

She was not, I suppose, a first-rate performer, but she more than satisfied me, and I was, I am afraid, a little incoherent in my thanks. A favourite composer with her was Gluck, and it was she who introduced me to Orfeo. She was generous to a

degree which nobody now living can measure, and she not
only gave money to necessitous friends, but took pains to serve
them. Years after I had left Chapman's I wrote to her asking if
she could assist a poor man of letters whom we both knew,
and she got work for him.

The first number of the *Westminster Review* under
Chapman's proprietorship appeared in January, 1852. It
was a good number, and Marian had every reason for pride
in it. It opened with an article on Representative Reform
by William J. Fox: a shrewd stroke of policy and a gra-
cious gesture, for this veteran writer had written the opening article for the very first number of the original *Westminster* (under James Mill) twenty-eight years before.
Other subjects faithfully dealt with ranged from shellfish,
and the relations between employers and employed, to the
"ethics of Christendom" and the latest continental theory
of legislation; and the contributors, all distinguished in
their day, and all writing anonymously, included James
Anthony Froude (on Mary Stuart), Francis William
Newman (brother of John Henry), James Martineau,
and George Henry Lewes. In their prospectus, printed at
the beginning of this first number, the editors undertook
to "unite a spirit of reverential sympathy for the cherished
associations of pure and elevated minds with an uncom-
promising pursuit of truth" and to discuss ecclesiastical
dogma and biblical criticism "without reservation, under
the conviction that religion has its foundation in man's
nature," having in mind "the pre-eminent importance of
a constructive religious philosophy, as connected with the
development and activity of the moral nature, and of
those poetic and emotional elements, out of which proceed our noblest aspirations. . . ." These ponderous plat-

itudes (but allowance must be made for the prose fashions
of the time) were the fruit of much anxious consultation,
much writing and rewriting: it was no doubt felt to be
necessary that a journal which aimed at undermining political and religious orthodoxy should maintain a massive
dignity of utterance, and where dignity is consciously
striven for, pompousness inevitably turns up. Later contributors were to include Giuseppe Mazzini, Herbert
Spencer, John Stuart Mill, Thomas Colley Grattan, and
some others equally eminent. Marian Evans herself, as
well as writing a large part of the summary of contemporary literature which appeared at the end of each number,
found time to contribute a review of Carlyle's *Life of
Sterling* in January, 1852, and six or seven very substantial
essays (in addition to regular reviewing) during the five
years that followed. Her editorial activities, however,
came virtually to an end when in October, 1853, she
moved from the Strand to lodgings at 21 Cambridge
Street, Edgware Road.

The success of the *Review*, in point of general esteem,
was never in doubt; but its finances were too hopelessly
entangled with those of Chapman's rapidly failing publishing business to admit of its succeeding in any other
sense. Chapman seems to have combined shrewdness and
rashness in equal parts. He was always in money difficulties, partly from ill luck and partly from his engaging
habit of taking impossible risks. He was the victim of his
own sanguine idealism and bad management: if he felt
that a book ought to be published, publish it he would,
regardless of profit and loss. He had friends and backers
and made ample use of them. G. H. Lewes, in the *Leader*,
the journal he ran with Thornton Hunt, warmly wel-

comed the new *Westminster* and defended it against subsequent attacks by the orthodox. But Chapman needed not only moral support but money, and not only money but someone capable of handling it sensibly, as he could not. An incorrigible optimist to the last, he eventually abandoned publishing for the practice of medicine, a profession for which he was very dubiously qualified. But his later history does not concern us here.

Toward the end of her life, anxious rather that certain of her early essays should not be reprinted than that some of them should, George Eliot selected seven and prepared them for ultimate publication. Four of these had originally appeared in the *Westminster Review*, the first in 1855, the last in 1857, the year in which her first piece of fiction saw the light. Evangelical teaching, as offered by a certain Dr. Cumming whose preachings and writings had attracted a huge public, provides the subject of the first of these occasional essays. It begins, in a vein of high satire:

Given, a man with moderate intellect, a moral standard not higher than the average, some rhetorical affluence and great glibness of speech, what is the career in which, without the aid of birth or money, he may most easily attain power and reputation in English society? Where is that Goshen of mediocrity in which a smattering of science and learning will pass for profound instruction, where platitudes will be accepted as wisdom, bigoted narrowness as holy zeal, unctuous egoism as God-given piety? Let such a man become an evangelical preacher; he will then find it possible to reconcile small ability with great ambition, superficial knowledge with the prestige of erudition, a middling morale with a high reputation for sanctity. Let him shun practical extremes and be ultra only in what is purely theoretic: let him be stringent on predestination, but latitudinarian on fasting; unflinching in insisting on the eternity of punishment, but diffident of curtailing the substantial comforts of time; ardent and imaginative on the pre-millennial advent of Christ, but cold and cautious towards every other infringement of the *status quo*. Let him fish for souls not with the bait of inconvenient singularity, but with the drag-net of comfortable conformity. Let him be hard and literal in his interpretation only when he wants to hurl texts at the heads of unbelievers and adversaries, but when the letter of the Scriptures presses too closely on the genteel Christianity of the nineteenth century, let him use his spiritualizing alembic and disperse it into impalpable ether.

This, though inferior as writing, is the kind of gay anger to which, in a later century, Mr. Shaw was to accustom us. The anger is exalted, but it is under control: it never degenerates into mere bad temper. And the discourse that follows is as scrupulously fair minded as it is severe. She is concerned not to controvert Christianity but merely to describe, with pitiless logic, the version of it which the object of her attack favors, the shameless unveracity with which he seeks to promote it, and the ignoble morality which it implies:

The only system he includes under the term Christianity is Calvanistic Protestantism. Experience has so long shown that the human brain is a congenial nidus for inconsistent beliefs, that we do not pause to inquire how Dr. Cumming, who attributes the conversion of the unbelieving to the Divine Spirit, can think it necessary to co-operate with that Spirit by argumentative white lies. Nor do we for a moment impugn the genuineness of his zeal for Christianity, or the sincerity of his conviction that the doctrines he preaches are necessary to salvation; on the contrary, we regard the flagrant unveracity found on his pages as an indirect result of that conviction—as a result, namely, of the intellectual and moral distortion of view which is inevitably produced by assigning to dogmas, based on a very complex structure of evidence, the place and authority of first truths. A distinct appreciation of the value of evidence—in other words, the intellectual perception of truth—is more closely allied to truthfulness of statement, or the moral quality of veracity, than is generally admitted. That highest moral habit, the constant preference for truth, both theoretically and practically, pre-eminently demands the co-operation of the intellect with the impulses —as is indicated by the fact that it is only found in anything like completeness in the highest class of minds. And it is commonly seen that, in proportion as religious sects believe themselves to be guided by direct inspiration rather than by a spontaneous exertion of their faculties, their sense of truth is misty and confused. . . . So long as a belief in propositions is regarded as indispensable to salvation, the pursuit of truth *as such* is not possible, any more than it is possible for a man who is swimming for his life to make meteorological observations on the storm which threatens to overwhelm him. The sense of alarm and haste, the anxiety for personal safety, which Dr. Cumming insists upon as the proper religious attitude, unmans the nature, and allows no thorough, calm thinking, no truly noble, disinterested feeling. . . . The fundamental faith for man is faith in the result of a brave, honest, and steady use of all his faculties.

This was George Eliot's own faith, and being what she was, a rationalist in the broader but not in the narrower sense of the term, we can be sure that when she said "all his faculties" she meant just that. Sympathy, the vital impulse of the heart, was for her the light of the world. Love guided by reason, but not originating in it, was the sum of her religious creed.

These early essays being hard to come by, lavish quotation is legitimate. In another one, to which in her selection she gave first place, she reveals not only her burning sense of human values, and her contempt for an unspiritual (because selfish and calculating) otherworldliness, but a sure and searching literary judgment. The subject is Edward Young, of the *Night Thoughts*, whose "religion exhausts itself in ejaculations and rebukes, and knows no medium between the ecstatic and the sententious. If it were not for the prospect of immortality, he considers, it would be wise and agreeable to be indecent, or to murder one's father; and, heaven apart, it would be extremely irrational in any man not to be a knave." It is this huckster morality, this contemptible contempt for disinterested goodness, that provokes her sharpest satire: she returns to it again and again. With all this, she says, "our new-made divine is an unmistakable poet. To a clay compounded chiefly of the worldling and the rhetorician, there is added a real spark of Promethean fire. He will one day clothe his apostrophes and objurgations, his astronomical religion and his charnel-house morality, in lasting verse, which will stand, like a Juggernaut made of gold and jewels, at once magnificent and repulsive." A poet he is, at moments, in spite of himself (she seems to imply) and in spite of his God. For the God of the *Night Thoughts*

is simply Young himself "writ large" . . . Young has no conception of religion as anything else than egoism turned heavenward; and he does not merely imply this, he insists on it. Religion, he tells us, in argumentative passages too long to quote, is "ambition, pleasure, and the love of gain," directed towards the joys of the future life instead of the present. And his ethics correspond to his religion. . . . Virtue, with

Young, must always squint—must never look straight towards
the immediate object of its emotion and effort. Thus, if a
man risks perishing in the snow himself rather than forsake
a weaker comrade, he must either do this because his hopes
and fears are directed to another world, or because he desires
to applaud himself afterwards! Young, if we may believe him,
would despise the action as folly unless it had these motives.
Let us hope he was not so bad as he pretended to be! The
tides of the divine life in man move under the thickest ice of
theory.

The conviction expressed in that last sentence is perhaps
the root of George Eliot's wide spiritual charity. However
much she may detest a man's opinions she is always ready
to believe the best of his humanity. This point links up
with what she has later to say about Cowper, in comparing
him with Young. Both men were attached to a dogmatic
Christianity, and on some grounds we might have antici-
pated a more morbid view of things from Cowper than
from Young, for Cowper's formal beliefs were actually
the more gloomy.

Yet see how a lovely, sympathetic nature manifests itself in
spite of creed and circumstance! . . . How Cowper's exquisite mind falls with the mild warmth of morning sunlight
on the commonest objects, at once disclosing every detail
and investing every detail with beauty! No object is too
small to prompt his song . . . and yet his song is never trivial,
for he is alive to small objects, not because his mind is narrow, but because his glance is clear and his heart is large. . . .
In Young we have the type of that deficient human sympathy, that impiety towards the present and the visible, which
flies for its motives, its sanctities, and its religion, to the remote, the vague, and the unknown; in Cowper we have the

type of that genuine love which cherishes things in proportion to their nearness, and feels reverence grow in proportion to the intimacy of its knowledge.

The comparison is useful and the contrast clear. But it is chiefly valuable to us for the light it throws, not on Cowper or Young, but on George Eliot. In such passages as this she reveals herself—her mind, her heart, her religious intuition—more luminously, because less deliberately and categorically, than in arguing for "a belief in necessity," urging "resignation to individual nothingness," and repudiating "hope unsustained by reason," as she does in a letter to Chapman. These phrases can all be defended. They are a salutary corrective to shallow philosophic complacencies. But they belong, as formulated, to the top layer of the mind; they are intellectual formulas which may suggest but cannot contain the ultimate truth; and it was not through them, it was in other and deeper channels, that the "tides of the divine life"—her own phrase—flowed in George Eliot.

## Chapter Three

## MARRIAGE WITH LEWES

### I

ARRIAGE it was, in every vital sense. To call it anything else would be the merest quibbling. In fact as in intention it was the coming together and living together of a man and woman for better for worse, for richer for poorer, in sickness and in health, till death them did part. And that is marriage.

The biographers of George Eliot have in general done something less than justice to Lewes. He is accorded perfunctory praise for his devotion (except by those who denounce him for his "selfishness"), and given credit for having been an entertaining talker; but it is too often implied, and occasionally stated, that both intellectually and morally he was no match for George Eliot. Now that is at least a debatable proposition. The true disparity between them is that she was a creative artist and he was not. She was destined to become, as he was not, a great figure in English literature. But I see no reason to suppose, as some have supposed, that she did not enjoy with him a rich intellectual companionship. As for their respective moral statures, here it was a question not of disparity but of difference, a difference in temperament, upbringing, and opportunity. Up to the time of their meeting she had lived a life of solemn if reluctant rectitude, and he (it is surmised, for nothing positive is known) had practiced as well as preached a high-flown doctrine of "free love";

but from that time onward his devotion was extravagant, his fidelity absolute. It is arguable that Lewes in maturity was none the worse, but merely the wiser, for his youthful follies; and certainly he paid in full for the fatuous ideal-ism which had led him to share house and wife with his friend, Thornton Hunt. For the rest, he was a first-rate journalist, a lively dramatic critic, a good judge of litera-ture, a brilliant talker, a lucid exponent of ideas, and a dili-gent field naturalist. He had nothing of George Eliot's creative gift, but he had qualities which she lacked and which were complemental to hers.

In his book on the Victorian age, G. K. Chesterton, re-butting a silly suggestion (which no one, so far as I know, had ever made) that George Eliot's novels were really written by Lewes, refers to Lewes' book on Robespierre as a "crushing opiate." The remark is just so far as it goes, but it would be still more just to add that the Robespierre is perhaps the flattest thing Lewes ever did. His dramatic criticism has a crisp and sparkling quality. His *Life of Goethe*, with all its faults, is still read and enjoyed. In short, he was not the libertine, the self-seeking adven-turer, the pretentious dullard, which he is sometimes rep-resented to have been. He was a man of considerable parts and tireless industry.[1] Let us glance at his personal history prior to his wooing and winning of Marian Evans.

George Henry Lewes, youngest son of John Lee Lewes, and grandson of the once-celebrated comic actor, Charles Lee Lewes, was born in London in April, 1817, two and a half years earlier than Marian Evans. His father had been manager for a while of the Theatre Royal at Liverpool, and was author of some memoirs of Charles Lee Lewes and

1. For specimen passages from Lewes' writing, see Appendix III.

two volumes of verse. His wife, George's mother, was of Devon stock. She outlived her first husband and married a second, a retired sea captain named Willim, and died at a great age in 1870, valued to the last by her one surviving son, George. George seems to have picked up his oddly miscellaneous education in a fashion that foreshadowed the diversity of his later career, going from school to school, in London, Jersey, Brittany, and finally Dr. Burney's school at Dulwich, as afterward he drifted from one occupation to another. His versatility and quickness of mind must have manifested themselves early, and it is not surprising if, with this kind of upbringing, he exhibited some wayward tendencies in his young manhood: the surprising thing is rather that so many of his several enthusiasms took such deep root.

After leaving school he was projected first into a notary's office, then into a merchant's countinghouse, and then, presumably by his own whim, into the study of anatomy. At an informal club which met in a tavern in Red Lion Square he consorted with other greatly aspiring young men. "The members," he wrote thirty years later,

were men whose sole point of junction was the Saturday meeting, or whose sole object was the admirable collision of contending views on subjects which at one time or other perplex and stimulate all reflecting minds. On every other day in the week their paths were widely divergent. One kept a second-hand bookstall, rich in free-thinking literature; another was a journeyman watchmaker; a third lived on a moderate income; a fourth was a bootmaker; a fifth "penned a stanza when he should engross"; a sixth [Lewes himself] studied anatomy and many other things, with vast aspirations

and no very definite career before him. . . . They came for
philosophic talk, and they talked.

Here we have the prototype of the workingmen's club
in *Daniel Deronda* to which George Eliot devoted some of
the most labored and lifeless pages that ever came from her
pen; and in Lewes' Jewish watchmaker, Cohn or Cohen
by name, we have unmistakably the model for her Mordecai. Lewes describes him as a calm, meditative, amiable
man, very poor, with weak eyes and chest, grave and
gentle in demeanor, and incorruptible even by the seduc-
tions of vanity. He adds:

I habitually think of him in connection with Spinoza, almost
as much on account of his personal characteristics as because
to him I owe my first acquaintance with the Hebrew thinker.
I venerated his great calm intellect. An immense pity and a
fervid indignation filled me as I came away from his attic in
one of the Holborn Courts, where I had seen him in the
pinching poverty of his home, with his German wife and
two little black-eyed children: indignantly I railed against
society, which could allow so great an intellect to withdraw
itself from nobler work and waste the precious hours in
mending watches. But he was wiser in his resignation than I
in my young indignation. Life was hard to him as to all of us;
but he was content to earn a miserable pittance by handi-
craft and keep his soul serene. I learned to understand him
better when I learned the story of Spinoza's life.

Lewes was already a zealot of science and an enemy of
supernaturalism, but Spinoza's vastly conceived mathe-
matical mysticism fascinated him, and it was perhaps Spinoza who prepared his mind for Auguste Comte's trium-
phal entry in later years.

Like all conspicuously talented young men, and like young men not so talented, he had his due share of "blooming gaseous folly" (Stevenson's phrase, quoted of himself by Bernard Shaw): his friend William Bell Scott, designer and poet, failed to persuade him that he was too young to be writing tragic dramas of love. He had also, however, an exuberant humor, a lively wit, and an astonishing flow of language. Naturally enough, in view of his ancestry, he was in love with the theater and never forgot seeing Macready play the part of Sardanapalus at Drury Lane. In his Red Lion Square days he seems to have enjoyed a sense of being frowned upon on account of his heterodoxy and had, he tells us, a rebellious sympathy with all outcasts. The problems of religion and philosophy were of absorbing interest to him: he read everything he could get hold of in these subjects, and in literature generally. He had moreover the luck to become acquainted with Leigh Hunt, that excellent talker and genial friend of aspiring youth, and father of the Thornton Hunt who was to play so significant a part in his later life. In 1838 he visited Germany, mastered the language, and saturated himself in German philosophy and literature; later he set up in London as a free-lance journalist and established friendly relations with (among others) John Stuart Mill, who treated him with great kindness and gave him excellent technical advice; and in 1841, at the age of twenty-three, he married his "child-wife" Agnes Jervis, who was then nineteen and "one of the loveliest creatures in the world."

The exact sequence of events thereafter is not known to us, but in 1842 we find the George Leweses, the Thornton Hunts, and other young couples, engaged together in an experiment in communal housekeeping in Bayswater, a "phalanstery" seeking to embody the doctrines of François Fourier (1772–1837). Thornton and his sister Jacinta having married, respectively, Kate Gliddon and her brother John, the Hunts and the Gliddons were doubly united; and the Leweses were united to both by the bonds of friendship and shared opinions. Eliza Lynn Linton, a forgotten novelist, has left an unsympathetic but not unilluminating account of this group. Her impressions are those of an easily shocked girl of eighteen (as she was when she first encountered these ardent Bohemians) remembered a lifetime later by the disappointed woman she became. Her evidence, in this as in the more important matter of Lewes' broken marriage and Thornton Hunt's part in it, must therefore be taken with more than a grain of salt. Nevertheless it tells us something. Eliza Lynn, as she then was, was evidently shocked by the libertarian opinions both of Thornton Hunt and of George Lewes; but Thornton she liked, in spite of those opinions, whereas for George she had evidently a strong antipathy. She dwells on his personal ugliness, and she was offended by the freedom of his manners.

To Lewes' ugliness there is abundant testimony, but a gay vivacity seems to have made amends for it. His skin was pitted by smallpox, but he had, says Francis Espinasse in his *Literary Recollections* (1893), a fine eye and an expressive countenance which when lighted up by a smile was far from disagreeable. Even the hostile Eliza Lynn speaks of the "wonderful expressiveness of his eyes" which, with his brightness and versatility, "made one forget the unlovely rest." The Carlyles, Thomas and Jane, dubbed him "The Ape." Carlyle found him tiresomely persistent, deprecated his iconoclasm, and had nothing good to say of his attempts at novel writing. Lewes as a young man was of an aggressively sanguine temper, genially boastful, somewhat pushing, and altogether too full of himself and his enthusiasms for sober, middle-aged tastes. Espinasse gives an amusing eyewitness account of how Lewes, having sent Carlyle a copy of his just-published *Rose, Blanche, and Violet*, interrupted a tête-à-tête between himself and the great man with no other object than to discover what he thought of the novel, and how Carlyle, by dint of ingenious digressions, avoided committing himself on the subject. Mrs. Carlyle privately pronounced the work "execrable"; and indeed neither fiction, which he soon abandoned, nor playwriting, which he tried later, was Lewes' strong suit. But both she and her husband were won over, in course of time, to a better opinion of him. After the collapse of his marriage he ceased to be "The Ape" for her and became—for a while at any rate —"poor dear Lewes." And Carlyle himself, after the establishment of the *Leader*, declared him to be "the prince of journalists."

The *Leader*, planned and largely created by George Lewes and Thornton Leigh Hunt, made journalistic history. It was the first of the English critical weeklies. From its beginning in 1850 till his elopement with Marian Evans in 1854 Lewes was its literary editor and a most copious contributor, writing book reviews, dramatic criticism, general articles, and, under the pseudonym of "Vivian," a great deal of high-spirited nonsense. He handled literature and the drama, science and philosophy, all with equal competence and assurance. He was a brilliant editor (as he was to prove again later on the *Fortnightly Review*) and secured the anonymous services of several of the good and great who were too respectable to wish their names to be associated with a radical paper, among them Marian's friend Herbert Spencer; but it is clear that he himself, George Henry Lewes, was the life and soul of the enterprise. Since we have it on Cross's authority that he had been wifeless for at least two years before the fateful July, 1854, it must have been during the early years of this tremendous journalistic activity that his marriage with "one of the loveliest creatures in the world" was drifting to disaster. To apportion blame is happily not our business, and certainly it is not necessary to blacken either Thornton Hunt or Agnes Lewes in order to exculpate Marian Evans. For she, Marian, had on any showing nothing whatever to do with it. Lewes himself can hardly escape some responsibility, since he apparently subscribed, with Thornton and others of the group, to the doctrine that love is a law unto itself, a doctrine which, however disastrous in practice, may be justly described as airy and idiotic rather than wicked or base. But what may well have begun in a spirit of generous and humorless idealism ended in unhappiness, at least for Lewes; and it was done, we are assured, with at any rate his nominal consent.

The admitted facts are that Agnes fell in love with Thornton and bore him two children while still living as Lewes' wife. The rest is largely conjecture. Whether Lewes allowed himself a similar latitude in sexual behavior is not positively known. Eliza Lynn fervently insists that he did, but Eliza, as we have seen, is a prejudiced witness, and one with an admitted grudge against George Eliot, whom she disliked at sight, when she first met her, and who had conspicuously succeeded where she, Eliza, had failed. What is both significant and important is that Lewes, the victim (if so it was) of his own crazy logic, had the dignity and justice to refrain from reproaches. It is true that Eliza Lynn sets herself to "redeem the character of Thornton Hunt from the undeserved reproaches cast on it by those whose interest it was to blacken him that another might be whitewashed," but I can find no record of these "reproaches," and Lewes' subsequent behavior toward Agnes, his unremitting interest in her welfare and that of her children by Hunt, makes it highly unlikely that they came from him. His only recorded complaints are concerned with Thornton's mismanagement (or worse) of Agnes' finances. Anna T. Kitchel, in her admirable study of the subject, says roundly that one can find no evidence of one side's blaming the other. "During years of utmost devotion to the woman chosen in his maturity for his mate, whose congeniality of mind and nobility of character he rested on, Lewes was not forgetful of the debt he owed to the woman who had been his girl-wife." [2] The statement is supported by a series of citations from Lewes' private diary, one of which, the entry for August 13, 1859, records how he "took Pug to Agnes, who was delighted with him, as were the children"—the children being, of course, Agnes' children by Thornton Hunt. Agnes outlived Thornton Hunt by twenty-eight years, and Lewes by twenty-four, dying in 1902 at the age of eighty. Marian herself continued the allowance to her after Lewes' death, and after Marian's death the Charles Leweses supported her. Of the four principals in the drama, Agnes was the last to make her exit.

2. Anna T. Kitchel, *George Lewes and George Eliot* (New York, John Day Company, 1933).

That Lewes in the early eighteen-fifties was an unhappy man, and that he confided his unhappiness and its cause to Marian Evans, is not in doubt. Whatever his theories, and whatever his precepts, it cannot have been pleasant to him to learn that his wife no longer loved him and that her child was not his. Some hint of reproach, however unjustified by logical consistency, might perhaps have been forgiven him. But there is no evidence that anything of the kind escaped him. "George Lewes and Thornton Hunt," writes Thornton's champion, Eliza Lynn,[3]

were essentially freethinkers—not only on theological questions, but on all moral and social matters whatsoever, beginning at the beginning and working upwards to the apex. Their views on marriage were those of Grant Allen and the modern school of New Hedonists. Love alone was the sole priest needed—confession and inclination made the one binding tie and ceremony. Legal obligation was to them the remnant of a foregone barbarism, and enforced permanency was unholy tyranny. I have heard this matter discussed and debated scores of times, and with ever the same intellectual weapons.

But, though their actions were identical, she continues, the two men were widely different. Thornton "loved where he should not, but so far as the intrinsic purity of a nature can redeem the wrong of an action, his nature redeemed his actions. His total freedom from grossness concentrated the blame attaching to him on the wrongheadedness of his principles." Not so Lewes. He, Lewes, had "nothing of that strain of asceticism leading to martyrdom which ran through his friend's character" and which presumably, by a somewhat circuitous route, led in fact to his becoming

3. Eliza Lynn Linton, *My Literary Life* (London, 1899).

the father of two children by Lewes' wife. Life to Lewes, this ingenuous witness declares,

meant love and pleasure; and he had that bright and expansive quality which makes pleasure and finds it everywhere. In work and in idleness, in the *sans façon* of Bohemianism and in the more orderly amusements of conventional society, in scientific discussion and in empty persiflage, he was equally at home; and wherever he went there was a patch of intellectual sunshine in the room.

## II

Such was the man whom, one day in 1851, Herbert Spencer took with him to call on Marian Evans at 142 Strand. "It was through him," wrote Lewes eight years later, "that I learned to know Marian—to know her was to love her—and since then my life has been a new birth. To her I owe all my prosperity and all my happiness." She, from a full heart, was to say as much of him, both in letters to friends and in inscribing to him the manuscripts of her successive books; but it is clear that she did not love him at sight. Their first casual encounter had happened earlier in the same year. "I was introduced to Lewes the other day in Jeff's shop—a sort of miniature Mirabeau in appearance." That was in September. In November, in a letter to the Brays, she reports Lewes as having said that his article on *Julia von Krüdener*, which he was writing for the *Westminster Review*, would be glorious: "He sat in the same box with us [Marian and Spencer?] at the Merry Wives of Windsor, and helped to carry off the dolorousness of the play." In March, 1853, she writes: "We had a pleasant evening last Wednesday. Lewes, as always, genial and amusing. He has quite won my liking, in spite of myself." And a month later: "People are very good to me. Mr. Lewes especially is kind and attentive, and has quite won my regard, after having had a good deal of my vituperation. Like a few other people in the world, he is much better than he seems. A man of heart and conscience wearing a mask of flippancy."

We know nothing in detail of the progress of this friendship, and its ripening into love; but clearly it was no sudden growth. In October, 1853, Marian removed from Chapman's house to lodgings at 21 Cambridge Street, Edgware Road. Here she was able to see Lewes with a freedom and frequency which they could not have enjoyed in the populous household at 142 Strand; and here, it is supposed, he confided to her the story of his ruined marriage. When the question of their going away together was first mooted, and for how long it was anxiously and conscientiously considered before a decision was reached, are also unknown to us. On these points they took no one into their confidence, then or later, so far as our evidence goes. Mrs. Bray, however, may well have had an uneasy feeling that something she would not approve of was in the wind; for she could hardly have failed to notice how often, in the spring of 1854, Lewes' name cropped up in her friend's letters, and was perhaps disturbed by the quasi-maternal color of these allusions.

Perhaps it was with the idea of tactfully preparing her friend for the worst that Marian mentioned her concern for Lewes in three successive letters during April and May. April 18:

I am rather overdone with the week's work, and the prospect of what is to come next. Poor Lewes is ill, and is ordered not to put pen to paper for a month; so I have something to do for him in addition to my own work, which is rather pressing. He is gone to Arthur Helps, in Hampshire, for ten days, and I really hope this total cessation from work, in obedience to a peremptory order, will end in making him better than he has been for the last year. No opera and no fun for me for the next month!

May 23: "Mr. Lewes is going on a walking excursion to Windsor to-day with his doctor, who pronounced him better, but not yet fit for work. However, he is obliged to do a little, and must content himself with an *approximation* to his doctor's directions." Later in May: "I expect to see Mr. Lewes back again to-day. His poor head—his only fortune—is not well yet; and he has had the misery of being ennuyé with idleness, without perceiving the compensating physical improvement. Still, I hope the good he has been getting has been greater than he is conscious of." July 10th, to Sara Hennell: "I shall soon send you a good-bye, for I am preparing to go abroad." And on July 20 comes the famous letter of farewell: "Dear Friends—all three—I have only time to say good-bye, and God bless you. Post restante, Weimar, for the next six weeks, and afterwards Berlin. Ever your loving and grateful Marian."

Had her carefully composed hints prepared them for the shock? For a shock it undoubtedly was, to these professedly emancipated spirits. The Brays made no secret of their disapproval, and Marian neither resented it nor reproached them for it. Her brother Isaac disowned her in disgust. Her sister Chrissie maintained a godly silence for five years, and then broke it to announce that she was ill (she was in fact dying of consumption). Marian accepted her cold-shouldering without complaint, as the price she must pay for being happy in her own way. She firmly believed that she was doing right, but was not so ingenuous as to imagine that the world would agree with her.

The entry in her journal for July 20, the day on which her new life began, reveals nothing of the tumult that must have possessed her. It records, without comment, that she said a last farewell to Cambridge Street and found herself on board the *Ravensbourne,* bound for Antwerp.

The day was glorious, and our passage perfect. The sunset was lovely, but still lovelier the dawn as we were passing up the Scheldt between two and three in the morning. The crescent moon, the stars, the first faint blush of the dawn reflected in the glassy river, the dark mass of clouds on the horizon, which sent forth flashes of lightning, and the graceful forms of the boats and sailing vessels, painted in jet-black on the reddish gold of the sky and water, made up an unforgettable picture. Then the sun rose and lighted up the sleepy shores of Belgium, with their fringe of long grass, their rows of poplars, their church spires and farm buildings.

A singularly unrevealing entry, and not even particularly good writing: any careful young lady composing a school essay could do as well. But epithalamiums were not in Marian's line, and it must be supposed that she did not confide her heart's secrets to her journal. We may be grateful for this, for the tender passages in her letters are apt to be cloying: she is at her best as an advocate, whether in defense or attack, or as pure narrator. Three months after leaving England with Lewes, that is on October 23, 1854, she had occasion to write to Charles Bray. The letter is of such extraordinary importance that it must be given entire. It was not printed by Cross.

62a Kaufgasse, Weimar.

Dear Friend,

I yesterday wrote to my brother to request that he would pay my income to you on the 1st of December. I also requested that, in future, he would pay my half yearly income into the Coventry and Warwickshire Bank, that I might order it to be sent to me wherever I wanted it, as he has sometimes sent me a cheque which I could not get cashed in London. Is there anything to be done—any notice given to the Bank in order to make this plan feasible?

It is possible that you have already heard a report prevalent in London that Mr. Lewes has "run away" from his wife and family. I wish you to be in possession of the facts which will enable you to contradict this report whenever it reaches you. Since we left England he has been in constant correspondence with his wife; she has had all the money due to him in London; and his children are his principal thought and anxiety. Circumstances with which I am not concerned, and which have arisen since he left England, have led him to determine on a separation from Mrs. Lewes, but he has never contemplated that separation as a total release from responsibility towards her. On the contrary he has been anxiously waiting restoration to health that he may once more work hard, not only to provide for his children, but to supply his wife's wants so far as that is not done by another. I have seen all the correspondence between them, and it has assured me that his conduct as a husband has been not only irreproachable, but generous and self-sacrificing to a degree far beyond any standard fixed by the world. This is the simple truth and no flattering picture drawn by my partiality.

I have been long enough with Mr. Lewes to judge of his character on adequate grounds, and there is therefore no absurdity in offering my opinion as evidence that he is worthy of high respect. He has written to Carlyle and Robert Chambers stating as much of the truth as he can without very severely inculpating the other persons concerned; Arthur Helps, who has been here since we came, already knew the whole truth, and I trust that these three rational friends will be able in time to free his character from the false imputations which malice and gossip have cast upon it.

Of course many silly myths are already afloat about me, in addition to the truth, which of itself would be thought matter for scandal. I am quite unconcerned about them except as they may cause pain to my real friends. If you can hear of anything that I have said, done, or written in relation to Mr. Lewes, beyond the simple fact that I am attached to him and that I am living with him, do me the justice to believe that it is false. Mr. and Mrs. Chapman are the only persons to whom I have ever spoken of his private position and of my relation to him, and the only influence I should ever dream of exerting over him as to his conduct towards his wife and children is that of stimulating his conscientious care for them, if it needed any stimulus.

Pray pardon this long letter on a painful subject. I felt it a duty to write it.

I am ignorant how far Cara and Sara may be acquainted with the state of things, and how they may feel towards me. I am quite prepared to accept the consequences of a step which I have deliberately taken and to accept them without irritation or bitterness. The most painful consequences will, I know, be the loss of friends. If I do not write, therefore, understand that it is because I desire not to obtrude myself.

Write to me soon and let me know how things are with you. I am full of affection towards you all, and whatever you may think of me, shall always be

Your true and grateful friend,

Marian Evans.[4]

4. Gordon S. Haight, *George Eliot and John Chapman.*

## III

Solemn discussion of the ethics of her situation, of whether she did right or wrong in consenting to marry Lewes without the help of clergy or registrar, is all but impossible today; and in the present climate of opinion, so different from that of a hundred years ago, it would seem to be unnecessary. It was declared so even in the eighteen-eighties, when Cross's ultradiscreet *Life* first appeared, but when those early critics and commentators pronounced the word "unnecessary" it was with an air of averting their eyes from a distasteful subject, of drawing a veil over the unmentionable: a difficult policy to defend, for since the fact was not in doubt the how and why of it could hardly be dismissed as irrelevant.

Few nowadays will be found to agree with R. H. Hutton that George Eliot's action constituted "a grave step downwards . . . a breach with a moral law which the great majority of men hold to be the essence of social purity": commenting upon which pronouncement an American writer in 1886 aptly says: "Clearly it was a breach of the civil law; but to make it also a breach of the moral law, must we not convict the parties of something like wrongful intent? What if on their part and in their own minds it was simply a refusal to identify the moral law with the law of Parliament? What if they simply meant to affirm that where the *fact* of separation is fully accomplished, the *decree* of separation, however desirable, is not vital?" Even the proposition that it was a breach of the civil law is perhaps questionable. If conceded, it leads to the amusing paradox that the only legal penalty provided for that breach was precisely the one which Lewes and Marian would most eagerly have welcomed, namely the dissolution by decree of Lewes' former marriage.

The truth surely is that the civil law of marriage is designed primarily for the protection of individuals against unscrupulous usage, and before Lewes and Marian Evans could be convicted of wrongdoing, it would have to be shown that some injury had been suffered by his wife and children. But in fact no one was injured, or even professed to be. The wife was deprived of nothing, and the children were provided with a foster mother who loved and cherished them as they did her. Greatly to the embarrassment and ill-concealed resentment of those who hold that the essence of marriage resides in its legality, which is like saying that the essence of being hanged resides in the proper enunciation of the death sentence, even the reprobators of Marian's action found themselves obliged to admit that from this "great evil"—as one writer calls it—there issued nothing but good to the persons most concerned: to Marian, to Lewes, to Lewes' children, and even, indirectly, to Lewes' wife.

"Since the publication of her life," wrote Margaret Lonsdale plaintively, "even silence is no longer left to us." And so, in the 'eighties, it becomes necessary for the admirers of George Eliot to take sides on this question. Those who condemn her do so more in sorrow than anger, and those who defend her weaken their case by special pleading. Mr. Lewes, we are told, must have possessed "a more than common share of the selfishness of men kind in general, or he could not have deliberately cast a moral and social blight upon George Eliot's life, by inducing her to stifle her womanly nature so far as to consent to live with him in dishonour." On the other hand we are asked to believe that George Eliot heroically sacrificed her good name for the sake of succoring, and saving from despair, an injured husband and his motherless brood.

Now whatever Lewes may have done he plainly did not induce Marian Evans to stifle her "womanly nature." On the contrary, he fulfilled that deepest need of her being for "someone who should be all in all to her and to whom she should be all in all." He advised and encouraged her, watched over her health, nursed and cosseted her talent, and, himself a writer, was content to live in the shadow of her larger glory. Equally certain is it, to my mind, that she entered into the relationship, not lightly indeed, and not without a consciousness of what social discomfort it might involve, but freely and willingly and with no sense of giving more than she received. What nettled the conventional moralists was not so much that she "sinned" as that her sinning was crowned with happiness.

To the mutual devotion of the pair there is abundant testimony. It flourished mightily for twenty years, till Lewes' death. They enjoyed an exceptionally happy marriage, and we need make no more of it than that. Irritated by the sentimentalities of the George Eliot cult, a reviewer of Cross's book in the periodical called *Temple Bar* justly remarks that her union with Lewes, "which her fame exalted into an epic poem, was a very simple, natural, and commonplace arrangement between two people who loved each other and who could not marry by any law of any land." If there was any sacrifice involved, it was as much on his part as hers. The reviewer just quoted, though animated by an hostility amounting to spite, has the fairness to admit, or rather to declare, that Lewes' life was one long act of devotion to Marian and their joint interests, "to making her as happy, and keeping her mind as tranquil, as her morbid temperament and frail health permitted; protecting her from every annoyance, making himself the fender to keep her free from the slightest shock or abrasion, surrounding her with a certain halo of almost sacred mystery, keeping her in a state of almost regal exclusiveness, and employing all his histrionic powers to perfecting the *mise en scene* and the attitude to be taken on the boards." This devotion, the article continues, "was a curious interlacing of selfishness and unselfishness. He [Lewes] made his own account by it, both pecuniarily and socially; but it shows the lovable side of the man as well as the more ignoble."

We notice, however, that this writer [5] is never more malicious than when pretending to a judicial impartiality. It had already been implied, earlier in the article, that Lewes had not "one touch of delicacy of conscience, of sensitiveness of fibre," and was ruthlessly intent on doing the best for himself, no matter at whose expense. This is the "ignoble side" of him which now, having taken due note of his twenty years of unremitting devotion, we are invited to remember. The phrase links up with the remark about his "pecuniary" profit and his "histrionic powers." The implication of "pecuniary" is that his love was not disinterested, that he seduced Marian Evans in order to possess himself of her earnings. Baldly stated this would be palpably false: therefore it is not baldly stated but merely insinuated, in the hope that we shall not notice the logical absurdity of it. Absurd it is, for the obvious reason

5. Anonymity was *Temple Bar's* rule, but the writer of this article is known to have been Eliza Lynn Linton, whose moral judgments we have had an opportunity of admiring earlier in this chapter.

that Lewes, not being possessed of supernatural knowledge, could not have foreseen the emergence of that talent
for fiction which was to make her a comparatively rich
woman in years to come. No sign of any such talent appeared until 1857, four years after the beginning of their
life together. His sustained devotion was "a curious interlacing of selfishness and unselfishness," was it? Possibly,
but only in the sense in which every true marriage can be
so described, and it was none the worse for that. In such
a context "selfishness" and "unselfishness" tend to lose
their meaning, shade off into each other, become inextri-
cably mixed. Is it unselfish for a man to devote himself to
a woman he loves? Is it selfish for him to receive unexpected material (as well as spiritual) benefits which she
delights to bestow? Had Lewes been more noble, less
selfish, what could he have done that he did not do? Could
he have demonstrated his nobility by breaking with her,
and breaking her heart, so soon as she was discovered to
be a source of revenue? Only so could he have avoided
sharing in her good fortune. As for this stage managing of
the situation, at which we are invited to curl the lip, that
can only be accounted to his credit. That he overdid it,
that he surrounded his protégée with an excess of dignity,
must be accounted to the credit of his heart, if not of his
judgment: it was his way, we must suppose, of offsetting
the social irregularity of her position. It was perhaps a
mistake; to us today it may seem unnecessary, pompous,
and lacking in humor; but we can hardly doubt that it was
what she wanted, nor deny that it argues in him just that
"delicacy of conscience" which we are told he lacked.

These contemporary moral judgments would hardly be
worth citing but for the opportunity they provide of

discussing the main points at issue. And they do, taken together, most beautifully cancel each other out. On the one hand it is contended, as we have seen, that Lewes deliberately cast "a moral and social blight" upon George Eliot's life, and on the other that he profited, not only "pecuniarily," but "socially," by the transaction. The talented fellow first destroys her socially and then basks in her social glory! We are entitled, moreover, to ask what sort of a social blight it was that allowed her, during the twenty years of her illicit union, to enjoy the friendship and esteem of such people as Herbert Spencer, T. H. Huxley, Frederic Harrison, Lord Houghton, Turgenev, Buxton Forman, Mark Pattison, Anthony Trollope, Lord Acton, F. W. H. Myers, W. K. Clifford, Edward Burne-Jones, Millais, Browning, and Tennyson.[6] Minor snubs and annoyances she may well have suffered in the early days, and certainly it irked her to be in a position that was in any way open to question, for we know she was almost morbidly sensitive to criticism. But a woman who is sought out and made much of by nearly all the distinguished men and women of her day can hardly be said to have lived a socially blighted life.

Discussion of this problem has continued at intervals into our own day. A French writer, M. Bourl'honne,[7] approaches it from the angle of a critic who, as the biog-

6. These, all but one, are a selection from thirty-nine names mentioned by Mathilde Blind, the first of the biographers. Twelve of the thirty-nine are women, and, for the assurance of the snobbish, there is a sprinkling of titles among them. The name I have added is that of Lord Acton, historian and Roman Catholic, who wrote, at the time of her death: "It seems to me as if the sun had gone out. You cannot think how much I loved her." (Quoted by Elizabeth S. Haldane, *George Eliot and Her Times* [London, 1927].)

7. P. Bourl'honne, *George Eliot: essai de biographie intellectuelle et morale.*

rapher primarily of her inner life, is concerned not so much to offer his own moral judgment upon George Eliot's action—though he does that too—as to discover to us what hers was. His conclusions are (1) that she was decisively influenced in favor of the alliance with Lewes by the doctrines of Feuerbach, whose *Das Wesen des Christenthums* she translated into English, (2) that she bitterly repented of it to her dying day, (3) that she suffered from a profound sense of moral guilt, and (4) that her work was a (conscious or unconscious?) attempt to expiate her "fault," the said "fault," which she "committed in 1853 in seeking her happiness," being "visibly written throughout her work." The first of these propositions has perhaps a certain plausibility, but the others would seem to be pure guesswork.

H. G. Wells's Mr. Polly had a rule of his own for the pronunciation of unfamiliar English words: it was, never to be misled by the spelling. M. Bourl'honne's rule in this particular piece of psychobiography is never to be misled by the evidence, or at any rate by the evidence that lies upon the surface. He thinks that George Eliot's biographers have been disingenuous in this matter, and he is inclined to suspect that the evidence on the surface has been (not invented but) carefully planted there, by herself and her friends, in the hope of placating the censorious. He dismisses as ill founded what he regards as an attempt to represent her misdemeanor as a conscious protest against oppressive and illiberal marriage laws, arguing, cogently enough, that however broad her views on marriage may have been, her general philosophy, tending so decidedly toward conservatism, must have disposed her rather to respect social institutions than to overthrow them.

True, but to rebut one piece of special pleading does not automatically justify another. There is no question but that Marian Evans would have married Lewes in due legal form had he been free. Her decision to live with him without legal marriage was determined not by doctrinaire considerations but by practical common sense. Her conservatism, her disposition to respect social institutions, was a matter not of principle but of temperament; and we have, I believe, no right and no reason to suppose that she was conscious, then or afterward, of wrongdoing. The most we can concede is that she was anxious lest her example should be seized upon by the light-minded as an excuse for sexual license. That is quite a different thing from feeling guilty. Nowhere in her general philosophy is there any suggestion that individual happiness must be at the mercy of arbitrary rules of conduct. In her immaturity, under the spell of a Calvinistic version of Christianity, she did indeed preach renunciation for its own sake; but that was a juvenile phase of opinion; and there is nothing in her later, adult philosophy inconsistent with the maxim that the individual has a right to seek (or at any rate to accept) his own happiness provided that in doing so he does not impair that of others.

But there is also, M. Bourl'honne contends, the evidence of her work, which he believes to have been "inspirée d'un sentiment de réparation par rapport à sa vie." I would amend this last sentence to read "par rapport à son exemple," and even so it would be an overstatement and an oversimplification of the truth. For she could not, I think, have disapproved of her example being followed in like circumstances and in all particulars: what she feared was that it might be, not followed, but misinterpreted—by people unacquainted with the whole story—as an encouragement to disorderly living. Her own life was in fact a model of decorum. Between her life and her work there is no moral inconsistency, and to represent her as haunted by a lifelong sense of guilt is melodramatic nonsense. One does not contend that George Eliot suffered no social discomfort whatever on account of her situation, or that there was no matter for regret. Being what she was she must certainly have regretted that she could not be legally married to the man of her choice. But, quite as certainly, so far as evidence goes, she did not regret having chosen and accepted him. No doubt a sense of her equivocal position, enhancing the personal diffidence from which she had always suffered, impelled her to embrace a life of comparative social seclusion. It was not pleasant to know that some of her oldest friends disapproved of her, and to make it a rule never to invite anyone to come and see her who did not ask for the invitation. It was mortifying to have to ask correspondents to address her as Mrs. Lewes. And it may be she was overeager to justify herself. But that she sought to justify herself to others does not prove, or necessarily suggest, that she felt any need to justify herself to herself. If I have committed an act which in ninety-nine cases is a felony and in the hundredth no worse than an indiscretion, does it argue a feeling of guilt in me that I should be eager to show that my case is the hundredth? If I endorse a check in another man's name, will it be held against me that I am in a great hurry to pay it into his account? And will it not be forgiven me that

I am a little loquacious about it? George Eliot was—how could she not be?—painfully conscious of having broken a social rule. But that does not imply that she believed herself to have committed a sin in doing so. She was a religious woman, and it is only the irreligious (whatever creed they profess) who accept *vox populi vox Dei* as their sole guiding principle. She lived according to her own lights, though she was very far from indifferent to the good opinions of others. This indeed was the crux of her situation. Far from indifferent though she was to the good opinion of others, she nevertheless lived by her own lights.

M. Bourl'honne freely admits, in a long footnote, that she found much happiness in her life with Lewes. She found first of all love, he says, and, what was not less necessary to her, someone who was absolutely devoted to "sa propre personne"; she found an intellectual and moral entente which, no less than the affection with which she felt herself to be surrounded, enabled her to surrender herself with a free mind to her artistic vocation and to the cultivation of spiritual values. But this entente, he adds, was not without a certain melancholy: Lewes (the argument continues) was morally inferior to George Eliot; his union with her was in all respects to his advantage; he broke with a past marked by levity, egoism, and sensuality, and he paid in love and devotion for the life of dignity which he was able to build up at her side. The sense that she was exercising a good influence on him must have been very sweet to her, M. Bourl'honne remarks, but—"elle ne pouvait guère s'empêcher d'éprouver une secrète tristesse qu'il en fût ainsi et de n'avoir pas rencontré en Lewes une âme qui ne le cédât en rien à l'esprit sous le rapport de la force et de la liberté."

Of that secret sadness I can find no jot of evidence. Are we to conclude that it was secret, in part, even from George Eliot herself? But if so it is secret also from us, unless we are willing to endow unbridled conjecture with the status of established fact. Psychological analysis cannot—and could not even though it were an exact science —hope to arrive at the whole truth about a woman who has been sixty years dead; and I conceive it to be the duty of George Eliot's biographer to resign himself, however sadly, to knowing not a great deal more of her inner life, whether conscious or subconscious, than she knew herself. She is beyond reach alike of our inquiry and of our correction. When she writes, on the manuscript of *Romola* and not for the eyes of the world, that Lewes' perfect love has been the best source of her insight and strength, when she inscribes to him the manuscript of *Middlemarch* "in this 19th year of our blessed union," when she declares to her intimate friend Barbara Bodichon that Lewes is "the prime blessing that has made all the rest possible to me," we cannot be at hand to explain to her how mistaken she is, to assure her that these loving tributes are merely the camouflage (if not positively the symptoms) of a "secrète tristesse," and that the happiness she imagines herself to have enjoyed with Lewes is nothing but the cloak of a bitter and abiding regret.

This counsel for the prosecution, who accuses George Eliot not merely of being guilty but of feeling so, frankly abandons himself to pure conjecture when he discusses, in another long footnote, her childlessness. Unfortunately, he says, we are here "en pleine hypothèse"; we know in fact absolutely nothing positive on this subject. Nevertheless he seems to be strongly attached to his hypothesis. It

is an elaborate one, and so purely fanciful that one wonders what purpose it can serve except to bolster up, by
insinuation, the scarcely less hypothetical theory which
we have just been considering, the theory that George
Eliot was hagridden to the day of her death by a deep
sense of guilt. The suggestion is that the prospect of becoming a mother must have weighed with her when she
decided to join her life with Lewes'. Her reading of Feuerbach would have disposed her to the view that, not only
sexual experience, but the experience of motherhood, was
necessary to the full flowering ("épanouissement") of her
womanly nature and to full, sympathetic communion with
her kind. If in the sequel she renounced maternity, and if
the renunciation was not imposed upon her by physiological causes, here is "une marque assez claire" of the
reprobation with which she regarded herself once the
union with Lewes was an accomplished fact. Before taking that fatal step (we are asked to suppose) she viewed
with enthusiasm the prospect of having children; but
afterward she must have realized that any children she
might have by Lewes would suffer the stigma and incon-
veniences of bastardy, and therefore she chose to be child-
less.

Thus far the hypothesis, and never in the history of
speculation was a hypothesis more hypothetical. It explicitly assumes—and it is a very large assumption—that
the decision whether or not to have children rested with
her and Lewes. It also assumes the very thing which it is
designed, as I think, to render plausible: that Marian began at once to experience a conviction of sin. But her decision to live with Lewes was made with full knowledge of
all the facts. Divorce was out of the question, and she

knew it. She cannot have entertained the least hope of being legally married to him, and it must have been obvious to her before the event, as well as after, that children born of such a union must be illegitimate. Supposition is piled on supposition: never once does the argument make contact with any established fact. Let us suppose she intended to have children by Lewes. Let us suppose she *could* have had children by Lewes. Let us suppose that in the sequel she decided *not* to have children by Lewes. And then let us suppose that this decision was the result of a changed attitude, a moral volte-face, a conviction of sin, and a resolve not to add "une seconde erreur à la première." Now, to suppose one thing for the sake of argument, in order to see where it will lead, is reasonable enough; but here is a series of unrelated suppositions; instead of one leading to another they are strung together quite arbitrarily; it is the apotheosis of the non sequitur. Yet the effect of the whole, upon an unwary reader, would be to suggest, by this juxtaposition of idle fancies, that George Eliot's not having had any children tends to show that she bitterly repented of her association with Lewes. Beginning with that unconfessed assumption, the argument, if so it can be called, not unnaturally ends with it too. This method of inquiry opens up a dazzling vista in the realm of biography. For Lewes and Marian Evans are not the only celebrated couple who, for one dark reason or another, have lived together in marriage without producing children to prove that they were not ashamed of themselves.

But, even though we reject his tentative answer, we may be grateful to M. Bourl'honne for asking a question which no other biographer has had the hardihood to ask out loud.

Why no children? It is reasonable to suppose that she would have been glad to have children, Feuerbach or no Feuerbach. Why, then, did she not? Either because the union with Lewes was naturally infertile, or because she felt she had no right to bring children into the world who would be at a social disadvantage. That by no means implies regret, disappointment, conviction of sin, or—most fantastic and gratuitous theory of all—that after the consummation of her union with Lewes she felt herself to be personally degraded. The palpably sincere and very moving letter which she wrote to Caroline Bray on September 4, 1855, fourteen months after the beginning of her life with Lewes, contains the fullest expression we have of her own point of view. "If there is any one action or relation of my life which is and always has been profoundly serious," she writes,

it is my relation to Mr. Lewes. It is, however, natural enough that you should mistake me in many ways, for not only are you unacquainted with Mr. Lewes's real character and the course of his actions, but also it is several years now since you and I were much together, and it is possible that the modifications my mind has undergone may be quite in the opposite direction of what you imagine. No one can be better aware than yourself that it is possible for two people to hold different opinions on momentous subjects with equal sincerity, and an equally earnest conviction that their respective opinions are alone the truly moral ones. If we differ on the subject of the marriage laws, I at least can believe of you that you cleave to what you believe to be good; and I don't know of anything in the nature of your views that should prevent you from believing the same of me. *How far* we differ, I think we neither of us know, for I am ignorant of your precise views; and apparently you attribute to me both feelings and opinions which are not mine. We cannot set each other quite right in this matter in letters, but one thing I can tell you in few words. Light and easily broken ties are what I neither desire theoretically nor could live for practically. Women who are satisfied with such ties do *not* act as I have done. That any unworldly, unsuperstitious person who is sufficiently acquainted with the realities of life can pronounce my relation to Mr. Lewes immoral, I can only understand by remembering how subtle and complex are the influences that mould opinion. But I *do* remember this: and I indulge in no arrogant or uncharitable thoughts about those who condemn us, even though we might have expected a somewhat different verdict. From the majority of persons, of course, we never looked for anything but condemnation. We are leading no life of self-indulgence, except indeed that, being happy in each other, we find everything easy. We are working hard to provide for others better than we provide for ourselves, and to fulfil every responsibility that lies upon us. Levity and pride would not be a sufficient basis for that. Pardon me if, in vindicating myself from some unjust conclusions, I seem too cold and self-asserting. I should not care to vindicate myself if I did not love you and desire to relieve you of the pain which you say these conclusions have given you. Whatever I may have misinterpreted before, I do not misinterpret your letter this morning, but read in it nothing else than love and kindness towards me, to which my heart fully answers yes. I should like never to write about myself again; it is not healthy to dwell on one's own feelings and conduct, but only to try and live more faithfully and lovingly every fresh day. I think not one of the endless words and deeds of kindness and forbearance you have ever shown me has vanished from my memory. I recall them often, and feel, as about everything else in the past, how deficient I have been in almost every relation of my life. But that deficiency is irrevocable, and I can find no strength or comfort except in "pressing forward towards the things that are before," and trying to make the present better than the past. But if we should never be very near each other again, dear Cara, do bear this faith in your mind, that I was not insensible or ungrateful to all your goodness, and that I am one amongst the many for whom you have not lived in vain. I am very busy just now, and have been obliged to write hastily. Bear this in mind, and believe that no meaning is mine which contradicts my assurance that I am your affectionate and earnest friend Marian.

IV

For a woman who had translated Strauss and Feuerbach, and for a man who intended to crown his long study of Goethe's works by producing the standard biography, Germany was the appropriate honeymoon resort. They were both deeply versed in the language and literature of that country, and knew how to value its massive contribution to culture; but the ponderous gravity of the German character was sometimes, it seems, a little too much for them.

It was too much even for Marian, who had her own full share of it: she notes in her journal that "during the whole seven months of our stay in Germany we never heard one witticism, or even one felicitous idea or expression, from a German." At Cologne, after breakfast on July 30, Dr. Brabant came to see them, bringing Strauss with him. Strauss seems to have made no great impression on Marian: she has nothing to record of him but that they had "a short interview." [8] The lovers then made their way to

8. Meeting him again, however, at Munich in 1858, she was "very agreeably impressed by him." He "looked much more serene, and his face had a far sweeter expression, than when I saw him in that dumb way at Cologne."

Weimar, Goethe's town. Here they were joined for a day or two by Arthur Helps, Lewes' friend of many years, and all three drove to Ettersburg, Helps enlivening the journey with anecdotes of his Spanish travels. Once, at a Spanish inn, he told them, he was embarrassed throughout his dinner by the presence of a handsome woman, who sat directly opposite him, resting on her elbows, and fixing her dark eyes on him with a fearful intensity of interest. She was the cook, anxious to be sure that her dishes pleased him, and under her terrible surveillance he did not dare to omit a single one of them.

Mountain ash, cherry trees, beechwoods, the opera, enjoying the *Fidelio*, finding *Lohengrin* wearisome, walks, drives, conversations about books, these and numerous social encounters form the texture of Marian's narrative of this time. They went to see the "tiny wooden house" which Goethe occupied on his visits to Ilmenau, and with ingenuous egotism they wrote their names "near one of the windows." By special permission of Frau von Goethe they saw also the studio and Schlafzimmer of Goethe's own house. They met Liszt and were charmed with him, the sweetness of his expression, the genius, benevolence, and tenderness that beamed (says Marian) from his whole countenance. They were specially delighted with the French Ambassador, the witty and genial Marquis de Ferrière, who, speaking of someone's published account of travels which he himself had shared, said: "It was untrue from beginning to end, but it was witty, paradoxical, amusing—in fine, everything that a journal should be." At Berlin Marian had the gratification of seeing her beloved George recognized and warmly greeted by Varnhagen, husband of a celebrated hostess. Varnhagen made much of them both. He proved to be "a real treasure" to George. He opened his house to them, introduced them to a number of distinguished men and women, and put them in the way of hearing much talk about Goethe. Marian, as we have seen, was intimately acquainted with German literature and art; Lessing, Schiller, Goethe, and Heine had already a permanent place in her mind; and this first of many visits to Germany was therefore full of interest and intellectual stimulus for her.

In short, as Cross remarks, they were "pleasant days these, at Weimar and Berlin, and they were working days." Lewes was endlessly busy collecting materials for his *Goethe;* and Marian, when she was not helping him, wrote articles for the *Westminster Review* and worked at her translation of Spinoza's *Ethics*. It was in Germany too that they formed that habit of reading aloud to each other which was to be one of the chief pleasures of their life together. They had a full, eventful, satisfying life abroad; and they arrived back in England, in March, 1855, very ready to enjoy a quieter mode of existence.

## Chapter Four

## THE NOVELIST EMERGES

### I

THE permanence of their union seems to have been never in doubt. There is never a hint of any personal disagreement. The only difficulties and setbacks they encountered were practical ones, not of their own making. Domestic stability, a first essential for people of literary habits, was not achieved all at once. In the March of their return from Germany we find Marian in lodgings for a few weeks at Dover, while Lewes is concluding some (unspecified) arrangements in London. In April they find lodgings at East Sheen and in May they move into them. In August Lewes and his three sons had a week's holiday at Ramsgate, and in September he and Marian spent a fortnight at Worthing before moving into new lodgings at 8 Park Shot, Richmond.

Richmond was to be their home for over three years, and they both worked very hard there, having to support not only themselves but Agnes and the three children. In the absence of any definite statement we may suppose that Thornton Hunt contributed something to the support of his own children by Agnes. Lewes and Marian had only one sitting room between them at Richmond, and she confided to Cross many years later that "the scratching of another pen used to affect her nerves to such an extent that it nearly drove her wild." Nevertheless she managed to get a good deal of work done, and so did the indefatigable Lewes. Lewes had relinquished the literary editorship of the *Leader*, but continued to write for it. Marian too wrote many articles during this year both for the *Leader* and for the *Westminster Review*.

Chapman from the first had heartily approved of her alliance with Lewes. His first act on hearing the news seems to have been to wish them happiness and propose to her that she should write an article for the October *Westminster*, then (July, 1854) in preparation. This she was glad to do. Seven months later, in answer to her note announcing her return to England, he had asked her to take on the Belles Lettres (reviewing) section at twelve guineas a number; and she did this job for eighteen consecutive months. Among her other *Westminster* contributions of this period was the one entitled "Evangelical Teaching: Dr. Cumming," which we glanced at in an earlier chapter: it was this essay which first suggested to Lewes that she possessed "genius" as well as great talent. Margaret Fuller, Mary Wollstonecraft, Heine, Carlyle, these were among the other subjects she tackled during 1855. She also read, enjoyed, and reviewed, Meredith's *The Shaving of Shagpat*. In the evenings she and Lewes read aloud to each other from such works as Gall's *Anatomie et physiologie du cerveau* and Carpenter's *Comparative Physiology*, as well as Sydney Smith, Boswell, Shakespeare, Heine, Gilbert White, and *The Odyssey*. She tries (she tells Sara Hennell) to fix some knowledge about plexuses and ganglia in her "soft brain": her life with Lewes is "intensely occupied" and "the days are far too short." The reading sessions were sometimes diversified by "very dramatic singing of Figaro, etc.," which, she thinks, "must alarm 'that good man, the clergyman,' who sits below us."

Meanwhile she continues at intervals to revise her Spinoza, and on the first day of November Lewes' book on Goethe triumphantly appears. Writing to Charles Bray she says: "I think you will find much to interest you in the book. I can't tell you how I value it, as the best product of a mind which I have every day more reason to admire and love." Evidently whatever breach there had been between herself and the Brays was now healed. Perhaps their poor opinion of her unregistered marriage had been due to mistaken notions about Lewes' character and to fear of the consequences to herself: these being removed, by her continuing happiness with him, they came round to a different way of thinking, we may suppose. In the spring of this year (1856) she is saddened by the idea of her friends' imminent removal from Rosehill. The ribbon trade was "a fluctuating concern at its best," Bray's wish for leisure in which to pursue his intellectual hobbies had increased, and so, as he tells us in his autobiography, having secured a small competency of about £400 a year he gave up manufacturing and turned his back on the prospect of making "a large fortune from inventions of my own." Since £400 must have been equal to something like £1600 today, his decision was eminently sensible. "I left my larger house," he says, "and went into a cottage of my own adjoining it, of about half the size, but with the same pleasant surroundings. Many people considered I had come down in the world, but in my opinion I had decidedly gone up."

Marian regretfully remembered summer days at Rosehill "when the bearskin was under the acacia." She and Lewes, she tells Bray, are flourishing in every way except in health. "Mr. Lewes's head is still infirm, but he manages, nevertheless, to do twice as much work as other people." She speaks of her own "muddled brains" and lack of literary facility. The need to make money was evidently much in her thoughts.

You don't know what a severely practical person I am become. . . . I keep the purse, and dole out sovereigns with all the pangs of a miser. In fact, if you were to feel my bump of acquisitiveness, I dare say you would find it in a state of inflammation, like the "veneration" of that clergyman to whom Mr. Donovan [a practicing phrenologist] said: "Sir, you have recently been engaged in prayer."

She is concerned about the education of Lewes' sons, and consults Bray about the possibility of John Sibree's taking them as private pupils. That project fell through, and the two elder boys, Charles and Thornton, were sent to a school at Hofwyl, near Berne. Early this summer she and Lewes visited Ilfracombe, whence a month later they went on to Tenby, "for the sake of making acquaintance with its molluscs and medusæ." These and later excursions resulted in Lewes' lively *Seaside Studies*, which he contributed to *Blackwood's Magazine* during 1856 and 1857 and published as a book in 1858.

The first hint of her becoming a novelist occurs in Marian's Journal on July 20, 1856. She is reluctant to undertake an article proposed to her by Chapman, because "I am anxious to begin my fiction-writing," and on August 18 "[I] talked with George of my novel." Nevertheless at the turn of the month, while George was in Switzerland settling his two boys at school there, she was busy on "Silly Novels by Lady Novelists," a somewhat heavily sarcastic effusion which was not among the essays she selected for possible publication in book form but which contains one particularly pertinent and perhaps half-prophetic remark: "The real drama of Evangelicalism, and it has abundance of fine drama for anyone who has genius enough to discern and reproduce it, lies among the middle and lower classes. Why can we not have pictures of religious life among the industrial classes in England, as interesting as Mrs. Stowe's pictures of religious life among the negroes?"

It must have been already in Marian's mind that she herself might attempt to supply the implied lack. The story of Amos Barton already existed in germ. It had always, she says, been a vague dream of hers that some time or other she might write a novel, but she never, until this September, 1856, got further than an introductory chapter describing a Staffordshire village and the life of the neighboring farmhouses; and as the years passed she lost hope that she would ever be able to write a novel, "just as I desponded about everything else in my future life." That last admission is significant, for it gives the measure of her debt to Lewes' faith in her talent. She thought she was deficient in dramatic powers, both of construction and dialogue, and Lewes was at first inclined to agree with her; but when during their stay in Berlin she showed him the "introductory chapter" mentioned above, which happened to be among the papers she had with her in Germany, he was so struck with it "as a piece of concrete description" that he advised her to try her hand at a novel. He began to say very positively: "You must try and write a story!" and later, when they were at Tenby together, he urged her to begin at once. With her habitual self-distrust, and because she had more immediate tasks in hand, she put off the attempt: but one morning as she was thinking what should be the subject of her first story (in bed, one infers, though she is too decorous to say so) she fell into a half-waking dream in which she imagined herself to be writing a story called "The Sad Fortunes of the Reverend Amos Barton." On waking she immediately told George about it; he exclaimed: "Oh, what a capital title!" and from that moment the subject of her first story was settled in her mind. Lewes was cautious in his encouragement. He allowed that she might fail but insisted that the experiment was worth trying. She had wit, description, and philosophy, he said: what remained to be seen was whether she had any talent for dramatic presentation. They decided that if the story turned out to be good enough they would send it to Blackwood; but Lewes, guarding her (one suspects) against a too bitter disappointment, "thought the most probable result was that I should have to lay it aside and try again." On their return from Tenby to Richmond she had, as we have seen, an article to write, and her monthly review of books for the *Westminster* to do; and so she did not begin the story till September 22:

After I had begun it, as we were walking in the park, I mentioned to George that I had thought of the plan of writing a series of stories, containing sketches drawn from my own observation of the clergy, and calling them "Scenes from Clerical Life," opening with *Amos Barton*. He at once accepted the notion as a good one—fresh and striking; and about a week afterwards, when I read him the first part of *Amos*, he had no longer any doubt about my ability to carry out the plan. The scene at Cross Farm, he said, satisfied him that I had the very element he had been doubtful about—it was clear I could write good dialogue. There still remained the question whether I could command any pathos; and that was to be decided by the mode in which I treated Milly's death. One night George went to town on purpose to leave me a quiet evening for writing it. I wrote the chapter from the news brought by the shepherd to Mrs. Hackit, to the moment when Amos is dragged from the bedside, and I read it to George when he came home. We both cried over it, and then he came up to me and kissed me, saying "I think your pathos is better than your fun."

Not everyone will agree with this particular judgment. But in the main Lewes was right, and posterity has endorsed his general verdict. With the completion of "Amos Barton," a new novelist was born into the world.

The manuscript went at once to John Blackwood, with a letter in which Lewes contrived to be at once truthful and disingenuous. The story, he says, "was submitted to me by a friend who desired my good offices with you," and he expresses the opinion that "such humour, pathos, vivid presentation, and nice observation, have not been exhibited (in this style) since *The Vicar of Wakefield*." Blackwood replied promptly, within a week: "I am happy to say that I think your friend's reminiscences of Clerical Life will do." He would like to see more of the series before making "any decided proposition," but declares this first specimen to be "unquestionably very pleasant reading." He puts his finger, gently enough, on certain faults, and ends by saying that he will probably have a more decided opinion of the merits of the story when he has looked at it again and thought over it, but "in the meantime I am sure that there is a happy turn of expression throughout, also much humour and pathos. If the author is a new writer, I beg to congratulate him on being worthy of the honours of print and pay. I shall be very glad to hear from you or him soon."

Almost any other first novelist would have been uplifted by such a letter from a man in Blackwood's position. Not so George Eliot, unless we are to regard Lewes' reply as a tactical maneuver: "I have communicated your letter to my clerical friend, who, though somewhat discouraged by it, has taken my advice, and will submit the second story to you when it is written. At present he has only written what he sent you. His avocations, he informs me, will prevent his setting to work for the next three weeks or so, but as soon as he is at liberty he will begin." There follows a reiteration of his former praise of the story, which evidently Blackwood had not praised enough to content him and his "clerical friend," and the letter ends, placatingly: "At the same time I told him that I thoroughly understood your editorial caution in not accepting from an unknown hand a series on the strength of one specimen." Blackwood's answer and the ensuing correspondence had best be given in full. They mark an epoch in the life of Marian Evans, now to become George Eliot ("George" because it was Lewes' name and "Eliot" because it was "a good mouth-filling, easily pronounced word"); and they exhibit all three in characteristic attitudes.

*John Blackwood to G. H. Lewes: November 18, 1856*

I was very far from intending that my letter should convey anything like disappointment to your friend. On the contrary, I thought the tale very good, and intended to convey as much. But I daresay I expressed myself coolly enough. Criticism would assume a much soberer tone were critics compelled *seriously to act* whenever they expressed an opinion. Although not much given to hesitate about anything, I always think twice before I put the decisive mark "In type for the Magazine" on any MS from a stranger. Fancy the intense annoyance (to say nothing of more serious considerations) of publishing, month after month, a series about which the conviction gradually forces itself on you that you have made a total blunder.

I am sorry that the author has no more written, but if he cares much about a speedy appearance, I have so high an opinion of this first tale, that I will waive my objections, and publish it without seeing more—not, of course, committing myself to go on with the other tales of the series unless I approved of them. I am very sanguine that I will approve, as in addition to the other merits of "Amos," I agree with you that there is great freshness of style. If you think also that it would stimulate the author to go on with the other tales with more spirit, I will publish "Amos" at once. He could divide into two parts. I am blocked up for December, but I could start him in January.

I am glad to hear that your friend is, as I supposed, a clergyman. Such a subject is best in clerical hands, and some of the pleasantest and least prejudiced correspondents I have ever had are English clergymen.

I have not read "Amos Barton" a second time, but the impression on my mind of the whole character, incidents, and feeling of the story is very distinct, which is an excellent sign.

### *G. H. Lewes to John Blackwood: November, 1856*

Your letter has greatly restored the shaken confidence of my friend, who is unusually sensitive, and, unlike most writers, is more anxious about *excellence* than about appearing in print—as his waiting so long before taking the venture proves. He is consequently afraid of failure, though not afraid of obscurity; and by failure he would understand that which I suspect most writers would be apt to consider as success—so high is his ambition.

I tell you this that you may understand the sort of shy, shrinking, ambitious nature you have to deal with. I tried to persuade him that you really *did* appreciate his story, but were only hesitating about committing yourself to a series; and your last letter has proved me to have been right—although, as he never contemplated binding you to the publication of any portion of the series to which you might object, he could not at first see your position in its true light.

All is, however, clear now. He will be gratified if you publish "Amos Barton" in January, as it will give him ample time to get the second story ready, so as to appear when "Barton" is finished, should you wish it. He is anxious, however, that you should publish the general title of "Scenes of Clerical Life"; and I think you may do this with perfect safety, since it is quite clear that the writer of "Amos Barton" is capable of writing at least one more story suitable to "Maga," and two would suffice to justify the general title.

Let me not forget to add that when I referred to "my clerical friend," I meant to designate the writer of the clerical stories—not that he was a clericus. I am not at liberty to remove the veil of anonymity, even as regards social position. Be pleased, therefore, to keep the whole secret, and not even mention *my* negotiation, or in any way lead guessers (should any one trouble himself with such a guess—*not* very likely) to jump from me to my friend.

*John Blackwood to George Eliot: December 29, 1856*

Along with this I send a copy of the January number of the Magazine, in which you will find the first part of "Amos

Barton." It gives me very great pleasure to begin the number with "Amos," and I put him in that position because his merits well entitle him to it, and also because it is a vital point to attract public attention to the *first* part of a series, to which end being the first article of the first number of the year may contribute.

I have already expressed to our friend Mr. Lewes the very high opinion I entertain of "Amos," and the expectations I have formed of the series, should his success prove equal to him, which I fully anticipate.

It is a long time since I have read anything so fresh, so humorous, and so touching. The style is capital, conveying so much in so few words.

Those who have seen the tale here are chiefly members of my own family, and they are all enthusiastic in praise.

You may recollect that I expressed a fear that in the affecting and highly-wrought scene of poor Milly's death, the attempt to individualise the children by reiterating their names weakened the effect, as the reader had not been prepared to care for them individually, but simply as a group—the children of Milly and the sorrow-stricken curate. My brother says, "No. Do not advise the author to touch anything so exquisite." Of course you are the best judge.

I now send proof of the conclusion of "Amos," in acknowledgment of which, and of the first part, I have the pleasure of enclosing a cheque for £52, 10s.—fifty guineas.

If the series goes on as I anticipate, there is every prospect that a republication as a separate book, at some time or other, will be advisable. We would look upon such republication as a joint property, and would either give you a sum for your interest in it, or publish on the terms of one half of the clear profits, to be divided between author and publisher, as might be most agreeable to you.

I shall be very glad to hear from you, either direct or

through Mr. Lewes; and any intelligence that the successors of "Amos" are taking form and substance will be very acceptable.

I shall let you know what the other contributors and the public think of "Amos" as far as I can gather a verdict, but in the meantime I may congratulate you on having achieved a preliminary success at all events.

### *George Eliot to John Blackwood: January, 1857*

Your letter has proved to me that the generous Editor and publisher—generous both in word and in deed—who makes the author's path smooth and easy, is something more than a pleasant tradition. I am very sensitive to the merits of cheques for fifty guineas, but I am still more sensitive to that cordial appreciation which is a guarantee to me that my work was worth doing for its own sake.

If the "Scenes of Clerical Life" should be republished, I have no doubt we shall find it easy to arrange the terms. In the meantime, the most pressing business is to make them worth republishing.

I think the particularization of the children in the death-bed scene has an important effect on the imagination. But I have removed all names from the "conclusion" except those of Patty and Dickey, in whom, I hope, the reader has a personal interest.

I hope to send you the second story by the beginning of February. It will lie, for the most part, among quite different scenes and persons from the last—opening in Shepperton once more, but presently moving away to a distant spot and new people, whom, I hope, you will not like less than Amos and his friends. But if any one of the succeeding stories should seem to you unsuitable to the pages of "Maga," it can be reserved for publication in the future volume, without creating any difficulty.

Thank you very warmly for the hearty acceptance you have given to my first story.

A writer who received today's equivalent of that fifty guineas for the serial rights of his or her first story, even though a comparatively long one, would have no cause for complaint; and one is relieved to find that even Lewes, so zealous for his "friend's" interests, was apparently satisfied with Blackwood's treatment of her.

## II

The "second story" referred to in the letter above was "Mr. Gilfil's Love Story," the first two parts of which went to Blackwood during February. He was delighted with it, and could not have failed to see that it was much better than "Amos Barton," upon the strength of which he had already made a proposal for the republication in book form of the whole series when it should be completed. Blackwood was indeed a prince among publishers. His dealings with George Eliot were marked by patience, critical discernment, and generosity. Despite Lewes' eulogium, it is not every publisher who would have given so warm a welcome to that first, comparatively crude attempt. Uncommon tact and skill were needed in the management of so shy, so nervous, so temperamental a horse as George Eliot, whose deep-seated self-mistrust took the form of an almost morbid sensitiveness to comment, let alone criticism, and who seems to have been always "ready to be dispirited on the slightest pretext."

The fuss about her pseudonymity was another symptom of that excessive self-consciousness. In the beginning she had a valid reason for secrecy, being afraid lest conspicuous failure as a novelist should impair her reputation (and therefore her earning capacity) as a literary journalist. But with the publication of the clerical series in *Blackwood's Magazine*, and the chorus of praise it evoked from Thackeray and others, that fear must have dwindled; and after their appearance in book form (January, 1858), which brought laudatory letters from Dickens, Froude, and Jane Welsh Carlyle, there was no further excuse for it. The success of *Adam Bede* in the following year was even more unequivocal. It was a resounding popular success as well as a literary triumph. Yet even then she was unwilling to confess to the authorship. Chapman, putting two and two together, came to the right conclusion. As early as January, 1857, when "Amos Barton" began its serial appearance, he had tried to secure her continued services for the *Westminster* (for she was already beginning to decline offers of work) by writing the following letter:

Dear Friend,

Of course it is impossible to adopt any scale of remuneration whereby I could graduate the payments to contributors to the W.R. so that each writer may be rewarded according to his (*or her*) merit. Still there are cases where a departure from the rule usually acted on would be so obviously just that I can have no hesitation as to the propriety of treating them as exceptional.

Your articles are so uniformly excellent that I desire to express my appreciation of their merit by paying for what you may hereafter contribute at the rate of £12.12.0 per sheet.

While paying you for the article on Young, as per agreement, both as to terms and length, I felt that you were inadequately remunerated; but knowing that the number, being a sheet and a half too long, would be a costly one, I acted according to *rule;* now, however, that I have read your article again with greatly increased delight, I shall not feel satisfied without sending you the enclosed, which, though when added to the £20 already sent on account of the article, will not represent its value, but which you will perhaps regard as an assurance of my high estimation of it, and of my hope that you will let the "Westminster" be the medium of publication of whatever quarterly review articles you may be able to write.

Yours faithfully,

John Chapman.[1]

After the publication, a year later, of the completed *Scenes,* all literary London was talking about the new, unknown author. Only three people besides herself were in the know: Lewes, Blackwood, and her old friend Herbert Spencer. One day in November Spencer went to dinner with the Leweses and brought with him "the unpleasant news" that Chapman had asked him point blank whether or not Marian Evans was George Eliot. Whereupon she wrote to Chapman, in terms which presumably hurt his feelings, for he let a month elapse before he acknowledged the letter. His answer, when it did come, failed to placate her. In a letter that begins, as usual, with "Dear Friend," and ends "Yours very sincerely," she expresses "much surprise" at certain of his observations and statements, but forbears commenting on them, "since it does not seem likely that further letter-writing would advance our mutual understanding." Three months later, *Adam Bede* having just appeared, Chapman repeated his crime of asking

1. G. S. Haight, *George Eliot and John Chapman.*

Spencer to confirm or deny the report that Marian Evans was the author. Spencer, having a punctilious regard for veracity, made no answer, and his silence amounted to an admission of the truth. It was now Spencer's turn to suffer the displeasure of this extraordinarily touchy pair; for when he told the Leweses what had happened they blamed him for not having given Chapman an explicit denial, and there was a coolness between them for some months. Lewes went even further. Apparently with Marian's "reluctant" consent he wrote to Chapman on February 12, 1859:

My Dear Chapman,
  Not to notice your transparent allusion in your last, would be improperly to admit its truth. After the previous correspondence, your continuing to impute those works to Mrs. Lewes may be *meant* as a compliment, but *is* an offence against delicacy and friendship. As you seem so very slow in appreciating her feelings on this point, she authorises me to state, as distinctly as language can do so, that she is not the author of "Adam Bede."
                    Yours faithfully,
                                    G. H. Lewes.[2]

This silly, pompous, and mendacious letter marks the end of Marian's relationship with John Chapman. In view of Chapman's sympathetic attitude to the Evans-Lewes alliance the reference to "Mrs. Lewes" is singularly inept and unfriendly. Tiresome he may have been, persistent he was, but with all his faults we cannot but feel that he deserved better of one to whom his friendship, if at first too deeply disturbing, had been a support, both moral and financial,

2. Haight, *op. cit.*

during a period of crisis. Chapman did not, however, write to inquire why she should resent being identified with the author of a book whose praises were in everyone's mouth. Nor did he claim, as perhaps he might have done, that considerations of "delicacy and friendship" might have persuaded her to confide her secret, from the first, to the man who, as editor of the *Westminster*, had provided her with regular breadwinning work during two momentous years. Despite Lewes' efforts, the identity between Marian Evans and George Eliot soon became generally known. And she would not have been a penny the worse if it had been known twelve months earlier.

### III

But we must return to 1858. On the second evening in that New Year, George Lewes arrived home from a week's visit to Vernon Hill saying: "I have some very pretty news for you—something in my pocket." It was the *Times* newspaper, and it contained a highly favorable review of Marian's first published book, the *Clerical Scenes,* for so she generally calls it in her letters and journal. Dear George had also a number of exciting conversations to report. Mrs. Nutt's curate had declared that the unknown author must be a High Churchman, like himself. Helps, when George Eliot's portrayal of children was mentioned, said: "Oh, he is a great writer!"

If we feel some embarrassment at the spectacle of a mature woman writing these things in her diary, it is only fair that we should read her own comment on them. She wonders how she will feel about "these little details" ten years hence. At present she values them as grounds for hoping that her writing may succeed, and so give point to her life. She values them as indications that she can touch the hearts of her fellow men "and so sprinkle some precious grain as the results of the long years in which I have been inert and suffering." She at once adds, however, with almost the gesture of one who touches wood: "But at present fear and trembling still predominate over hope." Three days later the book itself arrived, in two handsome volumes. And in another three days came news of the subscription: 580, with a probable addition of 25 for Longmans. George, the cautious fellow, had always said of the probable subscription: "I daresay it will be 250." She had had presentation copies sent to a number of well-known writers, some of whom wrote to her. The letter which gave her most pleasure, and made her regret, as well she might, the "iron mask of her incognito," was this one:

My Dear Sir,—I have been so strongly affected by the two first tales in the book you have had the kindness to send me, through Messrs. Blackwood, that I hope you will excuse my writing to you to express my admiration of their extraordinary merit. The exquisite truth and delicacy, both of the humour and the pathos of these stories, I have never seen the like of; and they have impressed me in a manner that I should find it very difficult to describe to you, if I had the impertinence to try.

In addressing these few words of thankfulness to the creator of the Sad Fortunes of the Rev. Amos Barton, and the sad Love-story of Mr. Gilfil, I am (I presume) bound to adopt the name that it pleases that excellent writer to assume. I can suggest no better one: but I should have been strongly disposed, if I had been left to my own devices, to address the said writer as a woman. I have observed what seemed to me such womanly touches in those moving fictions, that the assurance on the title-page is insufficient to satisfy me even now. If they originated with no woman, I believe that no man ever before had the art of making himself mentally so like a woman since the world began.

You will not suppose that I have any vulgar wish to fathom your secret. I mention the point as one of great interest to me—not of mere curiosity. If it should ever suit your convenience and inclination to show me the face of the man, or woman, who has written so charmingly, it will be a very memorable occasion to me. If otherwise, I shall always hold that impalpable personage in loving attachment and respect, and shall yield myself up to all future utterances from the same source, with a perfect confidence in their making me wiser and better.—Your obliged and faithful servant and admirer,

Charles Dickens

Forwarding this letter to Blackwood, with a proviso that it is not to be quoted in advertisements, she says that "there can hardly be any climax of approbation for me after this" and asks Blackwood to take any opportunity he may have of conveying to Dickens how deeply she feels about it. Why she could not have written to Dickens direct, as George Eliot, remains a mystery. No harm was done, however; for later the two met and became friends. Meanwhile she continued, stubbornly and with growing discomfort, to wear her iron mask. "When do you bring out your new poem?" she writes, in an ecstasy of irony, to Charles Bray.

I presume you are already in the sixth canto. It is true you never told me you intended to write a poem, nor have I heard anyone say so who was likely to know. Nevertheless I have quite as active an imagination as you, and I don't see why I shouldn't suppose you are writing a poem as well as you suppose that I am writing a novel. Seriously, I wish you would not set rumours afloat about me. They are injurious. Several people, who seem to derive their notions from Ivy Cottage [the Brays' new house], have spoken to me, of a supposed novel I was going to bring out. Such things are damaging to me.

Were they? Why and how? She was in fact well into her second work of fiction by this time. A letter arrived from Blackwood full of praise for the first part of *Adam Bede*, but wanting to see the rest of the story in outline before deciding on its serial publication. Apparently he was anxious to be sure that it would contain nothing that might offend the moral or religious susceptibilities of magazine readers. "I refused to tell my story beforehand, on the ground that I would not have it judged apart from my *treatment*, which alone determines the moral quality of art." This was a valid, indeed an unanswerable reason. Was there another one as well? Did she feel, as other writers have felt before and since, that a novel—of the kind she was concerned with—must be allowed, with limits, to develop in its own way, and that to commit herself to a synopsis would unduly restrict her imagination and at the same time dull her interest in the work? It is by no means certain that she did, for one gets the impression that she was sometimes overregardful of her plan. Plan of some kind there must be, but the living quality, the life illusion which the novel exists to create, is generated in the heat of actual composition, and many of the most "inspired" touches are as much a surprise to the writer as to the reader. Every imaginative writer will understand George Eliot's instinct for secrecy about the *content* of a work in progress, and may indeed wonder how she could bring herself to show it to her publisher in fragments: what is difficult to sympathize with is her unwillingness to let even old friends know that she was engaged in any such work. A normal and healthy woman does not take pains to hide the fact of her pregnancy: on the other hand she does, very naturally, keep hidden in her heart her secret ideas and hopes of what the child may be.

This year the Leweses paid another visit to Germany, and it was at Munich, about the middle of April, that Marian began writing the second volume of *Adam Bede*. Lewes, to whom the book was read chapter by chapter, expressed a fear that Adam's part throughout was too passive and suggested that he should be brought into more direct collision with Arthur Donnithorne. This doubt, she declares, haunted her, and out of it grew the scene in the wood between Arthur and Adam. The fight between them "came to me as a *necessity*." It does not, I suggest, strike the reader so. A critical appraisal of the novels will be attempted in later chapters; but here it may be said that this fight, forced on Donnithorne by Adam Bede, shows clear signs of having been forced on Adam Bede by his author. It is a useful piece of mechanism, but it is not, as narrated, consistent with Adam's character as we have learnt to know it. Nor does it achieve its purpose of showing that Adam was capable, like any other jealous man, of sudden anger and a hasty blow: his proceedings, far from being impulsive, are unnaturally deliberate. The book was finished at Richmond, and Blackwood at once offered £800 for four years' copyright in it, he and the author having agreed that it should be published without delay in book form and not serially.

She had promised herself, and Blackwood, that the new

book should be "a country story—full of the breath of
cows and the scent of hay." This remark was made before
she began the actual writing of *Adam Bede*, and it has a
special value for us as showing how the book in embryo
*felt* to her. Without suggesting that there exists any radical opposition between imaginative impregnation and deliberate plotting or planning, we recognize in that description the true germ of all that is best and most enduring
in the finished work. That sense of country things and
country people was the glowing nucleus of the whole.
The plot, the sequence of events, the complication and
unraveling, these though structurally important were secondary. The story of Hetty Sorrel was not indeed an
afterthought: it was the given subject. But it was given as
the bare outline of a story whose life was to consist, as the
life of a novel always must, in the feeling, the movement,
the moment-by-moment quality, flowing from the novelist's pen.

The notion that was to emerge as Hetty Sorrel had been
implanted in Marian's mind some twenty years earlier by
her ardently evangelical Aunt Elizabeth, wife of Samuel
Evans. The two were sitting together one afternoon at
Griff when it occurred to Aunt Evans to tell Marian how
she had once visited a condemned criminal, a very ignorant girl who had killed her child and refused to confess;
how she had stayed with her praying through the night,
till at last the poor creature broke down into tears and confession; and how she afterward went with her in the cart
to the place of execution. The story was told with great
feeling and made a deep impression. The stubborn stupid-
ity which insists on identifying fictional characters with
people who once lived in the flesh has had full play with

*Adam Bede*, and George Eliot's denial of these identifications has been sometimes put down to mere vanity, the vanity of an author anxious that her creative gift should not be depreciated. No doubt George Eliot had her share of vanity, but in this instance, I suggest, she was jealous not so much for her own reputation as for the art of fiction.[3] She resented the ingenuous assumption that a "living" character can be created by merely copying from nature. For in fact the very opposite is the truth. A novelist may, before he begins to write, have a model in mind; but if in the writing he relies on memory to the exclusion of imaginative invention he will produce either a lifeless dummy or at best a creature belonging to a different order of reality from that of the novel as a whole. It is sometimes said that the novelist borrows features from a diversity of remembered persons and creates of them a composite character; but this is rather less than half the truth. If painstaking fidelity to a model is fatal, the attempt to build up a character by a deliberate admixture of remembered persons, or by a deliberate selection from their personal idiosyncracies, is equally so. Observation is not enough. A fictitious character, whatever hints from "real life" it may incorporate, must be generated in the heat of imagination, must in short be "created" by the author, or it can have no more life than a still photograph. The persons and episodes in a novel that make the reader exclaim in admiration that these people must really have lived, these things

3. "I do feel more than I ought about outside sayings and doings, and I constantly rebuke myself for all that part of my susceptibility, which I know to be weak and egoistic; still what is said about one's art is not merely a personal matter—it touches the very highest things one lives for. . . . I never saw anything of my aunt's writing, and Dinah's words came from me 'as the tears come because our heart is full, and we can't help them.'" G. E. to John Blackwood, October 16, 1859.

must really have happened, are precisely those which the author has most vividly and freely imagined, with little or no reference to actual history.

The character of Dinah Morris, George Eliot says,

grew out of my recollections of my aunt, but Dinah is not at all like any aunt, who was a very small, black-eyed woman, and (as I was told, for I never heard her preach) very vehement in her style of preaching. She had left off preaching when I knew her, being probably sixty years old, and in delicate health; and she had become, as my father told me, much more gentle and subdued than she had been in the days of her active ministry and bodily strength, when she could not rest without exhorting and remonstrating in season and out of season.

Similarly, the character of Adam Bede, and one or two incidents connected with him, were suggested by Robert Evans' early life. "But Adam is not my father any more than Dinah is my aunt. Indeed, there is not a single portrait in *Adam Bede;* only the suggestions of experience wrought up into new combinations"—and inbreathed, we must add, with new life.

It is therefore a gross misuse of language to assert, as has been asserted, that Dinah Morris was Elizabeth Evans, that Seth Bede was Samuel Evans, that Adam Bede was Robert Evans, that Felix Holt was Gerald Massey, and so on and so on. If I seem to labor the point it is because the same kind of obstinate and uncritical identification is practiced in our own day, sometimes with painful results, as when Somerset Maugham was accused of maliciously portraying Thomas Hardy in the Edward Driffield of *Cakes and Ale*. The bare outline of Amos Barton's story was suggested by a sequence of actual events which the author remembered being told about in her childhood; personal memories are unquestionably incorporated (and transfigured) in *The Mill on the Floss;* it is highly probable that recollections of Dr. Brabant of Devizes furnished hints for Mr. Casaubon in *Middlemarch;* and no doubt the full catalogue of "suggestions from experience" would make a lengthy document. Nevertheless, Amos Barton, Mr. Casaubon, the Dodsons and Tullivers and Gleggs, are George Eliot's creations and live more by virtue of their fictional elements than by what little they derive from actual persons. "Mr. Tryan," she writes to John Blackwood, "is not a portrait of any clergyman, living or dead. He is an idea [i.e., imaginary] character, but I hope probable enough to resemble more than one evangelical clergyman of his day. If Mr. Jones's deceased brother was like Mr. Tryan, so much the better, for in that case he was made of human nature's finer clay."

And again, in a passage that disposes of the question once for all:

It is invariably the case that when people discover certain points of coincidence in a fiction with facts that happen to have come to their knowledge, they believe themselves able to furnish a key to the whole. That is amusing enough to the author, who knows from what widely sundered portions of experience—from what combination of subtle, shadowy suggestions, with certain actual objects and events—his story has been formed. It would be a very difficult thing for me to furnish a key to my stories myself. But where there is no exact memory of the past, any story with a few remembered points of character or of incident may pass for history.

IV

Marian Evans rejected Christianity in her twenties and never returned to it; but it is necessary to add that by Christianity is here meant, not the wisdom of Jesus, not the inspiration of his example, but the system of belief invented by a succession of theological committees during the four centuries that followed his death, and in particular the doctrine of the exclusive incarnation of God in an historical person who is also the Second Person of the Trinity. This, with all its elaborately expounded implications, she rejected. What she did not reject, what she never came within miles of rejecting, was the way of life demonstrated by Jesus, the need of "sacrifice" or self-giving, the profound paradox which affirms at once the littleness and the eternal significance of the individual human being, and the inescapable truth that we are members one of another.

"I dislike extremely," she tells Charles Bray,

a passage in which you appear to consider the disregard of individuals as a lofty condition of mind. My own experience and development deepen every day my conviction that our moral progress may be measured by the degree in which we sympathize with individual suffering and individual joy. The fact that in the scheme of things we see a constant and tremendous sacrifice of individuals is, it seems to me, only one of the many proofs that urge upon us our total inability to find in our own natures a key to the Divine mystery.

On the question of God and human immortality she was agnostic not from hostility to traditionalism as such but because she could not rest content with any facile solution of these mysteries, and because the constitution of the universe, the iron necessity in which she professed belief, seemed to her at variance with what was best in her own nature. Confronted by the Infinite Indifference, she could find refuge from that severe regard only in sympathy for her kind. Sympathy, compassion, toleration, these are the mainsprings of her mind as of her art. "My artistic bent is directed not at all to the presentation of eminently irreproachable characters, but to the presentation of mixed human beings in such a way as to call forth tolerant judgment, pity, and sympathy. And I cannot stir a step aside from what I *feel* to be *true* in character." That was written to Blackwood. And this too:

My irony, so far as I understand myself, is not directed against opinions—against any class of religious views—but against the vices and weaknesses that belong to human nature in every sort of clothing. . . . I should like to touch every heart among my readers with nothing but loving humour, with tenderness, with belief in goodness.

And to Sara Hennell, who had just published a rationalistic study of religion:

I am the more inclined to think that I shall admire your book, because you are suspected of having given undue preponderance to the Christian argument: for I have a growing conviction that we may measure true moral and intellectual culture by the comprehension and veneration given to all forms of thought and feeling which have influenced large masses of mankind—and of all intolerance the intolerance calling itself philosophical is the most odious to me.

Tolerance, however, is a word inadequate to describe Marian Evans' attitude to her fellow mortals. There is a tolerance, of a sort, that proceeds from a disdain of moral

GEORGE ELIOT IN 1865
BY SIR FREDERICK BURTON

values; there is a tolerance that regards all opinions other than one's own as equally beneath one's notice. Marian's was emphatically not of this kind. She was something of a stoic in her general philosophy; she had a powerful sense of duty, of the need for personal renunciations in the interest of the general good; and the moral burden of nearly everything she wrote was that the direct pursuit of one's own pleasure or happiness leads to disaster. But she had nothing of the stoic's (theoretical) indifference to the sins and sufferings of individual human beings. She was at once clear sighted and warmhearted, passionate and compassionate. Her tolerance was of the order of *caritas*, or loving-kindness. A moralist and an intellectualist, detesting certain types of behavior and keenly critical of many widely accepted beliefs, she was able not only to love the sinner while deploring his sin, but—what is sometimes a severer tax on patience—to regard with sympathy and respect certain traditional fancies and superstitions which, but for their human origin, she must have incontinently dismissed as merely ridiculous. Religious intolerance, religious arrogance, the dogmatic unspiritual temper that knowingly or unknowingly uses the forms of religion to cover its nakedness: these things she would ruthlessly attack, if they came her way. But for particular forms of religious belief, however little she might be able to share them, she had the respect and even the affection which she felt to be due to all human things. The intellectual errors of mankind, when they were not also morally or spiritually noxious, were in some measure sanctified for her by their humanity; and, whatever their opinions, she was always readier to find good than evil in individual men and women.

Her own emancipation as a young woman from evangelical Calvinism had been hastened by a simple piece of logic. As we have seen in an earlier chapter, she was deeply shocked and shaken when a coreligionist, convicted of barefaced lying, complacently remarked: "I don't feel that the Spirit is grieved overmuch." It then occurred to her that this woman and her own Aunt Samuel Evans professed precisely the same religious beliefs. The one was mendacious and self-deceived, the other she revered as a living embodiment of sincerity and goodness. Therefore, she argued, it is not her creed that makes my aunt good, for that is common to both: it is my aunt's innate goodness that sheds a glamour upon her creed. Rightly or wrongly Marian had no use for a religion divorced from morality, and, the distinction once made, she began to perceive that in point of human goodness, which was her chief concern, there was nothing to choose between the believers in a supernatural revelation and the unbelievers. From that moment, if not before, she was a humanist, heart and soul. Among contributory influences to this end must be reckoned the novels of Sir Walter Scott, for we may suppose that it was partly from Scott's glorious example of broad toleration and genial humanity, his Shakespearean delight in all sorts and conditions of men, that she learned to cultivate these virtues in herself. She began reading Scott when she was seven years old and continued her life long to "worship" him. During her last five or six years at Coventry she was able, she says, to make the evenings cheerful for her father by reading Scott's novels aloud to him. "No other writer would serve as a substitute for Scott, and my life at that time would have been much more difficult without him. It is a personal grief, a heart-wound to me, when I hear a depreciatory or slighting word about Scott."

The history of her attitude to Christianity is conveniently summarized in a letter to her excellent friends the D'Alberts, with whom she had lived so happily at Geneva in the interval between her father's death and her *Westminster Review* period:

I can understand that there are many pages in "Adam Bede" in which you do not recognize the "Marian" or "Minie" of old Geneva days. We knew each other too short a time, and I was under too partial and transient a phase of my mental history, for me to pour out to you much of my earlier experience. I think I hardly ever spoke to you of the strong hold evangelical Christianity had on me from the age of fifteen to two-and-twenty, and of the abundant intercourse I had had with earnest people of various religious sects. When I was at Geneva, I had not yet lost the attitude of antagonism which belonged to the renunciation of *any* belief; also, I was very unhappy, and in a state of discord and rebellion towards my own lot. Ten years of experience have wrought great changes in that inward self. I have no longer any antagonism towards any faith in which human sorrow and human longing for purity have expressed themselves; on the contrary, I have a sympathy with it that predominates over all argumentative tendencies. I have not returned to dogmatic Christianity—to the acceptance of any set of doctrines as a creed —a superhuman revelation of the unseen—but I see in it the highest expression of the religious sentiment that has yet found its place in the history of mankind, and I have the profoundest interest in the inward life of sincere Christians in all ages. Many things that I should have argued against ten years ago, I now feel myself too ignorant, and too limited in moral sensibility, to speak of with confident disapprobation.

On that questionn of our future existence to which you allude, I have undergone the sort of change I have just indicated, although my most rooted conviction is that the immediate object and the proper sphere of all our highest emotions are our struggling fellow-men in this earthly existence.

This "profoundest interest in the inward life of sincere Christians" is evident in all her fiction: nowhere more so than in the excessively tender portrayal of Dinah Morris in *Adam Bede*.

## v

The year 1859, though a year of triumph, brought ample opportunity for the exercise of this characteristic virtue, toleration. The Liggins affair, which began as something to laugh over, developed into a nuisance and a source of much irritation, especially, so Marian tells us, to Lewes, who "is of so sensitive a temperament, and so used to feeling more angry and more glad on my behalf than his own, that he has been made, several mornings, quite unable to go on with his work by this irritating correspondence." The first rumor of Liggins came in a letter from an old friend in Warwickshire [Bray?] asking Marian if she had read *Adam Bede* and whether she knew that the author was a Mr. Liggins.

A deputation of Dissenting parsons went over to ask him to write for the *Eclectic* [Review], and they found him washing his slop-basin at a pump. He has no servant, and does everything for himself; but one of the said parsons says that he inspired them with a reverence that would have made any impertinent question impossible. The son of a baker, of no mark at all in his town, so that it is possible you may not have

heard of him. You know he calls himself George Eliot. It
sounds strange to hear the *Westminster* doubting whether
he is a woman, when here he is so well known; but I am glad
it has mentioned him. They say he gets no profit out of
*Adam Bede*, and gives it freely to Blackwood, which is a
shame. We have not read him yet, but the extracts are irresistible.

Sending on this piece of news to John Blackwood,
Marian hopes he and his brother will "enjoy the myth."
But the myth gathered ground and ceased to be so amusing. George Eliot's letter to the *Times*, denying Liggins'
authorship, was not universally believed. She suggests that
Blackwood should write one too, because "we are bound
not to allow sums of money to be raised on a false supposition of this kind." A Mr. Quirk of Attleborough
takes up the cause of Liggins and has to be corresponded
with. Meanwhile the sales of the book are soaring so high
that Blackwood generously promises to pay the author
£800 in addition to the £800 agreed upon for the four
years' copyright, and, less agreeably, a publisher named
Newby announces a sequel entitled *Adam Bede Junior*.
A letter from Dickens describes some of the tricks that
are being used to push the book under the pretense of its
being the genuine work of George Eliot, and promises to
publish an article on the subject in *Household Words* "in
order to scarify the rascally bookseller," as Marian notes
in her Journal. It was probably their belief in Liggins that
persuaded her to unveil herself to the Brays and Sara Hennell, which she did on June 20, 1859, after she and Lewes
had heard Handel's *Messiah* in their company at the
Crystal Palace and afterward dined with them. They
seemed, she says, overwhelmed with surprise, a fact which

induced her to reflect upon "the ignorance in which we all live of each other."

But the Brays' surprise is perhaps not so very surprising. There seems to have been no contact between them and Marian, except by letter, since the beginning of her alliance with Lewes; she had not merely not told them, but had virtually denied, that she was writing fiction; and the discovery of her latent talent had been, after all, a surprise even to herself. Now she was able to talk to them about it, an expansiveness she doubtless enjoyed at the time but afterward, and characteristically, regretted. In a letter written ten days after the momentous reunion, in reply to one of theirs, she expresses her gratitude and her misgiving. She cared so much about her books that she was always alive to the dangers of vanity, egoism, and excessive self-regard. She was afraid of becoming intoxicated by a sense of her own achievement. The letter begins: "Dear Friends —all three of you—Thanks for your packet of heartfelt kindness. That is the best of your kindness—there is no sham in it." And continues:

It was inevitable to me to have that outburst when I saw you for a little while after the long silence, and felt that I must tell you then or be forestalled, and leave you to gather the truth amidst an inextricable mixture of falsehood. But I feel that the influence of talking about my books, even to you and Mrs. Bodichon, has been so bad to me that I should like to be able to keep silence concerning them for evermore. If people were to buzz round me with their remarks, or compliments, I should lose the repose of mind and truthfulness of production, without which no good healthy books can be written. Talking about my books, I find, has much the same malign effect on me as talking of my feelings or my religion.

She goes on to say once again that though there are things in *Adam Bede* about her father—that is, things her father had told her about his early life—there is no *portrait* in the book, either of him or of anyone else. She deprecated the search for "sources" as much as she had disliked speculation about the authorship. She was already, one may infer, wishing herself back in the refuge of her incognito. "The only safe thing for my mind's health is to shut my ears and go on with my work." It was perhaps this conviction, rather than mere wincing auctorial vanity, that led her to avoid reading, so far as she could, what the newspaper critics had to say about her subsequent books. She knew herself to be highly sensitive and suggestible, easily disturbed by either praise or censure, and she knew that once she allowed herself to take an active personal interest in the chattering of hack reviewers there would be no end to it, and her capacity for imaginative concentration would dwindle away.

This instinct was probably at the root of her wish not to be known to the world as the author of George Eliot's novels. To stand between her and her reviewers was one of the many devoted services which Lewes rendered her during their twenty years together. She had too much discouragement from within herself to be able to put up with it from outside. No sooner is she persuaded that the book she has written was "worth writing—worth living through long years to write" than she begins to think it impossible that she will ever write anything so good and true again. "I have arrived at faith in the past, but not at faith in the future." This kind of self-mistrust is a common enough feature of the artist's temperament: very few writers, and those not always the most gifted, are immune from its whispered insinuations. But in George Eliot it was more conspicuous than in most, unless by her complainings she made it seem so. She was always in need of reassurance, always avid for expressions of approval and friendship and love. And she never did arrive at faith in the future.

Among new friends made this year were Richard Congreve and his wife; of old friends, Herbert Spencer and Barbara Bodichon were among the most valued; Dickens was a frequent visitor; Mrs. Gaskell wrote her a "very beautiful letter." Marian was at work on her next book, *The Mill on the Floss;* she read Bunyan, Thomas à Kempis, and Darwin, the last aloud with Lewes; and in a letter to Lewes' son Charles she wishes she could find time to rub up her knowledge of algebra so that she might study it with him. The Brays and Sara Hennell, now fully restored to her by virtue of the June meeting, continue to receive long letters from her. She had also resumed contacts by letter with her sister Chrissey. Chrissey, in February, broke the long disapproving silence that had persisted since Marian's elopement with Lewes. "My object in writing to you is to tell you how very sorry I have been that I ceased to write, and neglected one who, under all circumstances, was kind to me and mine. *Pray believe* me when I say it will be the greatest comfort I can receive to know that you are *well* and *happy*. Will you write once more?" The letter went on to say that Chrissey had been suffering from tuberculosis for the past eighteen months, and it was followed next month by a note from her daughter Emily to say that she had been taken worse and could not live many days. Two years before, in April, 1857, we find Marian anxiously inquiring about Chrissey in a letter to Isaac, and arranging to send money to her through him;

but she seems not to have been kept in touch with the situation between then and February, 1859, and Chrissey's death, following so soon upon the happiness of reconciliation, was a grief to her. "I had," she tells Sara Hennell, "a very special feeling towards her—stronger than any third person would think likely."

*Chapter Five*

## YEARS OF ACHIEVEMENT

I

SHE was now, in 1860, fairly launched on her career
as George Eliot, a career that was to prove, in its
outward aspect, almost monotonously successful.
Behind this career was a life of planning and working,
triumph and despondency, anxiety and self-mistrust: the
triumphs sweetened and the despondency lightened by the
devoted companionship of that so "selfish" man who had
"deliberately cast a moral and social blight" upon her.
Every one of her manuscripts bears an inscription testify-
ing to her sense of his goodness, without which, she implies, her work could never have been accomplished; and
the most industrious research on the part of people with
moral axes to grind has failed to unearth any evidence of
major discord in her married life. She died at the end of
1880, having survived Lewes by two years and a month.
To say that her talent died with him would be misleading;
but it is true that the heart went out of her, and that she
wrote nothing of the smallest consequence after his death.
Her last volume, *The Essays of Theophrastus Such*, was
already with the publishers.

Of the last twenty years, the years of fulfillment and
achievement, there is little to tell but that she accomplished
then the work by which she is now remembered, from
*Scenes of Clerical Life* in 1857 to *Daniel Deronda* in 1876.
The *Scenes* were followed by *Adam Bede* in 1859, *The*

*Mill on the Floss* in 1860, *Silas Marner* in 1861, *Romola* in 1862–63, *Felix Holt,* 1866, *The Spanish Gypsy,* 1868, and *Middlemarch,* 1871–72. Of all these some account will be given in later chapters. After years of storm and stress and much inward misgiving, in middle life she had found her true haven with Lewes and discovered her literary destiny. To argue from the comparative uneventfulness of this later time (as some have done) that her life was impoverished, starved of social pleasures, virtually over, is singularly shallow. She lived for a while in a certain seclusion, and was no doubt uneasily conscious of being disapproved of; but in general it must be obvious that the most contented as well as the most fruitful period of her existence began when, purged of personal frustrations and freed from economic cares, she was able at last to devote herself to imaginative writing. "It was never a trial to me," she writes to Mrs. Peter Taylor in 1861, "to have been cut off from what is called the world, and I think I love none of my fellow-creatures the less for it." She adds, however, that she must always retain a peculiar regard for those few who showed her any kindness in word or deed at that time, "when there was the least evidence in my favour." There follows, it is true, a more strident, a painful passage:

For the last six years I have ceased to be "Miss Evans" for any one who has personal relations with me—having held myself under all the responsibilities of a married woman. I wish this to be distinctly understood; and when I tell you that we have a great boy of eighteen at home who calls me Mother, as well as two other boys, almost as tall, who write to me under the same name, you will understand that the point is not one of mere egoism or personal dignity, when I request that any one who has a regard for me will cease to speak of me by my maiden name.

Poor Marian! So quick, in moments of uneasiness, to resort to pompousness! But it would be a mistake to make much of that; it was no more than a limp or a stammer, and it does not hide her real simplicity of heart. We can surely forgive her too for being a little oversolemn about her work, since after all it was good work. She entreats Sara Hennell not to think of reading *Silas Marner* just because it is come out.

I hate *obligato* reading and *obligato* talk about my books. I never send them to anyone, and never wish to be spoken to about them, except by an unpremeditated spontaneous propheting. They are written out of my deepest belief, and as well as I can, for the great public—and every sincere strong word will find its mark in that public.

She did indeed, one cannot deny it, make something of a fuss of herself and her Muse. She must not be distracted by hearing what the critics say about her. She is reluctant to venture out of her private paradise, for "only by re-nouncing all social intercourse but such as comes to our own fireside" can she escape sacrificing the "chief objects of life"—which we may presume to have been domestic happiness and the writing of books.

The "great boy of eighteen" was Charles Lewes; and the two others, who wrote to her from school, were Thornton (named after Thornton Hunt) and Bertie. They called her in fact not "Mother" but—uncomfortable compromise, one would have thought—"Mutter." A certain fulsomeness in the expression of affection seems to have been current in the Lewes household, if we may judge from the letters [1] that passed between the boys and their father and adoptive mother. Charles, on the eve of his betrothal, is "very glad to hear how much better the little Mutter is," and adds: "I long so to kiss her." Mutter responds in kind, sometimes resorting to the nauseous device of writing of herself, playfully, in the third person. Lewes in her letters is nearly always "the little Pater," and there are kisses in plenty.

But these are private family letters, written with no view to publication, and whether one likes them or not they afford clear evidence of the mutual regard between Marian and Lewes' sons. Anthony Trollope, always a good friend, helped Charles to get a job in the post office, in which department he himself was a senior official. Lewes and Marian, enjoying their shared solitude, had looked forward with some misgiving to having him always with them, but he proved to be, Lewes says, a comfort and delight and never caused them any anxiety. In 1865 he married a granddaughter of Dr. Southwood Smith, distinguished physician and pioneer of sanitary reform. Thornton, adopting a "colonial career," went to Natal, where Bertie, who chose to be a farmer, presently joined him. Only Charles survived his father, Bertie dying at the age of twenty-nine, and Thornton, perhaps the most engaging personality of the three, while still virtually a boy. In May, 1869, three years after his going, Thornton came home ill, lingered in pain for six months, and died. Agnes Lewes, his mother, came and sat with him for two hours soon after his arrival home; but it was Lewes and Marian who watched over him, day after day, in fluctuating hope

1. Arthur Paterson, ed., *George Eliot's Family Life and Letters* (London, 1928).

and fear, throughout that terrible summer and autumn.

Lewes' own health gave frequent cause for anxiety, and it is likely that Marian's proneness to depression had physical as well as mental causes. They both worked very hard, she at her fiction and her reading, he at his studies in what was then called physiological psychology. Visits to the coast were undertaken only partly for pleasure, and partly for the sake of the marine specimens which Lewes so industriously collected and of which, as already noted, he gives an account in his *Seaside Studies*. But if they seldom enjoyed perfect health, it was not for lack of holidays. Marian confides to her Journal that she had looked forward for years to visiting Italy: "rather with the hope of the new elements it would bring to my culture," adds the earnest self-improver, "than with the hope of immediate pleasure." It was perhaps in this spirit that she explored the byways of Florence: rather with the hope of filling her notebooks with local color than for the sake of mere enjoyment. The result was *Romola*, a work with which it is difficult indeed to associate enjoyment. "Mr. Lewes," she writes to Blackwood, "is kept in continual distraction by having to attend to my wants—going with me to the Magliabecchian Library, and poking about everywhere on my behalf—I having very little self-help about me of the pushing and inquiring kind."

It is clear that Lewes consistently spoiled her, running errands, looking up references for her, sifting the reviews of her books so that no wounding word should catch her eye, and coddling her egoism in every conceivable way. Not that his devotion was unreciprocated: her frequent, admiring, affectionate allusions to "Mr. Lewes"—why could she not sometimes say simply "George"?—show

that she was almost as interested in his projects as he in
hers. Almost, I think, is a necessary qualification; but she
did appreciate his mind, as well as delighting in his company and being grateful for his endless solicitude. "Mr.
Lewes"—this to Sara Hennell, one of her most intimate
friends—

has been mending ever since we went to Malvern, and is
enjoying life and work more than he has done before for
nearly a year. He has long had in his mind to write a history
of science—a great, great undertaking, which it is a happiness
to both of us to contemplate as possible for him. And now he
is busy with Aristotle, and works with all the zest that belongs to fresh ideas.

They both had the habit of writing in their diaries a summary judgment on each year as it reached completion.
Lewes' for 1861 begins: "One more year of deep wedded
happiness . . ."

## II

Much reading, much writing, family anxieties, concerts,
the opera, piano playing, visits abroad (Italy, France, Germany, Spain) and holidays at home, correspondence with
friends old and new, and "deep wedded happiness" with
a man who shared her interests and whose interests she
shared: this was her life in these last twenty years. "My
trouble now is George's delicate health [August, 1864:
he is "George" at last]. He gets thinner and thinner. He
is going to try what horseback will do, and I am looking
forward to that with some hope." In the same letter: "Our
boy's love-story runs smoothly, and seems to promise
nothing but good. His attraction to Hampstead gives

George and me more of our dear old *tête-à-tête*, which we can't help being glad to recover." In the following month, again to Sara Hennell, she writes from Scarborough: "Mr. Lewes, in spite of a sad check of a few days, is strengthened beyond our most hopeful expectations by this brief trial of fresh conditions." On Christmas Day, 1864, she reads the Third Act of *The Spanish Gypsy* to George, who praises it highly. In the following February she tells Sara Hennell: "We are very happy. . . . I am beginning to feel it an heroic effort when I make up my mind to invite half-a-dozen visitors. But it is necessary to strive against this unsocial disposition, so we are going to have some open evenings." But her Journal entry for February 21 runs: "Ill and very miserable. George has taken my drama away from me." Illness is a recurring theme. A month later: "Dear George is all activity, yet is in very frail health. How I worship his good humour, his good sense, his affectionate care for every one who has claims on him! That worship is my best life."

She had need of George's buoyancy, having none of her own. She was constantly beset with fears and doubts of herself. "Horrible scepticism about all things paralysing my mind. Shall I ever be good for anything again? Ever do anything again?" All artists know this mood of spiritual exhaustion, but in George Eliot it was perhaps related to her general disposition and her personal philosophy. She suffered her life long from an excess of taking thought. To "live without opium" was her resolve, by opium meaning the consolations of conventional religion and what we nowadays call wishful thinking; and she could not see that if self-deception is opium, persistent dwelling on the darker aspects of mortal life is poison of a more lethal kind.

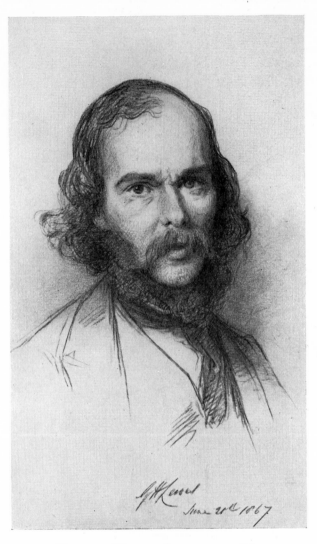

GEORGE HENRY LEWES IN 1867
BY RUDOLF LEHMANN

She seems to have had almost no capacity for unreflecting joy. She was an inveterate moralizer even of her pleasures. In work she could sometimes forget herself, and live; but her mind in repose was apt to be "sad"—not necessarily with sorrow, but with the heavy sadness of an ill-cooked cake. To regard her bleak outlook on life as the result of her change over from Christian theism to agnostic fatalism, as Bernard Shaw seems inclined to do in his Postscript to the World's Classics edition (1946) of *Back to Methuselah*, is, I think, to oversimplify the matter. Between the Calvinism of her youth and the determinism of her later years there is little to choose. Either, if *felt* as well as intellectually accepted, is deadly: belief in the first means the abandonment of justice, and belief in the second implies the denial of reason. The cause of George Eliot's "sadness" must lie deeper than any mere opinion. Her philosophy— not her views but her view, her habitual way of looking at life—was rather the symptom than the cause of her sad condition. One does not deny that her view was often colored, or deprived of color, by an obsession with the idea of necessity; but many men and women, however inconsistently, have accepted and preached that barren half truth without any appreciable loss of vigor and hope in their personal outlook.

The ancient opposition between freedom and necessity is fundamentally a false one, the problem insoluble only because it is stated in terms that beg the whole question. The only way out is to accept the vital paradox that though we are conditioned, and so far determined, we have yet an ineradicable sense of free choice. To deny that sense, to try to act as though determinism were absolute, is at once a logical contradiction and a form of death. It is

a logical contradiction because if we are wholly determined, our thoughts are determined, the reasoning process
is nothing but a fond illusion, and the theory of determinism, being itself determined, cannot be known to be
true. Both "reason" and "knowledge" become irrational
fictions. And it is a form of death because it makes everything, including our own thinking, a mindless mechanism.

George Eliot did not think so far as this, or she would
have seen that a belief that denies the validity of reasoning
can hardly be called reasonable.[2] Nor did she, we may be
sure, feel herself and her own actions to be the product of
mechanical necessity. Her dreary insistence, in her fiction,
on the inevitability of consequence, the theme that what a
man sows that shall he also reap, is moral rather than, in
the strict sense, philosophical. The gray outlook, merci-
fully lightened by flashes of humor and affection, is the
result not of her opinions but of her unbuoyant temperament, the hidden psychological causes of which are now
beyond our finding.

Large resignation and acceptance of the inevitable (her
own words) are all that she is able to commend to us. True
and salutary so far as it goes; but if human life is nothing
but a sad asylum of invalids bravely awaiting their doom,
the sooner we dispatch ourselves the better. Happily, she
assures us, there is more.

Love, pity, constituting sympathy, and generous joy with
regard to the lot of our fellowmen, comes in—has been grow-

2. Rationalism and an unqualified belief in determinism are mutually
exclusive. The attempt of some professed determinists to eat their cake
and have it reminds one of the solipsist for whom the truth of his doctrine was so self-evident that he was astonished when others did not
see it.

ing since the beginning—enormously enhanced by wider vision of results—by an imagination actively interested in the lot of mankind generally; and these feelings become piety— i.e. loving, willing submission and heroic Promethean effort towards high possibilities, which may result from our individual life.

She continues:

There is really no moral "sanction" but this inward impulse. The will of God is the same thing as the will of other men, compelling us to work and avoid what they have seen to be harmful to social existence. Disjoined from any perceived good, the divine will is simply so much as we have ascertained of the facts of existence which compel obedience at our peril. Any other notion comes from the supposition of arbitrary revelation.

Here surely is the *reductio ad absurdum* of arid rationalism, the displacement of living experience by thought, the deification of rational deduction. Is the love that binds mother to child or man to woman born of the rational reflection that love on the whole is a good thing for humanity in general, something ordained by "the will of other men"? Does a flower grow its own way into beauty according to a rational recipe? It should have been obvious, even to a converted Calvinist, that life and the joy of life come first, and reason a helpful but not infallible second. George Eliot the thinker, shying away like a frightened horse from the (quite unnecessary) "supposition of arbitrary revelation," could make this colossal blunder. As an artist she knew better. The gossips in the Rainbow Inn have a more robust vitality, and a more searching common sense, than she was willing to allow to herself.

F. W. H. Myers,[3] at whose invitation she and Lewes visited Cambridge, has left an account of her which, despite its portentous style, is illuminating:

I remember how at Cambridge I walked with her once in the Fellows' Garden of Trinity, on an evening of rainy May; and she, stirred somewhat beyond her wont, and taking as her text the three words which had been used so often as the inspiring trumpet-call of men—the words God, Immortality, Duty—pronounced with terrible earnestness how inconceivable was the first, how unbelievable the second, and yet how peremptory and absolute the third. Never, perhaps, have sterner accents affirmed the sovereignty of impersonal and unrecompensing Law. I listened, and night fell; her grave, majestic countenance turned towards me like a sibyl's in the gloom; it was as though she withdrew from my grasp, one by one, the two scrolls of promise and left me the third scroll only, awful with inevitable fates. And when we stood at length and parted, amid that columnar circuit of forest trees, beneath the last twilight of starless skies, I seemed to be gazing, like Titus at Jerusalem, on vacant seats and empty halls —on a sanctuary with no Presence to hallow it, and heaven left lonely of a God.

Duty, "stern daughter of the voice of God"—she is not to be neglected, and she is a true guide in dark places. But must we be forever thinking about her?

### III

They had had several changes of residence since their first coming together, but in November, 1863, George Lewes and George Eliot moved house for the last time.

3. (1843–1901) author of *Human Personality and Its Survival of Bodily Death.*.

Their new home was known as The Priory, 21 North Bank, Regent's Park. On the day of the removal Marian was only half recovered from a severe attack of influenza, which had caused her, she says, more terrible pains in the head and throat than she had known for years. The crisis past, however, she is able to enjoy her new situation. "Mr. Owen Jones has been unwearied in taking trouble that everything about us may be pretty. He stayed two nights till after twelve o'clock, that he might see every engraving hung in the right place." But he did more than that; for she amusedly confesses that she is wearing "a grey moire antique" in consequence of a severe lecture from him on her "general neglect of personal adornment."

Charles Lewes' twenty-first birthday fell on the day when they were at last properly settled in, which made the housewarming "a doubly interesting epoch"—what a genius she had for ponderosity in personal letters!

I am glad to have got over this crisis of maternal and house-keeping duty. My soul never flourishes on attention to details which others can manage quite gracefully without any conscious loss of power for wider thoughts and cares. Before we began to move, I was swimming in Comte and Euripides and Latin Christianity: *now* I am sitting in puddles, and can get no sight of deep water. *Now* I have a mind made up of old carpets fitted in new places, and new carpets suffering from accidents; chairs, tables, and prices; muslin curtains and down-draughts in cold chimneys. I have made a vow never to think of my own furniture again, but only of other people's.

One is tempted to think that a few weeks in the England of the nineteen-forties might have been a salutary spiritual experience for this pampered housewife. But before long she is thoroughly enjoying our new house—enjoying its quiet and freedom from perpetual stair-mounting—enjoying also the prettiness of colouring and arrangement, all of which we owe to our dear good friend Mr. Owen Jones. He has determined every detail, so that we can have the pleasure of admiring what is our own without vanity. And another magnificent friend has given me the most splendid reclining chair conceivable, so that I am in danger of being envied by the gods, especially as my health is thoroughly good withal.

In this house she was to write her last three novels and her poems; and it was here that she and Lewes began "receiving" on Sunday afternoons. These receptions were famous in their day. They were stage managed by Lewes; but whether it was he or her own morbid sense of duty that persuaded her to sit in her shop window and placate the curiosity of the pilgrims, we do not know. It must certainly have been Lewes who, with his geniality and facile wit, kept the conversation going; for she had no talent for that kind of thing. Her notion of talk, and a very good notion it is, was the interchange of real thought between intimate friends. In personal intercourse of the less intimate kind she had no lightness of touch. Her seriousness disdained the graces and pleasant artifice of literary small talk, and in the atmosphere of the *salon* she was like a whale out of water. From what we know of her, as she is revealed in her letters and her fiction, we may be sure, I think, that she did not willfully or willingly assume the airs of a sibyl; but this unfortunately was the impression she made on some. In private she was a good friend and wise counsellor to young men and women who came to her with their troubles and difficulties. She was gentle, deeply sympathetic, and quite unassuming, giving all her attention to anyone whose need levied a claim on her. And it was not her fault, but her misfortune, if on more public occasions her aloofness gave her the effect of an oracle. Among the young men of letters who resorted to her was Oscar Browning, and his account of these Sunday afternoons [4] provides us with valuable firsthand evidence:

Few houses in London have been the scene of stronger and more interesting emotions. The visitor on Sunday afternoon rang at the gate, entered the porch of the house, turned along the passage to the left, passing by the dining-room and Mr. Lewes's study, and entered the drawing-room by the door at the end of the passage. It was a double drawing-room without folding doors, decorated by Owen Jones, and hung with Leighton's drawings for the illustration of *Romola*. A bow window, with casements down to the ground, looked on to the garden. Mrs. Lewes generally sat in an armchair at the left of the fireplace. Lewes generally stood or moved about in the back drawing-room, at the end of which was the grand piano, on which, as far as I am aware, she never played during these receptions. In the early days of my acquaintance the company was small, containing more men than women. Herbert Spencer and Professor Beesly were constant visitors. The guests closed round the fire and the conversation was general. At a later period the company increased, and those who wished to converse with the great authoress whom they had come to visit took their seat in turns at the chair by her side. She always gave us of her best. Her conversation was deeply sympathetic, but grave and solemn, illumined by happy phrases and by thrilling tenderness, but not by humour. Although her features were heavy, and not well-proportioned, all was forgotten when that majestic head bent slowly down, and the eyes were lit up with a penetrating and

4. Oscar Browning, *Life of George Eliot* (London, 1890).

lively gaze. She appeared much greater than her books. Her ability seemed to shrink beside her moral grandeur. She was not only the cleverest, but the best woman you had met. You never dared to speak to her of her works; her personality was so much more impressive than its product. At a later time the string of visitors became fatiguing to those who remembered the old days. The drawing-room was enlarged to hold them; and three fashionably dressed ladies, sweeping in, occupied the sofa, and seemed to fill the room. These Sunday afternoon receptions were a great strain upon her strength. When the last visitor had departed she would, if the weather were fine, seek refreshment in a brisk walk to dispel her headache, and to call back the circulation into her feet, the icy coldness of which was one of her perpetual trials.

And now another, a somewhat less sympathetic witness, takes up the tale: a young *Athenæum* reviewer,[5] whose "gushing defence" of *Daniel Deronda* (the phrase is his own) provoked an invitation from Lewes. He went, he says, with all the feelings of the neophyte at the shrine for the first time; and, inevitably, he was disappointed. He was struck by the contrast between "the boisterous Bohemian bonhomie" of George Lewes and the "almost old-maiden-ish refinement" of George Eliot. He tried to lead her to talk of his own criticism, but was met by the quiet parry: "I never read criticisms of my own works." He had occasion to visit her again, after Lewes' death; found the house in gloom and herself in depression; and on this occasion was struck by the massiveness of her head as contrasted with the frailty of her body.

When she was seated one thought her tall: such a head should have been propped up by a larger frame. The long thin hands

5. Joseph Jacobs, Introduction to *Essays and Reviews* (London, 1891).

were those of a musician. The exquisite modulations of the voice told of refinement in every well-chosen phrase. . . . She spoke of one of her favourite themes, the appeal of the circle in which one is born even if one has in certain ways grown beyond or outside it.

It would be difficult for a young man to suppose that a woman in George Eliot's position could be shy of him at a first encounter; but that is how I read her remark that she never read criticisms of her own works. It was not a snub but an evasion prompted by diffidence. For it was not strictly true. She did, for example, read R. H. Hutton's article on *Romola*, and wrote to him, at once appreciatively, gratefully, and with the genuine humility of an artist ready to recognize her own faults. "You have correctly pointed out the reason why my tendency to excess in this effort after artistic vision makes the impression of a fault in *Romola* much more perceptible than in my previous books. And I am not surprised at your dissatisfaction with Romola herself." There was no unkindness in her, and though "there lay undoubtedly a deep gloom in the recesses of her own nature," her personal influence, says Oscar Browning, was stimulating. One summer afternoon in Windsor Park, he found himself alone with her, and "ventured to pour into her ears the difficulties which were then assailing me, the struggle between the demands of the life of self-culture and the life of self-sacrifice, which is the common malady of youthful minds." Whereupon she turned to him "with the eager glance of a prophetess" and said: "I know all you mean. I have felt it all myself." And then talked to him in a way that put an end to his unrest and "laid the germs of content." Here, and in her work, not in the solemn Sunday afternoon sessions, was the real George Eliot.

## IV

The death of Lewes was a shattering blow to her. The prop and mainstay of her life was gone. "Here I and sorrow sit," she writes in her Journal. It is possible to imagine, and hardly possible to exaggerate, her desolation. She roused herself, after some weeks of stupor, to receive a few friends again and to become busy with plans for the foundation of a George Henry Lewes Studentship in which his memory should be perpetuated.

Among the first friends to be granted audience was John Walter Cross, whom she and Lewes had first met in 1869, at Rome. She was then fifty, and Cross twenty-nine. His eldest sister and her husband, who were on their honeymoon, had become friendly with Lewes and George Eliot, and when Cross arrived with his mother and another sister the three of them went by invitation to call on the illustrious couple. It was a tremendous experience for young Mr. Cross: he was "better acquainted with George Eliot's books than with any other literature" and evidently cherished a profound veneration for her. He recalls, fifteen years later,

the low, earnest, deep musical tones of her voice . . . the fine brows, with the abundant auburn-brown hair framing them, the long head broadening at the back, the grey-blue eyes, constantly changing in expression, but always with a very loving, almost deprecating, look at my mother, the finely-formed, thin transparent hands, and a whole *Wesen*, that seemed in complete harmony with everything one expected to find in the author of *Romola*.

Their next encounter was in the August of the following year, when Lewes and George Eliot visited the Crosses at Weybridge.

Mr. and Mrs. Lewes were in deep trouble, owing to the illness of Thornton Lewes; we were also in much anxiety as to the approaching confinement of my sister with her first child; and I was on the eve of departure for America. Sympathetic feelings were strong enough to overlap the barrier (often hard to pass) which separates acquaintanceship from friendship. A day did the work of years. Our visitors had come to the house as acquaintances, they left it as lifelong friends. . . . Within a month my sister had died in child-birth, and her death called forth one of the most beautiful of George Eliot's letters.

This was the sister who, on this same Weybridge occasion, had moved George Eliot to tears by her rendering of one of the songs from *The Spanish Gypsy:* she moved quickly to the piano, says Cross, and "kissed Mrs. Bullock very warmly in her tears." Cross tells us little of his subsequent friendship with George Eliot and Lewes, and that little is all we know. He deeply admired her genius and personality; and no doubt she and Lewes thought him a very sympathetic and discerning young man. There was no more to it than that.

John Walter Cross was born in 1840, the son of a London merchant. Before he was out of his teens he had joined his father's firm, Dennistoun Cross and Company, of Cannon Street; and it was probably as an agent or representative of that firm that he spent twelve years, from 1857, in New York. At the time of his marriage (1880) to George Eliot he was in his fortieth and she in her sixty-first year. That event, had it been foretold eighteen months before, would have seemed to her utterly incredible: to us, who can watch its approach in her letters, it has a certain painful inevitability. Seven weeks after Lewes' death, she writes in a letter to Cross: "Some time, if I live, I shall be able to see you—perhaps sooner than anyone else—but not yet. Life seems to get harder instead of easier." A week later, in answer to his further importunity: "When I said 'some time' I meant still a distant time. I want to live a little time, that I may do certain things for his sake. So I try to keep up my strength, and I work as much as I can to save myself from imbecility. But that is all at present. I can go through anything that is mere business. But what used to be a joy is joy no longer, and what is pain is easier because he has not to bear it." A week later (February 7, 1879):

I do need your affection. Every sign of care for me from the beings I respect and love, is a help to me. In a week or two I think I shall want to see you. Sometimes, even now, I have a longing, but it is immediately counteracted by a fear. The perpetual mourner—the grief that can never be healed—is innocently enough felt to be wearisome by the rest of the world. And my sense of desolation increases. Each day seems a new beginning—a new acquaintance with grief.

This sequence of letters suggests that she was already, with the clinging dependency that was central in her character, beginning to turn to Cross for the indispensable "someone to lean upon." As Charles Bray has recorded, she was "not fitted to stand alone"; and moreover she was apparently incapable of even trying to do so. Cross was allowed to visit her on February 23. In April she writes to him: "I am in dreadful need of your counsel. Pray come to me when you can—morning, afternoon, or evening." And from that time he saw her constantly.

A week after Lewes' death Cross had lost his mother, to whom he had been much attached; and it may be that subconsciously he was looking for someone who should take her place. Driven by his bereavement to seek new interests, he had begun to read Dante; and now, during the next twelve months, George Eliot read with him, not, he says, in a dilettante way, but with minute and careful examination of every sentence. "The divine poet took us into a new world. It was a renovation of life. At the end of May I induced her to play the piano at Witley for the first time; and she played regularly after that whenever I was there, which was generally once or twice a week." A year later, on May 6, 1880, they were married at St. George's, Hanover Square; and that pillar of righteousness, Marian's brother Isaac, was placated at last. Breaking his long silence of disapproval he sent her "kind words of sympathy," and doubtless thanked his dreary god that someone at last had made an honest woman of Isaac Evans' sister. The stain on an illustrious family was all but rubbed out.

One can scarcely resist the suspicion that in some obscure corner of her heart Marian Evans felt that too. The child Mary Ann that was still alive in her somewhere may perhaps have recalled to her the honest, industrious, and rigidly respectable father whose opinions had once been her law; may even have toyed with the fancy that as she went up the aisle with her bridegroom elect, an aging woman with a man twenty years her junior, Robert Evans from his front pew in heaven was watching with stern approval her slow, belated appoach to respectability. But even if Marian entertained such fancies, George Eliot, we may be sure, did not. I refrain from the impertinence of pretending to know her mind at that moment, but it is difficult to suppose that she did not think somewhat of her beloved Lewes. This new marriage, she writes to Barbara Bodichon, is a "wonderful blessing falling to me beyond my share, after I had thought that my life was ended. Deep down below there is a hidden river of sadness, but . . . I shall be a better, more loving creature than I could have been in solitude." To Isaac, returning thanks for his so brotherly letter, she says: "The only point to be regretted in our marriage is that I am much older than he. But," she adds, with a truly wonderful complacency, "his affection has made him choose this lot of caring for me rather than any other of the various lots open to him." The same note is heard in an earlier letter to Barbara Bodichon in which she announces her intention to marry. "I am going to do what not very long ago I should myself have pronounced impossible for me, and therefore I should not wonder at any one else who found my action incomprehensible. . . . Mr. J. W. Cross, who, you know, is a friend of years, a friend much loved and trusted by Mr. Lewes, and who, now that I am alone, *sees his happiness in the dedication of his life to me*. . . ." The italics are mine: she perhaps would not have seen the point of them.

Any summary account of this affair, which followed so soon upon the extravagant mourning for Lewes, must do scant justice to the inner truth of it. It has all the distortion of a cartoon and will suggest, quite falsely, that her grief was shallow and her protestations a species of hysteria. But if the clamor of the wedding bells in Hanover Square breaks upon us with the effect of an almost ludicrous anticlimax, we must remind ourselves of two things. The decision to marry Cross was finally taken, after much doubt and struggle, only a fortnight before the event. It is true that hardly eighteen months had passed since Lewes' death; but anyone who has suffered a bereavement of that magnitude knows that a lifetime of agony can be lived in eighteen months. The second fact to be taken into account is one that has already, and perhaps tediously, been insisted on: to be all in all to someone was an absolute necessity of George Eliot's existence. Nor need we grudge her the sunset gleam that lightened her last days; for within eight months of this odd marriage she was dead.

*Part II*

HER BOOKS

## Chapter Six

# THE RUSTIC NOVELS

I

WE HAVE glanced at her life and letters: let us now look at her art, her art of fiction. George Eliot presents the unusual spectacle of a first-rate imaginative artist who was also an abstract and analytical thinker. She can enter intuitively into the lives of her dramatis personæ, feeling their joys and sorrows and imaginatively sharing (a greater feat) their intellectual limitations, while at the same time remaining a little aloof, ready to relate all human experience to a general philosophy. In this she stands almost alone among the novelists of her time. Dickens, with his immense gusto and super-abundant energy of creation, remained to the end a brilliantly precocious child, seeing everything larger than life. Thackeray, despite his wider culture and his habit of sententiousness, has nothing of philosophy to offer us but a blend of genial satire and easy sentiment. Trollope, copious and kindly, with an art wonderfully adequate to the tasks he set it, was wisely content to leave the depths un-plumbed. And it is a commonplace of criticism that Jane Austen, who came nearest to perfection of them all, achieved that near perfection within a narrow scope. The Brontës had fire and passion, as these had not; but the Brontës too were limited in range, to the exceptional, the eccentric, the outrageous; they do not, as George Eliot does, seek to invest the commonplace with a universal significance.

But the power of abstract philosophizing carries with it, for the artist, a penalty, or at any rate a danger. It is the artist's business to find the universal in the particular, and the habit of generalization must be sparingly indulged in or it becomes a vice. George Eliot's chief minor fault as a novelist is her insistence on pointing the moral, her failure at times to let her imaginative creation speak for itself. Sometimes, as in her earliest work, she obtrudes herself clumsily; sometimes she interpolates her comment with tact; but always, except in moments of highest inspiration, she is aware of herself and her "message." Nearly all the Victorians indulged in didactic asides to the reader, but with George Eliot the habit was something more than a mere following of literary fashion. It arose from something in her character which, whether innate or acquired, was ineradicable: an ingrained Puritanism, an excess of conscientiousness, a felt need to give to the practice of art a moral justification. This anxious ethicalism, this deification of duty, had dominated her from her earliest years. In her adolescence it had worn the garb of an evangelical and Calvinistic Christianity, and it remained with her to the end, quite unaffected by her change of creed. It is arguable that even her laborious quest of culture, her voracious reading and her learning of six or seven languages, had been pursued in this same spirit of dutiful self-justification, and that the lust to achieve moral excellence, which for a while took the form of a girlish ambition for sainthood, was rooted not in vanity but in a pathological self-dislike. The attempt to relate it to her flouting of convention in 1854 cannot be sustained, since even in the psychological field effects do not precede their causes; but that her preoccupation with the ideas of duty and sacrifice and personal renunciation implies a sense of something that may almost be called "guilt" is undeniable. It is part of the paradox of her enigmatic personality that she who repudiated the doctrine of original sin remained infected with a sense of it. Among the great novelists of her time she alone, who theologically speaking denied its existence, was deeply concerned with the human soul.

Often in her treatment, and sometimes in her general plan, we find the thinker in George Eliot at odds with the artist. In treatment the dichotomy is very apparent, and for that reason the more easy to allow for. When she forgets herself she can write like an angel, with wit and humor and unforced tenderness, and with a buoyancy that was singularly lacking in her personal character; but when she recalls herself to the duty (as she conceives it) of instructing and edifying as well as entertaining the reader, she not only falls into didacticism but narrowly escapes falling into pedantry. In her letters she does *not* escape that disaster. In her letters, because she is always aware of herself and her intellectuality, there is scarcely one passage of sustained, uncareful, spontaneously good writing. No one, on the evidence of those letters, could have predicted that she had it in her to be a good novelist. Art is not achieved without effort, but the art begins when the effort ends, when the creative power generated by disciplined meditation takes command of hand and brain. At the height of her power George Eliot's fiction does indeed exhibit this quality of effortless creation, but there is hardly one novel of hers in which effort does not make itself felt sooner or later, and the blemishes in her work arise not from carelessness but from an excess of care. From first to last, from *Clerical Scenes* to *Deronda*, you may find examples both of near pedantry in the choice of words and of the resolve to be edifying. They are grossest, as we should expect, in the very first story of all, "Amos Barton," where we read of church walls that are "as smooth and innutrient as the summit of the Rev. Amos Barton's head, after ten years of baldness and supererogatory soap," of a child's "alphabetic erudition" (meaning that he had mastered the alphabet), and of a "lacteal addition" to a cup of tea. Vile writing this, and none the better for being half facetious. Still more difficult to suffer patiently are the several passages in which the author argues and moralizes with the reader about her characters, in the very worst schoolma'am style:

Depend upon it, you would gain unspeakably if you would learn with me to see some of the poetry and the pathos, the tragedy and the comedy, lying in the experience of a human soul that looks out through dull grey eyes, and that speaks in a voice of quite ordinary tones. In that case, I should have no fear of your not caring to know what farther befell the Rev. Amos Barton, or of your thinking the homely details I have to tell at all beneath your attention. As it is, you can, if you please, decline to pursue my story farther, since I learn from the newspapers that many remarkable novels, full of striking situations, thrilling incidents, and eloquent writing, have appeared only within the last season.

The wonder is not that George Eliot could bring herself to write like that in her first attempt, but that she should have let such passages stand in all subsequent printings. They can be defended, theoretically, on the ground that in these *Scenes from Clerical Life* she was writing in the character of a man recalling the scenes and personages of his boyhood, and since this convention does give to the stories the warmth and actuality of reminiscence, it would be merely tiresome to ask how he is able to record conversations at which he was not present and disclose thoughts which were never confided to him. Those who read the book when it first appeared have the advantage of us here: the author being unknown to them, they were spared the trouble of remembering that the narrator is not, in logic, to be identified with Marian Evans. The relevance of this defense may be questioned, however; for even in the later novels, done with a maturer and far more delicate art, and with no fictitious narrator interposed between author and reader, George Eliot does not hesitate to obtrude herself from time to time.

But if the faults to be found in her first comparatively crude attempt can be found again in a refined form, later, so too the qualities that startle us into admiration of *Adam Bede* and *Middlemarch* are to be found, if less frequently, in the *Clerical Scenes*. There is development in her work, and a growing mastery, but no fundamental change either of method or outlook. From the very first she had the knack of quick and humorous characterization that gives us a scene or a person in a few strokes of the pen. "While this greeting was going forward, Mr. Bridmain and Jet the spaniel looked on with the air of actors who had no idea of by-play." Again: "Mr. Bridmain had put his neck under the yoke of his handsome sister, and though his soul was a very little one—of the smallest description indeed—he would not have ventured to call it his own." So the most minor of minor characters is made, by his very nullity, amusing. Then there is Mr. Luke Byles, a mere chorus part in the story in which he figures, but who "piqued himself on his reading, and was in the habit of asking casual acquaintances if they knew anything of Hobbes." By virtue of that one sentence the man stands before us, a familiar acquaintance. And of Amos Barton himself: "His very faults were middling—he was not *very* ungrammatical. It was not in his nature to be superlative in anything; unless, indeed, he was superlatively middling, the quintessential extract of mediocrity." These, too, are author's comments; but they are slipped in, not obtruded, and so they pass for direct description. They are, however slightly, a foretaste of good things to come. So, too, the brilliant pictures of provincial life, sketched in with the confident ease of a master, and tinged with humor and light irony; and so, too, above all, those passages of homely, racy, character-revealing dialogue which foreshadow not only George Eliot's later triumphs in this kind but those of her great successor, Thomas Hardy.

In view of her implied disdain of "striking situations" and "thrilling incidents" in the passage quoted above, it is amusing that she nevertheless found it necessary to provide herself with such things in the *Clerical Scenes*, which are a mixture of melodrama, sentimental pathos, acute characterization, and quiet rural comedy. There are wife-beatings, dipsomania, lingering consumption, sudden death, scarlet sins, and dramatic conversions, for such as want them; there is the time-honored situation of a wife being turned out of the house in her nightshift by a brutal husband. The second piece, "Mr. Gilfil's Love Story," is the most shapely of the three; but it is in parts of the third, "Janet's Repentance," that we find the clearest promise of what George Eliot was to become. She is at her best when most at home and most at ease. She is at her best when, escaping from the domination of her predetermined plot, she concerns herself with background and atmosphere, and deals at leisure with incidentals. Nothing in the two earlier stories is so satisfying as her sketch, in the third, of the town she calls Milby, described not in terms of bricks and mortar but as an assemblage of human souls. It has the warmth and flavor of intimate reminiscence, but the "remembering," we must remember, is part of the fiction. The whole chapter, amounting to some thousands of words, is irradiated with a kind of affectionate irony that at moments recalls Jane Austen. This, for example, of Milby's two medical men:

Pratt was middle-sized, insinuating, and silver-voiced; Pilgrim was tall, heavy, rough mannered, and spluttering. Both were considered to have great powers of conversation, but Pratt's anecdotes were of the fine old crusted quality to be procured only of Joe Miller; Pilgrim's had the full fruity flavour of the most recent scandal. Pratt elegantly referred all diseases to debility, and, with a proper contempt for symptomatic treatment, went to the root of the matter with port-wine and bark; Pilgrim was persuaded that the evil principle in the human system was plethora, and he made war against it with cupping, blistering, and cathartics. They had both been long established in Milby, and as each had a sufficient practice, there was no very malignant rivalry between them; on the contrary, they had that sort of friendly contempt for each other which is always conductive to a good understanding between professional men; and when any new surgeon attempted, in an ill-advised hour, to settle himself in the town, it was strikingly demonstrated how slight and trivial are theoretic differences compared with the broad basis of common human feeling. There was the most perfect unanimity between Pratt and Pilgrim in the determination to drive away the obnoxious and too probably unqualified intruder as soon as possible.

Better still, and more evidently in Jane Austen's manner, is this later passage on the same theme:

The doctor's estimate, even of a confiding patient, was apt to rise and fall with the entries in the day-book; and I have known Mr. Pilgrim discover the most unexpected virtues in a patient seized with a promising illness. At such times you might have been glad to perceive that there were some of Mr. Pilgrim's fellow-creatures of whom he entertained a high opinion, and that he was liable to the amiable weakness of a too admiring estimate. A good inflammation fired his enthusiasm, and a lingering dropsy dissolved him into charity. Doubtless this crescendo of benevolence was partly due to feelings not at all represented by the entries in the day-book; for in Mr. Pilgrim's heart, too, there was a latent store of tenderness and pity which flowed forth at the sight of suffering. Gradually, however, as his patients became convalescent, his view of their characters became more dispassionate; when they could relish mutton-chops he began to admit that they had foibles, and by the time they had swallowed their last dose of tonic he was alive to their most inexcusable faults. After this, the thermometer of his regard rested at the moderate point of friendly back-biting, which sufficed to make him agreeable in his morning visits to the amiable and worthy persons who were yet far from convalescent.

But, inevitably, seriousness breaks in. Lest we should take her gentle malice too seriously, and be persuaded against her wish into adopting a cynical view of human nature, George Eliot is at pains to assure us that Milby undoubtedly had, in greater abundance than was visible on the surface, "that salt of goodness which keeps the world together." She elaborates the point in one of her more acceptable passages of commentary:

To a superficial glance, Milby was nothing but dreary prose: a dingy town, surrounded by flat fields, lopped elms, and sprawling manufacturing villages, which crept on and on with their weaving shops, till they threatened to graft themselves on the town. But the sweet spring came to Milby notwithstanding: the elm-tops were red with buds; the churchyard was starred with daisies; the lark showered his love-music on the flat fields; the rainbows hung over the dingy towns, clothing the very roofs and chimneys in a strange transfiguring beauty. And so it was with the human life there, which at first seemed a dismal mixture of griping worldliness, vanity, ostrich feathers, and the fumes of brandy: looking closer you found some purity, gentleness, and unselfishness, as you may have observed a scented geranium giving forth its wholesome odours amidst blasphemy and gin in a noisy pothouse. Little deaf Mrs. Crew would often carry half her own spare dinner to the sick and hungry; Miss Phipps, with her cockade of red feathers, had a filial heart, and lighted her father's pipe with a pleasant smile; and there were grey-haired men in drab gaiters, not at all noticeable as you passed them in the street, whose integrity had been the basis of their rich neighbours' wealth.

Of the many pieces of dialogue which "remind" one of Hardy's rustic choruses we shall find examples enough and to spare in the novels of her artistic maturity. But here is one, meanwhile, from the first story in that first book of all:

"I never saw the like to parsons," Mr. Hackit said one day in conversation with his brother churchwarden, Mr. Bond;

"they're al'ys for meddling with business, an they know no more about it than my black filly."

"Ah," said Mr. Bond, "they're too high learnt to have much common sense."

"Well," remarked Mr. Hackit, in a modest and dubious tone, as if throwing out a hypothesis which might be considered bold, "I should say that's a bad sort of eddication as makes folks unreasonable."

And one from the second, "Mr. Gilfil":

"Some folks can't a-bear to put off their colours," she [Mrs. Higgins] remarked; "but that was never the way i' *my* family. Why, Mrs. Parrot, from the time I was married, till Mr. Higgins died, nine year ago come Candlemas, I niver was out of black two years together!"

"Ah," said Mrs. Parrot, who was conscious of inferiority in this respect, "there isn't many families as have had so many deaths as yours, Mrs. Higgins."

Mrs. Higgins, who was an elderly widow, "well left," reflected with complacency that Mrs. Parrot's observation was no more than just, and that Mrs. Jennings very likely belonged to a family which had had no funerals to speak of.

This is as English as Shakespeare, and the resemblance to Hardy, who is in the same great tradition, can scarcely be missed. It is perhaps most marked in what may be termed the stage directions. Mr. Hackit utters his truism "as if throwing out a hypothesis which might be considered bold." The tone of Mrs. Parrot's remark is indicated by saying that she was "conscious of inferiority" in the matter of funerals. So Hardy's Joseph Poorgrass in *Far from the Madding Crowd* makes himself small while talking, "apparently from a meek sense of undue prominence":

"Such a modest man as he is!" said Jacob Smallbury. "Why, ye've hardly had strength of eye enough to look in our young mis'ess's face, so I hear, Joseph?"

All looked at Joseph Poorgrass with pitying reproach.

"No—I've hardly looked at her at all," simpered Joseph, reducing his body smaller whilst talking, apparently from a meek sense of undue prominence. "And when I seed her, 'twas nothing but blushes with me!"

And so Shepherd Gabriel Oak, when the great age of Jacob's father is the subject of admiring discussion:

"Shepherd would like to hear the pedigree of yer life, father, wouldn't ye, shepherd?"

"Ay, that I should," said Gabriel, with the heartiness of a man who had longed to hear it for several months . . .

That stage direction ("with the heartiness," etc.) is exactly in George Eliot's manner.

II

That is not to say, however, that her dialogue is always "right." We shall find, I think, that it is most right when she does not trouble to make it so. *Adam Bede* represents an immense advance on its predecessor. It is a book which, taken as a whole, cannot be spoken of except in terms of high respect. The warm rural coloring, the shrewd humor, the diversity of characters, the deep human feeling, the power and the amplitude and the patient workmanship, these things can hardly be praised too much. England is most English in those midland shires, and George Eliot gives us the England she knew as a child, knew not by deliberate study but by unconscious innocent assimilation, the England that existed before the industrial revolution and the coming of the machine age. Her rural scenes, her pictures of life in farmhouse and field, remain unsurpassed, unless by Hardy himself, whose description of his own *Under the Greenwood Tree* can be fitly applied to much in *Adam Bede:* "a rural painting of the Dutch school."

And it is not, for all its charm, an idealized picture: notwithstanding a certain complacent conservatism natural in the daughter of Robert Evans, a man who by his own efforts had risen in the feudal scale, she is as little blind to social injustice as to individual human faults, though she lays no undue stress on either. It is her evident resolve to tell the whole truth as she sees it that gives to her fiction that powerful illusion of actuality, an illusion that triumphantly survives her moralizing, her excess of showmanship, her lavish use of the historic present. For she is always the showman, always pointing at her characters and telling us what we ought to think of them, with a persistency which in a writer of inferior genius would be fatal. Luckily her fictions are for the most part too firmly grounded in imagination to succumb to these assaults on their reality. *Adam Bede* survives even Adam Bede.

If you are a character in a George Eliot novel, the chief thing you have to fear is your author's unqualified moral approval. If that cannot destroy your pretension to reality, nothing can. Not only by commentary, but in the subtler process of characterization, by the very speeches she puts into your mouth and your mind, she will do her best to expose you for what you are, or what you would be but for her own imaginative power, a walking shadow, a garrulous embodiment of qualities she is resolved to admire. Thus Adam. Thus at moments, despite all the praise lav-

ished on her by contemporaries, Dinah Morris. With these
two, with Adam's brother Seth, and with Rufus Lyon and
Ezra Cohen in later books, George Eliot is like a proud
mother at a baby show. They are never presented except
for our unqualified admiration, with the result that Adam,
the honest carpenter, conscientious and sagacious, in skill
and integrity far above the average of his excellent kind,
begins and ends his paper existence as a mere bundle of
moral qualities, a prig in homespun. We do not complain
that he is sententious, for that is his author's conception of
him; but must he be sententious and nothing else? And is
this a sententious carpenter speaking his mind, or is it
George Eliot herself, very transparently disguised?

*Adam Bede*

"Nay, Seth, lad; I'm not for laughing at no man's religion.
Let 'em follow their consciences, that's all. Only I think it
'ud be better if their consciences 'ud let 'em stay quiet i' the
church—there's a deal to be learnt there. And there's such a
thing as being over-speritual; we must have something beside
Gospel i' this world. Look at the canals, an' th' aqueducs, an'
th' coal-pit engines, and Arkwright's mills there at Cromford;
a man must learn summat beside Gospel to make them things,
I reckon. But t' hear some o' them preachers, you'd think
as a man must be doing nothing all 's life but shutting 's eyes
and looking what's a-going on inside him. I know a man
must have the love o' God in his soul, and the Bible's God's
word. But what does the Bible say? Why, it says as God put
His sperrit into the workman as built the tabernacle, to make
him do all the carved work and things as wanted a nice hand.
And this is my way o' looking at it: there's the sperrit o' God
in all things and all times—weekday as well as Sunday—and
i' the great works and inventions, and i' the figuring and the
mechanics. And God helps us with our headpieces and our
hands as well as with our souls; and if a man does bits o' jobs

out o' working hours—builds a oven for 's wife to save her from going to the bakehouse, or scrats at his bit o' garden and makes two potatoes grow istead o' one, he's doing more good, and he's just as near to God, as if he was running after some preacher and a-praying and a-groaning."

Both Adam and Dinah are examples of George Eliot's thoroughness overreaching itself. Everything the man says is painstakingly characteristic. There are no vitalizing inconsistencies in his behavior. He cannot even lose his temper except laboriously; and his private thoughts, carefully put into words for us, are as full of moral maxims as his public speech. "There's nothing but what's bearable as long as a man can work," he is represented as saying to himself. "The nature o' things doesn't change, though it seems as if one's own life was nothing but change. The square o' four is sixteen, and you must lengthen your lever in proportion to your weight, is as true when a man's miserable as when he's happy; and the best o' working is, it gives you a grip hold o' things outside your own lot." Dinah, too, full of good words and good works, and embodiment of Christian loving-kindness, is attractive as goodness must always be; but she is at best an ideal figure, with scarcely a touch of individuality, and at her less than best she is too conscious of her author's partiality. Nor is she altogether free from sanctimoniousness: " 'How do you do, Adam Bede?' said Dinah, in her calm treble, pausing from her sweeping, and fixing her mild grave eyes upon him. 'I trust you feel rested and strengthened again to bear the burden and heat of the day.' " One could hardly object to sanctimonious unction in a character portrayed quite objectively. A scrupulous portrait painter will put in the warts as well as the dimples. But the whole tone of

Dinah's portrait is one of unqualified admiration, and the warts—admittedly only little ones—seem to be offered as additional graces.

It will be remembered that George Henry Lewes, who saw the book chapter by chapter while it was being written, expressed a fear that Adam's part in the story was too passive, and suggested that he should be brought into dramatic conflict with his rival Arthur Donnithorne, Hetty's secret lover. The fight in the wood, unconvincing in itself but useful as a piece of plot mechanism, was a direct result of this advice. So, too, was Dinah's marriage with Adam a direct result of Lewes' wish that she should be, and remain to the end, the principal figure. But Adam's part is a passive one because Adam is not a vital character. Nor does putting him through the motions of fighting Donnithorne make him so. Adam is a moral concept, the sense of duty personified, an automatic machine from which, every time you insert your penny, you get a moral maxim. And that nothing can make Dinah the principal figure, not even her palpably contrived espousal of a man whose only sign of life was that he was amorously inclined rather to prettiness than to moral worth, is proved by the utter collapse of interest from the moment Hetty Sorrel has been bundled out of the book. The *narrative* strength of *Adam Bede* is in the Hall Farm scenes on the one hand, and in Broxton Vicarage and the Squire's household on the other. The main *dramatic* interest is provided by the simple story of Hetty and Arthur. The Poysers, man and wife and domestics, infect the whole book with their rich, ordinary humanity. Mrs. Poyser is a masterpiece of comic realism, and the emphasis is on the realism: she is a natterer, and incidentally a shrew, as well as a good wife and fond mother and the immortal embodiment of rustic, racy, kindly common sense. She is drawn with the same scrupulous fidelity to nature as went to the portrayal of Lisbeth Bede. In fine she is not an idealized character. Irwine, the rector, to some extent *is;* but he too succeeds in being both a type—the kindly, tolerant, well-bred, easygoing Anglican clergyman—and an individual: he survives even his author's strong moral approval, as Adam and Dinah do not. Arthur Donnithorne, a very average specimen of good-natured, erring humanity, and Hetty herself, the pretty victim of her own shallowness and his far from vicious passion, have ten times as much life and artistic truth in them as those laboriously studied "principal figures."

Theirs is not a new story: it is one of the oldest stories in the world, the theme of a hundred ballads. But it is given new life and a deeper significance by the art and sympathy with which it is treated. Arthur means no harm to Hetty; and Hetty, fond of herself though she is, is artless enough in her response to his gentle attentions. There is love, as well as some little vanity, on both sides. The artist triumphing over the moralist, George Eliot gives us, not a "seduction scene," in which the Squire's son takes cynical advantage of simple innocence, but an idyll of first love, presented with delicacy and understanding. She does this not because she wishes to gloss over the "wrongness" or at any rate the unwisdom of their indulging such feelings, but because as an artist she is concerned for once with what they felt, not with what we, sitting in judgment, ought to think about it. To themselves, this shy approach to love was a miracle of delight: it is right, therefore, that it should be so presented. And because, knowing what is to come, we are all the while conscious of the pity of it—that the seed of ultimate doom is hidden in this moment of beauty—the two chapters which contain this woodland idyll are perhaps the most moving in the whole book, more so than the prison scenes, more so than the trial and the sentence.

Before we leave *Adam Bede* a word more must be said about Dinah. We may regret the afterthought (prompted by Lewes) which persuaded George Eliot to try to make Dinah dominate the book. We may think that Dinah has had more than her share of praise and that her portrait is too partial. We could not, however, do without her, for she represents an important feature of that broad vision of human life, that conception of the mystery and diversity of human nature, which, over and above any explicit di-dacticism, the book as a whole seeks to embody. An artist projects upon his canvas the characters that exist in himself. He is not to be identified with any one of them, but there is a sense in which all that he creates is created of his own psychological substance: not of something that is peculiarly his own, not his own personal character, but of that mass of potentiality which we may call the common human heart. Individual character is the effect of a (largely unconscious) process of selection, the realization of some potentialities and the necessary exclusion of others. Human nature is not an abstraction: it is the well of being upon which we all draw, and upon which the imagination of the artist can draw freely, to the limit of his art's ca-pacity. The greatness of George Eliot is seen in the range of her imaginative sympathy, her intuitive sense of char-acter, and in the effect she gives, *beyond her conscious intention*, of having dramatized, in individual human figures, the conflicting elements that are in every human soul. Where such an aim is consciously pursued the result is apt to be crude allegory, a parade of lifeless abstractions like the figures in a morality play. But with George Eliot, as with some other and greater novelists, and as (preëminently) with Shakespeare, no such intention exists. With them the sense of a universal significance, of an implicit "criticism of life" as Matthew Arnold unhappily phrased it, comes to us as an incidental, an accidental, effect of the whole work, and is something that cannot be expressed except in the work as a whole.

We oversimplify the truth if we say that Quixote is pure spirit and Sancho Panza the flesh to which he is bound. Yet something of the sort must be said. Dinah, all sweetness and light, a selfless dedicated spirit, and Mrs. Poyser, with her head full of housewifely details and her mouth of homely proverbs, form a pair of beautifully contrasted characters. They are both good women in their different ways, and each gains from their juxtaposition. No two human souls could be outwardly more different; but they appreciate each other, and their author equally appreciates them both, and we are conscious, on reflection, that what they have in common, their simple, kindly humanity, is more radical and enduring than the differences that divide them. Moreover, the reader who grows weary of Dinah's somewhat stilted perfection finds relish and relief in hearing Mrs. Poyser give voice to his own impatience. Mrs. Poyser is forever urging Dinah to leave her native country, called (a little too appropriately) Stonishire, and to make her home at the Hall Farm and "leave off that preaching, as is ten times worse than anything your aunt Judith ever did." She elaborates the theme in her own garrulous fashion:

". . . And even if you'd marry Seth Bede, as is a poor wool-gathering Methodist, and 's never like to have a penny be-forehand, I know your uncle 'ud help you with a pig, and very like a cow, for he's allays been good-natur'd to my kin, for all they're poor, and made 'em welcome to th' house; and 'ud do for you, I'll be bound, as much as ever he'd do for Hetty, though she's his own niece. And there's linen in the house as I could well spare you, for I've got lot's o' sheeting and table-clothing, and towelling, as isn't made up. There's a piece o' sheeting I could give you as that squinting Kitty spun—she was a rare girl to spin, for all she squinted, and the children couldn't abide her; and, you know, the spinning's going on constant, and there's new linen wove twice as fast as th' old wears out. But where's the use o' talking, if ye wonna be persuaded, and settle down like any other woman in her senses, instead o' wearing yourself out with walking and preaching, and giving away every penny you get, so as you've nothing saved against sickness; and all the things you've got i' the world, I verily believe, 'ud go into a bundle no bigger nor a double cheese. And all because you've got notions i' your head about religion more nor what's i' the Catechism and the Prayer-book."

"But not more than what's in the Bible, aunt," said Dinah.

"Yes, and the Bible too, for that matter," Mrs. Poyser re-joined, rather sharply; "else why shouldn't them as know best what's in the Bible—the parsons and people as have got nothing to do but learn it—do the same as you do? But, for the matter o' that, if everybody was to do like you the world must come to a standstill; for if everybody tried to do with-out house and home, and with poor eating and drinking, and was allays talking as we must despise the things o' the world, as you say, I should like to know where the pick o' the stock, and the corn, and the best new-milk cheeses 'ud have to go. Everybody 'ud be wanting bread made o' tail ends, and everybody 'ud be running after everybody else to preach to 'em, instead o' bringing up their families, and laying by against a bad harvest. It stands to sense as that can't be the right religion."

"Nay, dear aunt, you never heard me say that all people are called to forsake their work and their families. It's quite right the land should be ploughed and sowed, and the precious corn stored, and the things of this life cared for, and right that people should rejoice in their families, and provide for them, so that this is done in the fear of the Lord, and that they are not unmindful of the soul's wants while they are caring for the body. We can all be servants of God wherever our lot is cast, but he gives us different sorts of work, according as he fits us for it and calls us to it. I can no more help spending my life in trying to do what I can for the souls of others, than you could help running if you heard little Totty crying at the other end of the house; the voice would go to your heart, you would think the dear child was in trouble or in danger, and you couldn't rest without running to help her and comfort her."

"Ah," said Mrs. Poyser, rising and walking towards the door, "I know it 'ud be just the same if I was to talk to you for hours. You'd make me the same answer at th' end. I might as well talk to the running brook, and tell it to stan' still."

We thank heaven for Mrs. Poyser. Without her crisp common sense to relieve our feelings, Dinah's oracular spirituality would be intolerable. But Dinah, or what she represents, is equally necessary to our full appreciation of Mrs. Poyser; for undiluted Poyser would be almost as insipid as undiluted Dinah. The mixture is stimulating and it is more than that. It both adds to our enjoyment of each character and affirms by implication the rich complexity of human nature. For the mixture was in George Eliot, and, in whatever varying proportions, it is in every human soul.

### III

The creation of living characters is not the whole of the novelist's art, nor the manner of their presentation the only problem of treatment which he has to solve; but, that proviso granted, it is scarcely possible to exaggerate the importance of these two things. Two things in theory, in practice they turn out to be one thing, for it is in the process of presentation that characters "come to life," as we say, not merely for the reader but in some sense for the author as well. They are conceived in his imagination, but they are brought to birth, externalized, given body and definition, at the end of the pen. The best characters of Scott, of Dickens, of Jane Austen, like those of Shakespeare himself, *talk* themselves alive, as Logan Pearsall Smith has pointed out. The same is true of George Eliot and of all other good novelists of the central English tradition. Even Sterne, whose aim is rather to tease and entertain us with digressions than to tell a story, clearly belongs to this tradition so far as his characterization is concerned. Virginia Woolf, in whose fiction everything is subordinated to a delicate poetic impressionism, as clearly does not; nor do some other modern novelists who, as didactic and direct as she is subtle and evocative, prefer to people their novels with embodied points of view instead of with vital, individualized, unpredictable persons.

In novels of the central tradition, from (say) Richardson and Fielding at the middle of one century to Meredith and Hardy at the end of the next, characterization is of first importance. The quality of characterization is determined in part by many intermediate things: by choice of method, technical skill, narrative tempo, tone of voice, style, and the degree in which the author possesses an eye for significant features and an ear for idiosyncrasies of speech, especially the last. But behind and within all these, as the animating principle of the whole enterprise, is something of which not even the novelist himself (or herself) is always fully aware, namely, his own attitude to the creatures of his imagination. That it must be one of sympathy is self-evident, insofar as sympathy, imaginative sympathy, is a prerequisite of understanding: the products of pure satire are apt to be either mechanical monsters, mere caricatures of humanity, or gigantic figures of fun. But sympathy, though necessary, is not enough: sympathy unmixed with detachment is likely to result in a self-identification of author with creature in which the outlines of character are lost and characterization, properly so called, gives place to mere subjectivism and a species of special pleading. I have tried to show that George Eliot sometimes comes very near to falling into this trap in *Adam Bede;* and she does so again in later novels, most conspicuously in the last one of all, *Daniel Deronda*, where not only are some of the comparatively minor characters sentimentalized in this way, such as Mrs. Meyrick and her daughters, but some of the principals as well, Mirah Cohen, her brother Mordecai (intolerably overdone), and to a large extent Deronda himself.

In every novel of the kind we are considering the characters fall roughly into one of two classes: (*a*) the chief persons of the drama, whose inner life, from time to time, is directly revealed to us, and (*b*) the "chorus parts," as we might call them, whose function it is to suggest the world at large, to create in the reader a sense of the animated human environment in which this particular drama moves. We sometimes, of course, encounter borderline cases; but it is true in general that a character belongs either to (*a*) or (*b*), is either intimately presented, and endowed with as much complexity as the author's purpose may require and his imagination compass, or is drawn in swift, bold strokes and with complete objectivity. In the first case we learn to know the character's mind and heart, in the second we are content to know what he looks like and sounds like. It is enough that a minor character, a chorus part, should be recognizably "good" or "bad" or morally neutral, should be comic or pathetic or anything you like, so long as he is recognizably human; but a principal character presented in such simple terms cannot engage the interest or persuade the imagination of a reader who knows how inadequate they are to express the complex truth of any human soul. George Eliot's failures in characterization are never to be found among her chorus parts: there is no novelist who can more dexterously suggest the human environment of a story, by peopling her background with small, significant, representative figures who have nothing to do with the main action: her failures are those among her chief characters whose virtues she too urgently and tediously insists upon. They are the victims of their author's partiality.

There are no such failures in her second novel, *The Mill on the Floss*. It is not her best work; it is not nearly her best; it lacks indeed some indefinable quality that gave color and warmth to *Adam Bede;* but it does mark an advance in this one respect, that sympathy and detachment are well-nigh perfectly blended. True, we might guess, if we did not already know, that there is a good deal of the earlier Marian Evans in George Eliot's portrayal of Maggie Tulliver; but though there is tenderness in the portrait, and an element of self-pity, it cannot be contended that it is in any relevant sense a partial portrait. Maggie's faults and weaknesses are forgiven by her author but not glossed over, not held up for admiration. Something very near to strict justice is dealt out to her, as it is, and more surprisingly, to Tom. More surprisingly, because in Tom she succeeded in depicting a detestable person without ever, even for a moment, seeming to feel detestation.

If there is excess of anything in her characterization of these two, it is an excess of consistency, an anxious underlining of the dominant characteristic of each, lordly assertiveness in young Tom, clinging emotional dependency in Maggie. The effect, at moments, is of slavish conformance with a psychological formula. Here again it is only the chief, the intimately studied characters that suffer from this excess of consistency. The Dodson sisters, Maggie's aunts especially, in whose portrayal realism is spiced with satire, actually gain from it, gain in definition and therefore in memorableness, as minor characters are apt to do. And here again, in this overstressing of Tom's Tomhood and Maggie's Maggieness, George Eliot was doing something which she was to do again and again, the most glaring example being the early chapters of *Deronda* in which Gwendolen Harleth's selfishness and vanity are insisted on to the total exclusion of any other human quality. It is nearly always in the early chapters that George Eliot dis-

plays this weakness. In the early chapters, because she lacks
confidence, because her imagination has not warmed up,
she is too painstakingly faithful to her conscious design
and tries to make statement and emphasis do the work that
belongs to suggestion and imaginative persuasion. Later,
the heat generated by the effort of beginning softens the
hard core of her intention and gives her some measure of
ease, though seldom the careless ease of some other major
novelists and of many small garrulous ones.

Critics in her own time were united in admiration of
George Eliot's children; and it is true that except when
she uses a child in our (*b*) category, as a piece of sentimental decoration, she brings to her studies of children
the same instinct for psychological realism that she brings,
at her best, to other principal characters. Her portrayal of
Tom and Maggie as children, though their style of conversation has sometimes a synthetic air, is remarkable not
only for its general truth but for a certain ruthless fidelity
to the least amiable feature of childish psychology, its ingenuous and peremptory egoism. Tom is a masterful, self-
satisfied, and boastful little monster, and Maggie is the
adoring little sister insatiably greedy for affection: he has
no "feminine" virtues and she no "masculine" ones. Nothing could be truer to unregenerate human nature, nothing
could more sharply dramatize the different (but comple-
mentary) characters of these two, than the scene in which
Tom shares his jam puff with Maggie. He cuts the puff
into two halves and bids her shut her eyes:

"Now, which'll you have, Maggie—right hand or left?"

"I'll have that with the jam run out," said Maggie, keeping
her eyes shut to please Tom.

"Why, you don't like that, you silly. You may have it if

it comes to you fair, but I shan't give it you without. Right or left—you choose, now. Ha-a-a!" said Tom, in a tone of exasperation, as Maggie peeped. "You keep your eyes shut, now, else you shan't have any."

Maggie's power of sacrifice did not extend so far; indeed, I fear she cared less that Tom should enjoy the utmost possible amount of puff than that he should be pleased with her for giving him the best bit. So she shut her eyes quite close, till Tom told her to "say which," and then she said, "Left-hand."

"You've got it," said Tom, in rather a bitter tone.

"What! the bit with the jam run out?"

"No; here, take it," said Tom firmly, handing decidedly the best piece to Maggie.

"O, please, Tom, have it; I don't mind: I like the other: please take this."

"No, I shan't," said Tom, almost crossly, beginning on his own inferior piece.

Maggie, thinking it was no use to contend further, began too, and ate up her half puff with considerable relish as well as rapidity. But Tom had finished first, and had to look on while Maggie ate her last morsel or two, feeling in himself a capacity for more. Maggie didn't know Tom was looking at her; she was seesawing on the elder bough, lost to almost everything but a vague sense of jam and idleness.

"O, you greedy thing!" said Tom, when she had swallowed the last morsel. He was conscious of having acted very fairly, and thought she ought to have considered this, and made up to him for it. He would have refused a bit of hers beforehand, but one is naturally at a different point of view before and after one's own share of puff is swallowed.

Maggie turned quite pale. "O, Tom, why didn't you ask me?"

"*I* wasn't going to ask you for a bit, you greedy. You

might have thought of it without, when you knew I gave you the best bit."

"But I wanted you to have it—you know I did," said Maggie, in an injured tone.

"Yes, but I wasn't going to do what wasn't fair, like Spouncer. He always takes the best bit, if you don't punch him for it; and if you choose the best with your eyes shut, he changes his hands. But if I go halves, I'll go 'em fair—only I wouldn't be a greedy."

There is no maternal sentimentalism here, such as one too often finds in portraits of children. Nor is there any censoriousness. The two children are set before us, without comment, precisely as the author's imagination pictures them.

When we regard the book as a whole, I think it must be accounted a fault, if a minor one, that though George Eliot admirably succeeds in being fair to Tom she cannot contrive, despite allusions to manliness and blue eyes, to make us even for a moment find him lovable, as Maggie does. This, in however negligible a degree, diminishes not only his reality for us but Maggie's as well; or at any rate it diminishes the intimacy of our knowledge of them. We have some difficulty in sympathizing fully with Maggie's distresses when Tom's coldness or hostility is the cause of them, because, though we are told again and again that she loved him dearly, we ourselves are given no chance of doing so; with the result that her love of him, because we cannot imaginatively feel it with her but must needs take her word for it, looks to us almost like a piece of perverseness, an aberration.

But perhaps this is not a minor fault after all: perhaps it affords a clue to the reader's feeling of dissatisfaction when at last he lays the book down, and his total failure to feel any tragic exultation in the final specious reconcilement between brother and sister in that hastily contrived last scene of all. "The boat reappeared, but brother and sister had gone down in an embrace never to be parted: living through again in one supreme moment the days when they had clasped their little hands in love, and roamed the daisied fields together." This passage has not lacked for admirers, but to my mind it will not bear examination: its falseness is apparent. Coming from the agnostic George Eliot, what does "never to be parted" mean? Heaven being not among the possibilities she envisaged, one is tempted to retort with the gravedigger in *Hamlet* that "your water is a sore decayer of your whoreson dead body" and will dissolve all embraces. And the words that follow, what are *they* but a device to bring the story full circle by carrying one's mind back to its beginning? Legitimate enough if it can be done without cheating, but here it fails even of that purpose, or, if it succeeds, succeeds only in prompting the reflection that what in fact we remember of that shared childhood is less the clasping of little hands in love than the filling of little eyes with tears, masterful egoism on the one side and a frustrated eagerness for affection on the other. These things were dramatized in scene after scene: the hours of harmonious companionship, the roaming of daisied fields, we were merely told about, briefly, between quarrels.

This ending, with its "supreme moment," is a clear sign of the importance attached by the author to this Tom-Maggie theme. It is true that a great deal of the main action has no direct bearing on it—Tulliver's willful blundering to his ruin, Tom's rebuilding of the family fortunes, and the rest—but this nevertheless is the theme that contains the book as a line contains a circle. The title-page quotation is another clear pointer: "In their death they were not divided." Without falling into the silly impertinence of treating the *Mill* as factual autobiography, it is easy to see that Marian Evans, who had doted on her brother Isaac in childhood and been cast off by him in early middle age, had a special emotional interest in the brother and sister theme and in her delineation of Maggie was drawing largely on her own psychological experience. Maggie's emotional dependency, her need for someone "to whom she should be all in all" (as Cross said of George Eliot), is exactly in line with what we know of Marian herself. So, too, Maggie's passionate nature and the spirit of zealous self-mortification by which she tried to subdue it.

Maggie is afraid, as young Marian had once been, even of the most "innocent" pleasures. Wandering in her favorite Red Deeps was "a pleasure she loved so well, that sometimes, in her ardours of renunciation, she thought she ought to deny herself the frequent indulgence in it." Philip Wakem, who loves her, sounds the note of warning, and it is clear that George Eliot herself speaks with his voice when he tells Maggie that she is shutting herself up in a narrow self-delusive fanaticism, which is only a way (he adds) of escaping pain by starving into dullness all the highest powers of her nature. Joy and peace are not resignation, he goes on: resignation is the willing endurance of a pain that is not allayed, that you don't expect to be allayed. "It is stupefaction to remain in ignorance—to shut up all the avenues by which the life of your fellow-men might become known to you. You are not resigned:

you are only trying to stupefy yourself." Later in the same conversation he utters a more pointed warning, in retort to Maggie's hope that she will have strength given to her to pursue her chosen course. "No, you will not, Maggie: no one has strength given to do what is unnatural. It is mere cowardice to seek safety in negations. No character becomes strong in that way. You will be thrown into the world some day, and then every rational satisfaction of your nature that you deny now, will assault you like a savage appetite." When that prophecy is fulfilled, temptation takes the form, not indeed of a savage appetite, but of deep, physical enchantment and an overmastering desire for "easy delicious leaning on another's loving strength" (which was precisely George Eliot's everlasting demand and her peculiar conception of married bliss).

Those who believe that Marian repented of her association with Lewes, a theory which is in plain conflict with all the available evidence,[1] may imagine they find support in the story of Maggie's falling in love with Stephen Guest, he being half committed to her cousin Lucy, and Maggie herself half committed to Philip Wakem, for whom she entertains not passionate love but a tranquil affection. R. H. Hutton, an able critic but one with whom it is often a pleasure to disagree, convinced himself that George Eliot "intended her work as an authoress to be expiatory of, or at least to do all that was possible to counterbalance, the effect of her own example." The truth, I have suggested, is that she was anxious lest simple or light-minded people,

1. The manuscript of *The Mill on the Floss* bears the following inscription: "To my beloved husband, George Henry Lewes, I give this MS of my third book, written in the sixth year of our life together . . ."

knowing only the bare outline of her personal history, knowing nothing of the peculiar circumstances, should misinterpret her "example" as a plea for moral laxity and the easy breaking of faith. That anxiety may possibly have had some influence on her choice of theme. Hutton did not, so far as I know, develop his thesis, or support it by citing chapter and verse; but he may well have had, among other things, Maggie Tulliver in mind.

But the points of difference between Maggie's problem and Marian's are clear and very significant. Maggie and Stephen's predicament arose from a conflict of human loyalties. Each owed loyalty both to Lucy and to Philip, whom, if they married each other, they must deeply hurt. Marian and Lewes, as we have seen, hurt nobody by their coming together. It is significant, too, that George Eliot was careful not to confuse the issue by introducing legalistic or semilegalistic considerations: there was no question even of breaking promises, of dishonoring the plighted word, for Stephen was not formally betrothed to Lucy, nor Maggie to Philip. The problem is stated in terms of human kindness, and it proves insoluble. George Eliot is clear on the duty of self-renunciation when the happiness of others is at stake. She is equally clear that when two people are in love with each other they cannot give others, in marriage, the happiness they renounce for themselves. The question is argued with painful force in the scene in which Maggie finally resolves not to marry Stephen. We feel her decision to be wrong. We may even feel, with Stephen, that it is cruel and perverse. Yet we know, too, that had she decided otherwise, her marriage with Stephen, she being what she was, would have been poisoned by remorse. The deadlock was absolute, the problem insoluble, in art as in life. And so, in desperation, Maggie was hurried by her author to a premature death.

Bulwer-Lytton, and afterward Swinburne, were pained that George Eliot had allowed serious, sensitive Maggie to fall in love with Stephen Guest. If we are to believe, says Swinburne,

that a woman of Maggie Tulliver's kind can be moved to any sense but that of bitter disgust and sickening disdain by a thing—I will not write a man—like Stephen Guest; if we are to accept as truth and fact, however astounding and revolting, so shameful an avowal, so vile a revelation as this; in that ugly and lamentable case our only remark, as our only comfort, must be that now at least the last word of realism has surely been spoken, the last abyss of cynicism has surely been sounded and laid bare.

This is the language of hysteria. Stephen Guest is in fact a very ordinary young man of the world, neither better nor worse than the average of his class and kind. But even if Swinburne's estimate of him were just, it could still be contended that Maggie's falling in love was psychologically true; for when nature rebels, reason is overthrown, and we act "out of character." The enchantment into which Maggie fell was no doubt largely an affair of the senses. She did not, as presumably Swinburne would have had her do, arrive at her passion for Stephen by striking a balance between his merits and his faults and deciding that on the whole he deserved her. She merely fell in love with him, as he (quite sincerely) with her, and the conspicuous irrationality of the proceeding is precisely the point of it: it represents the nemesis that lies in wait for those who, whether in fear or spiritual pride, willfully starve themselves of happiness.

It is possible that George Eliot herself did not realize quite how faithfully in this instance her imagination had served her. "Maggie's position towards Stephen," she wrote to John Blackwood, July 9, 1860, "is too vital a part of my whole conception and purpose for me to be converted to the condemnation of it." She does not say, perhaps does not consciously know, what that purpose was. But she knows, beyond argument, that she was right. "If I am wrong there," she adds,

if I did not really know what my heroine would feel and do under the circumstances in which I deliberately placed her, I ought not to have written this book at all, but quite a different book, if any. If the ethics of art do not admit the truthful presentation of character essentially noble, but liable to great error—error that is anguish to its own nobleness—then, it seems to me, the ethics of art are too narrow, and must be widened to correspond with a widening psychology.

IV

So far, in this chapter, I may seem to have dwelt with undue emphasis on what I conceive to be mistakes or imperfections in the early novels of George Eliot, and more particularly on her habit of too zealously dotting the i's and crossing the t's of her moral intention. But admiration of the whole has always (I hope) been clearly implied, and nothing said that would call in question a novelist's right to *have* a moral intention (in the broadest sense) and to carry it out, so long as he can do so without injury to his artistic effect. One is not pleading that art should or can be unmoral, unrelated to the human values by which we live, but only that those values are better served by purely imaginative art than by didactic statement. There is more spiritual nourishment in one perfect lyric than in a dozen pages of moral homily. But it is by results, not by any rule of thumb, that a work of art must be judged. A novelist, like any other artist, makes his own "rules," and can break them too, with impunity, if he is artist *enough*. To pose the problem in terms of moralism versus imagination would be moreover a gross simplification: the dissonance, when it occurs, is rather between conscious intention (which may or may not be specifically moral) and what for want of a better word we may call "inspiration," namely, that which is given, that which presents itself, heaven knows how or whence, to the imagination.

There are two among George Eliot's seven novels, one long and one comparatively short, where intention and inspiration run so beautifully together that a critic is glad to forego his fault finding and indulge himself in the pleasure of unstinted applause. *Silas Marner*, next in order of writing to *The Mill on the Floss*, falls only a little short of perfection. "It came to me first of all quite suddenly," she told Blackwood, "as a sort of legendary tale, suggested by my recollection of having once, in early childhood, seen a linen weaver with a bag on his back; but as my mind dwelt on the subject I became inclined to a more realistic treatment." The result is the happiest blend of romantic allegory with homely realism. One is conscious, in the very first chapter, of the author's imaginative saturation in her subject, conscious of her new ease and confidence as well as of the precise carefulness to which she has accustomed us in earlier work. The seed, as she makes clear in the above-quoted letter to Blackwood, though apparently without realizing the full significance of what she says, had been long maturing in her subconscious mind; and we see it blossom into a work of art which, because her fine intelligence is content to serve instead of interfering, has the integrity of a natural growth. True, there are bits of palpable contrivance, but we readily forgive them. Perhaps only once, in the penultimate paragraph of Part One, are we definitely jarred, by a comment that makes needlessly explicit what has already been abundantly implied.

*Silas Marner* represents, indeed, the distilled essence of George Eliot's art as a novelist: all the elements that went to the making of her earlier books are here, the penetrating sympathy, the rustic chorus, the genial bustle and humor (rooted in character) of provincial life, and the author's commentary. Yes, the commentary is here too, but done with infinitely more tact, and in a more acceptable proportion to the whole, than hitherto. Like most other novelists, it may be said of George Eliot that in her most characteristic work it is always the same novel she is writing: or rather that all her novels are more or less successful approximations to an ideal unwritten novel that haunts her imagination and constitutes her personal vision of human life. If she could realize it, if she could capture it whole and embody it perfectly, once and for all, in a book, her work as a writer would be done. This too is perhaps a universal truth. The same pattern, the same themes, even the same characters (only a little disguised) recur throughout her work. There is a distinct family resemblance between Captain Wybrow in "Gilfil" and Grandcourt in *Deronda*, and between Arthur Donnithorne and Godfrey Cass, and a less obvious but more significant spiritual resemblance, unaffected by the social contrast, between Hetty Sorrel and Gwendolen Harleth. A diligent reader will have no difficulty in extending the catalogue. Each of these pairs are variations on some recurring theme. The theme embodied in the two young women is a prime favorite with George Eliot: it is that of vanity and self-seeking egoism bringing about its own inevitable punishment.

The story of the weaver of Raveloe was intended, said its author, to "set in a strong light the remedial influences of pure, natural human relations." Fortunately it does much more than that. By reciting the plot it would be easy to make it sound merely sentimental, which in the hands of a lesser artist it must have been. There is indeed some sentimentalization, in the sense of wishful thinking, at the end of the story, where everything bends to the author's resolve that Silas shall enjoy a blissful old age; but the book as a whole is truly and simply conceived. Marner engages our sympathy at once. A cruel sequence of events having shattered his faith in God and man, his loving, which is a need of every human nature, must find a non-human object; and his delight in his hoarded gold is as innocent as that of a child in pretty things. When he is robbed of this treasure he is desolated, unmanned. When, waking from a sick daydream, he thinks it has suddenly been restored to him, he is wrong and he is right, deceived by the coincidence that the straying child who has taken refuge with him has hair the color of his lost gold, and not yet knowing that here is indeed his treasure translated into responsive human form, something upon which his love may spend itself not vainly but fruitfully, to the release of his pent spirit and the enrichment of his starved life. "Thought and feeling were so confused within him, that if he had tried to give them utterance he could only

have said that the child was come instead of the gold—
that the gold had turned into the child."

Throughout this book we see George Eliot's gifts, of
humor, of pregnant utterance, of lightning characterization, in their highest perfection. She speaks of "that wide-
gazing calm which makes us older human beings, with our
inward turmoil, feel a certain awe in the presence of a
little child, such as we feel before some quiet majesty or
beauty in the earth or sky." She shows Squire Cass's pride
in his son Bob, "whom he repeatedly declared to be just
like himself in his young days in a tone that implied this
to be the very highest stamp of juvenile merit." She gives
us, in addition to the main dramatis personæ, such richly
humorous characters, sketched in with light irony, as
Priscilla Lammeter, Mr. Macey, and Mr. Kimble, the
apothecary. When Godfrey Cass, at the New Year's Eve
party, has engaged Nancy for a dance, Kimble is moved
to facetiousness:

"Ah, well, you're a lucky fellow, Godfrey," said uncle
Kimble; "but you're my godson, so I won't stand in your
way. Else I'm not so very old, eh, my dear?" he went on,
skipping to his wife's side again. "You wouldn't mind my
having a second after you were gone—not if I cried a good
deal first?"

"Come, come, take a cup o' tea and stop your tongue, do,"
said goodhumoured Mrs. Kimble, feeling some pride in a
husband who must be regarded as so clever and amusing by
the company generally. If he had only been not so irritable
at cards!

And there, in a hundred words, Mr. Kimble is set before
us, very much alive, a minor but memorable character. As
for Dolly Winthrop, with her staunch practical kindliness

and her theological dispositions about Them Above; as for old Macey, the parish clerk, and Dowlas, the farrier, and their fellow worthies at the Rainbow Inn; these have been much praised and can never be praised too much. That immortal chapter of talk at the Rainbow, which Marner's frantic entry interrupts, is nowhere excelled in our literature, and in fiction hardly matched unless by Hardy himself, with whose pages of rural comedy the resemblance here is so strong that a reader might be forgiven if he turned back to the title page to make sure that Hardy did not in fact write it. The scene is so rich in humor, and of an excellence so brilliantly sustained, that if one began to quote from it one would end by quoting the whole.

*Chapter Seven*

## INTENTION VERSUS INSPIRATION

### I

INTO her next English novel, *Felix Holt*, she put some of her very best writing. It has never, I think, been a general favorite, nor is it likely to become so: not for the reason alleged by the *Athenæum* reviewer in 1879, but because here as elsewhere the major theme proposed to herself by George Eliot makes a slighter mark on the imagination than the secondary theme or story with which it is linked. Our grandfathers were informed by the *Athenæum* that this book's "unsavoury motif places it out of competition": which is as fine an example of really puerile Victorian prudery as the wholesale denouncers of that great period of English literature can wish for. So changed are the times, and in this sole respect for the better, that a modern reader has to search his memory with some care in order to discover to which part of the story the disdainful phrase can refer. To him it will seem that the one conspicuous (and not fatal) failure in *Felix Holt* is the earnest, honest young man who gives his name to the book, and whose "radicalism," so deeply tinged with his author's conservative moderation, must have struck even contemporary readers as very mild medicine for the prevailing social ills.

Here once again, as later in *Deronda*, we have trivial selfishness and high moral endeavor isolated and dramatized in two persons. Holt begins by despising Esther

Lyon, who, much against her will, falls in love with him. He talks to her, as she aptly says, like an angry pedagogue; but her reluctant admiration of him, and (once again, and again to be repeated in Gwendolen Harleth) her "need for someone to lean on," work a moral revolution in her. Esther is a "living" character enough, presented with full knowledge and understanding; but Felix, in whom there is no fault, remains at best something of a stick, at worst the mere mouthpiece for unexceptionable opinions. The strength of the book lies in the living warmth and fidelity of the Midlandshire background, of which the superb introductory chapter gives us a comprehensive panorama, and in the firm, sensitive, acute characterization of Mrs. Transome, her husband, her son Harold, her maid Denner, her brother the Reverend John Lingon, and Jermyn, the sleek lawyer.

Seldom, indeed, has a novel opened more propitiously; nowhere, except in a work to be considered later, is George Eliot's skill more impressive than in these first three chapters of *Felix Holt* in which not only are these several persons put vividly before us but a situation of high dramatic interest is tactfully indicated. The next chapters, which introduce what the title advertises as the principal theme, come with the effect of frustration, not because the Transome story has been interrupted and the scene changed, for the double plot is a familiar convention, but because the story we have now to begin is less compelling, and the worthy persons we are now meeting seem in a fair way to be killed by kindness. Rufus Lyon is not many miles removed from Dinah Morris, and Felix Holt is no very distant cousin of Adam Bede. We admire, in passing, the noise and bustle of the election scenes; we weary of the legal complications involved in Esther's claim to the Transome estate (upon which George Eliot sought and obtained help from Frederic Harrison); and so we come back to our point of departure, to Mrs. Transome alone with her bitter secret, and aged, pitiful Mr. Transome who has not the full use of his wits. "Your father has slept there for years," Mrs. Transome tells her son, returned to her after fifteen years abroad. "He will be like a distracted insect, and never know where to go, if you alter the track he has to walk in." All the bitterness of her long frustration is distilled in that remark. And what comfort can she hope for from Harold?

He was at once active and luxurious; fond of mastery, and goodnatured enough to wish that every one about him should like his mastery; not caring greatly to know other people's thoughts, and ready to despise them as blockheads if their thoughts differed from his, and yet solicitous that they should have no colourable reason for slight thoughts about *him*. The blockheads must be forced to respect him.

The opening dialogue between this young gentleman and his mother is full of point, sharp with dramatic irony. His blindness to what does not interest him, namely, his mother's feelings, is perfect: every other sentence he utters rubs salt in her wincing wound. Lawyer Jermyn he despises and suspects him, with good reason, of crooked dealing in his management of the family estates. This Jermyn

was grey, but still remarkably handsome; fat, but tall enough to bear that trial to man's dignity. There was as strong a suggestion of toilette about him as if he had been five-and-twenty instead of nearly sixty. He chose always to dress in black, and was especially addicted to black satin waistcoats, which carried out the general sleekness of his appearance; and this, together with his white, fat, but beautifully-shaped hands, which he was in the habit of rubbing gently on his entrance into a room, gave him very much the air of a lady's physician. Harold remembered with some amusement his uncle's dislike of those conspicuous hands; but as his own were soft and dimpled, and as he too was given to the inno-cent practice of rubbing those members, his suspicions were not yet deepened.

Curious, the reader begins to say to himself, that a gently-born young fellow like Harold Transome should be en-dowed by his author with the same mannerism as "one of your middle-class upstarts who want to rank with gentle-men and think they'll do it with kid gloves and new fur-niture," as Uncle John Lingon put it. But before the thought is born there dawns another notion, in the light of which the coincidence is seen to be not so curious after all. That is good storytelling. John Lingon, the comfort-loving Rector, with beaming eyes and a mouth full of smooth reasons for turning his coat and being loyal to no one but himself, is a portrait worthy of Jane Austen. And then, for companion piece and contrast, there is Denner, the little peering waiting woman, round featured and of pale mealy complexion from her youth up, between whom and her "tall, eagle-faced, dark-eyed lady" there was some-thing which she herself would never have presumed to call friendship, "a tacit understanding that Denner knew all her mistress's secrets" and the habit of plain, unflatter-ing speech. Yet she "never said anything which Mrs. Transome could feel humiliated by, as by a familiarity from a servant who knew too much"; for she identified her own dignity with that of her mistress. "What are your pleasures, Denner," asks Mrs. Transome in despondent mood, "besides being a slave to me?" Denner's answer is a telling piece of self-characterization:

"Oh, there's pleasure in knowing one's not a fool, like half the people one sees about. And managing one's husband is some pleasure; and doing all one's business well. Why, if I've only got some orange flowers to candy, I shouldn't like to die till I see them all right. Then there's the sunshine now and then; I like that as the cats do. I look upon it, life is like our game at whist, when Banks and his wife come to the still-room of an evening. I don't enjoy the game much, but I like to play my cards well, and see what will be the end of it; and I want to see you make the best of your hand, madam, for your luck has been mine these forty years now. But I must go and see how Kitty dishes up the dinner, unless you have any more commands?"

At the end of that eventful day, the day of Harold's return to England and Transome Court, Mrs. Transome says to herself that the best happiness she will ever know will be to escape the worst disaster. But she does not escape even that; and it is her story and Harold's, not Felix Holt's, that gives life and depth to the book.

## II

Between *Silas Marner* and *Felix Holt* there comes, in order of composition, a work upon which George Eliot lavished enormous pains, at great cost both to herself and to the reader's patience. She herself said of *Romola*, which occupied nearly two years of her life, that she began it a young woman and finished it an old one. To call it sheer waste of labor would no doubt be going too far, but few readers who persevere to the end without skipping will hesitate to confess that it is an arduous and aging experience. The scene, industriously peopled with scholars and politicians and talkative worldlings, is fifteenth-century Florence; the chief persons of the drama are the beautiful high-minded Romola and the speciously charming Tito Melema who marries and betrays her, and betrays, incidentally, nearly everyone else he has dealings with; and the dominant theme, as usual, is the contrast and conflict between unscrupulous opportunist egoism and self-sacrificing devotion to duty. The formidable figure of Savonarola crosses the stage at intervals, to exercise a commanding influence on the plot; and the personal story, such as it is, is smothered in historical color. The diligently compiled background of Renaissance scholarship and Florentine politics is forever pushing its way into the foreground, converting what might have been a tolerable piece of studied conventional fiction into a species of historical treatise. It goes without saying that there is much literary skill displayed in the book, but its few flashes of wit are merely academic, its attempts at colloquial humor are forced, its flow is turgid and its eloquence pompous: it is full of learning but empty of life. Magnificent in intention, it stands as a huge, dull monument to the author's laborious industry, and marks the total (temporary) eclipse of creative inspiration by a planning, plodding intelligence. It was produced not from true imaginative experience but from notebooks, and occasional "natural" touches do not compensate for the prevailing lifelessness, the air of conscious contrivance.

In a book full of talk it is a fatal defect if the speech idiom is merely "literary." George Eliot does indeed in a sense "understand" her *Romola* characters, from a distance; but her endeavor to feel with them and in them, to think and express their intimate thoughts, is a pathetic if gallant failure. She knows about them but she does not know them. They do not "talk themselves alive": they talk themselves dead. Romola's middle-aged cousin, Monna Brigida, is perhaps the most human thing among them, precisely because she bears some family resemblance to the homely, sensible people, Poysers and the rest, whom her author had unconsciously observed in her childhood; for the imaginative saturation which must precede the writing of a good novel is a long, slow, and largely unconscious process, not something that can be crammed into a few months of diligent research. The tremendous experience you had last week may some day furnish material for a work of art; but it will not be today or tomorrow; it must be allowed to percolate into the subconscious, slowly in its own time, and stay there perhaps for years all but unnoticed, to undergo a subtle enrichment and transformation and emerge ultimately in the guise of a new creation. "She has that way of walking like a procession," remarks Monna Brigida of Romola. And one wonders whether George Eliot half knew that here is a shrewd judgment not only of Romola the woman but of *Romola* the book. For Romola, with all her noble beauty of person and character, is not much more than a cardboard figure. If she walks like a procession, she talks like a proclamation: which in fact she is, the proclamation of her author's ethical ideas. George Eliot's despondency during and just after the writing of this novel has perhaps no critical significance, for she was apt to despond at intervals about all her work; but did she perhaps suspect, in her secret heart, that for all her long and painful labor she had nothing to show but a stillborn child?

*Romola* (1863) is the first conspicuous example, in George Eliot's work, of what happens when a novelist willfully insists on writing against the grain of his true genius. A less intellectual artist, or shall we say an artist with more intellectual humility, would hardly have made such a mistake, or at any rate not on so grand a scale. For despite her habit of self-depreciation it must be recognized, I think, that George Eliot had too high an esteem for her own opinions and was too apt to believe, or to act as if she believed, that a vital work of art can be produced by intelligence alone. In *Felix Holt* (1866), upon which she had begun meditating before *Romola* was thought of, she tapped imagination at a deeper level, returning to scenes which for almost as long as she could remember had been part of her mental world; but in the five or six years that followed she was again busying herself with tasks for which, as time's verdict has made clear, she was essentially unfitted. The novel *Romola* and the drama in blank verse called *The Spanish Gypsy*, as well as a great part of *Daniel Deronda* (her last novel, published 1876), illustrate with painful force the thesis which so persistently crops up in our study of her art and gives a title to the present chapter. Of the origin of *The Spanish Gypsy* she wrote a most explicit account, an account which very carefully, and very significantly, puts the cart of intention before the horse of inspiration. The subject, she says, was suggested to her by a picture she saw in Venice, an Annunciation, said to be by Titian:

It occurred to me that here was a great dramatic motive of the same class as those used by the Greek dramatists, yet specifically differing from them. A young maiden, believing herself to be on the eve of the chief event of her life—marriage—about to share in the ordinary lot of womanhood, full of young hope, has suddenly announced to her that she is chosen to fulfil a great destiny, entailing a terribly different experience from that of ordinary womanhood. She is chosen, not by any momentary arbitrariness, but as a result of foregoing hereditary conditions: she obeys. "Behold the handmaid of the Lord." Here, I thought, is a subject grander than that of Iphigenia, and it has never been used. I came home with this in my mind, meaning to give the motive a clothing in some suitable set of historical and local conditions. My reflections brought me nothing that would serve me except that moment in Spanish history when the struggle with the Moors was attaining its climax, and when there was the gypsy race present under such conditions as would enable me to get my heroine and the hereditary claim on her among the gypsies. I required the opposition of race to give the need for renouncing the expectation of marriage. I could not use the Jews or the Moors, because the facts of their history were too conspicuously opposed to the working out of my catastrophe. Meanwhile the subject had become more and more pregnant to me. I saw it might be taken as a symbol of the part which is played in the general human lot by hereditary conditions in the largest sense, and of the fact that what we call duty is entirely made up of such conditions; for even in cases of just antagonism to the narrow view of hereditary claims, the whole background of the particular struggle is made up of our inherited nature. Suppose for a moment that our conduct at great epochs was determined entirely by reflection, without the immediate intervention of feeling which supersedes reflection, our determination as to the right would consist in an adjustment of our individual needs to the dire necessities of our lot, partly as to our natural constitution, partly as shares of life with our fellow-beings. Tragedy consists in the terrible difficulty of this adjustment. . . . Looking at individual lots, I seemed to see in each the same story, wrought out with more or less of tragedy, and I determined the elements of my drama under the influence of these ideas. . . . A tragedy has not to expound why the individual must give way to the general: it has to show that it is compelled to give way, the tragedy consisting in the struggle involved, and often in the entirely calamitous issue in spite of a grand submission. Silva presents the tragedy of entire rebellion: Fedalma of a grand submission, which is rendered vain by the effects of Silva's rebellion: Zarca, the struggle for a great end, rendered vain by the surrounding conditions of life.

No doubt they do, and there is no *a priori* reason why characters in a drama should not present such ideas, provided they also create the illusion of life. But the sad thing is that this prose prospectus is on the whole rather more readable than the work of art it relates to. And what, we must ask, is Fedalma but Romola all over again? As for the medium, it is capable of uninspired blank verse, apt in imagery, with many a neatly turned phrase, but monotonously regular, with little variation of pause interval: the kind of blank verse which any man or woman of letters can turn out by the yard, with far less expenditure of effort than good prose demands. That there was a rich vein of poetry in George Eliot is apparent in many fine passages of her descriptive prose. But she was not, for all that, a poet; and her stubborn endeavor to be one has made no mark on our literature, has produced nothing more remarkable or enduring than the nine sub-Wordsworthian lines (out of a poem containing forty-three) which are sometimes to be met with in anthologies:

O may I join the choir invisible
Of those immortal dead who live again
In minds made better by their presence: live
In pulses stirred to generosity,
In deeds of daring rectitude, in scorn
For miserable aims that end with self,
In thoughts sublime that pierce the night like stars,
And with their mild persistence urge man's search
To vaster issues.
                    So to live is heaven . . .

This is perhaps as near as George Eliot ever got to poetry, in her blank verse. It is not very near.

### III

But the poems, as such, do not properly belong to our subject: *The Spanish Gypsy* is relevant only in so far as it touches on George Eliot's art as a storyteller. Even *Romola* can be left out of our account of the conflict between intention and inspiration (that is, between conscious contrivance and the living creation which mysteriously wells up from a hidden source) if, as I have suggested, it represents the total eclipse of the one by the other, for so there is no conflict. It is in the last novel of all that the conflict can most clearly be seen.

*Daniel Deronda* has found friends only among those who appreciate, as most readers do not, its fervid espousal of Jewish Zionism; and the apocalyptic figure of Mordecai Cohen has distracted attention from the book's high merits. Critics have for the most part concurred in dismissing it as a total failure, evidence of declining power. But it is emphatically not that. The truth about *Deronda* is that it gives us, between one pair of covers, the best and the worst that George Eliot can do. More astonishing still, the good and the bad exist not blended together but side by side in almost complete isolation. The book reads like a collaboration between two writers who are at odds with each other, the one a great artist, the other a sentimental enthusiast inflated with large, vague ideas about racial continuity and expounding them with all the embarrassing extravagance of the convert. Each has her own different story to tell, each her own theme, and the two stories are nowhere joined except in the person of Daniel Deronda himself. To say that the one is very good and the other very bad may seem an absurd simplification. But it is true. The Gwendolen Harleth theme, her willful egoism, her walking open eyed into a loveless marriage, her bitter reaping of what she has sown, and her ultimate regeneration by suffering, this is entirely admirable and very characteristic George Eliot. It shows her at the very height of her powers. As a morality it is impressive, and it is done with searching and sensitive art. Except for quite minor blemishes, such as the undue harping on Gwendolen's selfishness in the early chapters, it is as consistently good as the other story—the encounter with Mirah, the advent (as from heaven) of Mordecai, and Deronda's profound satisfaction in discovering himself to be a Jew—is consistently forced and false. Mirah, Mordecai, the Meyrick women, all are presented in that spirit of uncritical admiration which not only wearies the reader but—and this is far more important—tends to diminish his belief in their existence.

Deronda, too, suffers from his author's partiality and "comes to life" only at intervals: nearly always in his passages with Gwendolen, often when the lively Hans Meyrick is talking to him, and conspicuously on one particular occasion when we discover, to our relief, that this paragon of virtue and wisdom has at least one of the weaknesses common to erring humanity, for "he was conscious of that peculiar irritation which will sometimes befall the man whom others are inclined to trust as a mentor—the irritation of perceiving that he is supposed to be entirely off the same plane of desire and temptation as those who confess to him." In short, his concern for Mirah's welfare was not entirely disinterested, and he was ready to be jealous of Hans's emotional appropriation of her. In that moment he is human. Hans Meyrick himself, the artist, is a minor character engagingly drawn: his letter to Deronda, amusing in itself, is as excellent a piece of characterization as one could wish for.

For here again George Eliot exhibits an unconscious mastery in her handling of minor episodes: here again, when she does not seem to be trying very hard, she succeeds to admiration. Herr Klesmer, the great musician, is brilliantly done; and the scene between him and Catherine Arrowpoint in which they declare themselves to each other is delicate and moving, not the less so because they speak in a prim and formal style. She is an heiress of supposedly good family, he merely a talented foreigner and in her family's estimation beyond the matrimonial pale. He announces to her that he must go off to St. Petersburg. There is no answer. He says, with some irritation: "You agree with me that I had better go?" She answers that she had never thought of his consenting to come to them, to be her tutor, as anything but a sacrifice. "Why should I make the sacrifice?" he says, seating himself at the piano and letting his fingers run over the keys:

"That is the mystery," said Catherine, not wanting to affect anything, but from mere agitation. From the same cause she was tearing a piece of paper into minute morsels, as if at a task of utmost multiplication imposed by a cruel fairy.

"You can conceive no motive?" said Klesmer, folding his arms.

"None that seems in the least probable."

"Then I shall tell you. It is because you are to me the chief woman in the world—the throned lady whose colours I carry between my heart and my armour."

Catherine's hands trembled so much that she could no longer tear the paper: still less could her lips utter a word. Klesmer went on—

"This would be the last impertinence in me, if I meant to found anything upon it. That is out of the question. I mean no such thing. But you once said it was your doom to suspect every man who courted you of being an adventurer, and what made you angriest was man's imputing to you the folly of believing that they courted you for your own sake. Did you not say so?"

"Very likely," was the answer, in a low murmur.

"It was a bitter word. Well, at least one man who has seen women as plenty as flowers in May has lingered about you for your own sake. And since he is one whom you can never marry, you will believe him. That is an argument in favour of some other man. But don't give yourself for a meal to a minotaur like Bult. I shall go now and pack. I shall make my excuses to Mrs. Arrowpoint." Klesmer rose as he ended, and walked quickly towards the door.

"You must take this heap of manuscript, then," said Catherine, suddenly making a desperate effort. She had risen to fetch the heap from another table. Klesmer came back, and they had the length of the folio sheets between them.

"Why should I not marry the man who loves me, if I love

him?" said Catherine. To her the effort was something like the leap of a woman from the deck into the lifeboat.

"It would be too hard—impossible—you could not carry it through. I am not worth what you would have to encounter. I will not accept the sacrifice. It would be thought a *mésalliance* for you, and I should be liable to the worst accusations."

"Is it the accusations you are afraid of? I am afraid of nothing but that we should miss the passing of our lives together."

Catherine's courage and Klesmer's dignity in this scene make the heart leap.

### IV

In October, 1872, George Eliot wrote to her publisher from Hamburg:

The Kursaal is to me a hell, not only for the gambling but for the light and heat of the gas, and we have seen enough of its monstrous hideousness. . . . The saddest thing to be witnessed is the play of a young lady, who is only twenty-six years old, and is completely in the grasp of this mean, money-making demon. It made me cry to see her young fresh face among the hags and brutally stupid men around her.

Here, evidently, is the seed of suggestion which flowered into Gwendolen Harleth, whom Deronda sees, in just such a situation, at the very beginning of the book. "Was she beautiful or not beautiful? and what was the secret of form or expression which gave the dynamic quality to her glance?" Attracted by the enigma she presents to his imagination, he takes it upon himself to restore to her, anonymously, the diamond necklace which she loses in play, not knowing that he is destined to meet her months later, in England, and to become, in effect, her priest and confessor and her only hope of salvation. For this is the young woman who, from motives partly mercenary and wholly misguided, is to marry his distant kinsman Henleigh Grandcourt. She is a spoilt child, vain, imperious, self-seeking. She is a sophisticated Hetty Sorrel. In the early stages of our acquaintance with her she is made too precisely according to formula, but as the story develops we begin to feel her fascination. Gwendolen has wit as well as beauty; there is a certain grace even in her insolence; and her assumption that the universe exists solely for her personal benefit excites our compassion, once it becomes apparent that she is drifting to disaster. Drifting is perhaps hardly the word, for everything she does is carefully calculated, everything she plans is constructed logically, upon false premises. To watch her contriving her own doom is to be reminded of Greek tragedy in which the action is at once willful and predetermined, and the end foreknown by all but those who must endure it.

Grandcourt has been misrepresented by some critics as a mere figure of melodrama. He is much more than that. Though slighter in stature, and strikingly different in character, he is of the same order of artistic creation as Emily Brontë's Heathcliff: the demonic order. His inhumanness makes him not smaller than life, but larger and more terrible. Moreover, recent history (1935–45) has enlarged our conception of how satanical human beings can be. Heathcliff is redeemed in the last resort by the consuming fire of his passion. Grandcourt is ice cold in his egoism, ice cold and self-sufficient, a walking death. His lust is for power; he desires nothing for its own sake but only as a tribute from the universe to its center, which is himself. His own will is the one law of his being. He is a pure egoist, and therefore incapable of love. If Gwendolen could but have seen him as he was, as we are allowed to see him, he might have served as a hideous warning of what she, by persisting in egoism, might one day become. For Grandcourt carries Gwendolen's self-regarding philosophy to its logical extreme. She too had always taken it for granted that she must have her own way, and it is this very assumption which persuades her to her ruin. The dramatic irony in such a sequence of events needs no underlining, and again one is reminded of classical models. Gwendolen is a tragic figure in the Aristotelian mode: she herself, in blind, hubristic folly, works her undoing. She thinks that Grandcourt will serve her purpose well enough, and fondly imagines that when they are married her dominion over him will be absolute and all will be well. She has not the wit to see that the egoism she perceives in him is of the same nature as her own. Here is her first sight of him, at the moment of their introduction to each other:

He was slightly taller than herself, and their eyes seemed to be on a level; there was not the faintest smile on his face as he looked at her, not a trace of self-consciousness or anxiety in his bearing; when he raised his hat he showed an extensive baldness surrounded with a mere fringe of reddish-blond hair, but he also showed a perfect hand; the line of feature from brow to chin undisguised by beard was decidedly handsome, with only moderate departures from the perpendicular, and the slight whisker too was perpendicular. It was not possible for a human aspect to be freer from

grimace or solicitous wrigglings; also it was perhaps not possible for a breathing man wide awake to look less animated.

The correct Englishman, drawing himself up from his bow into rigidity, assenting severely, and seeming to be in a state of internal drill, suggests a suppressed vivacity, and may be suspected of letting go with some violence when he is released from parade; but Grandcourt's bearing had no rigidity, it inclined rather to the flaccid. His complexion had a faded fairness resembling that of an actress when bare of the artificial white and red; his long narrow grey eyes expressed nothing but indifference. Attempts at description are stupid: who can all at once describe a human being? even when he is presented to us we only begin that knowledge of his appearance which must be completed by innumerable impressions under differing circumstances. We recognize the alphabet; we are not sure of the language. I am only mentioning the points that Gwendolen saw by the light of a prepared contrast in the first minutes of her meeting with Grandcourt: they were summed up in the words "He is not ridiculous." But forthwith Lord Brackenshaw was gone, and what is called conversation had begun, the first and constant element in it being that Grandcourt looked at Gwendolen persistently with a slightly exploring gaze, but without change of expression, while she only occasionally looked at him with a flash of observation a little softened by coquetry.

Consistently with his cold and insolent assumption that whatever he wants he must infallibly have, Grandcourt announces his intention to marry her before a word of that possibility has been so much as hinted between them. Their meeting is the coming together of two worldlings, each secretly intent on getting the better of the other; and their wooing is elegant and artificial, a mimic fencing match, a scene from ballet, in which Gwendolen holds her own quite prettily. "He is very proud," she tells her mother, the day after accepting his proposal. "But so am

I. We shall match each other. I should hate a man who went down on his knees, and came fawning on me. He really is not disgusting." And later, irony piled on irony, answering her mother's remark that he will expect to be first with her, she says airily: "Rather a ridiculous expectation. However, I don't mean to treat him ill, unless he deserves it." Because from our own point of vantage we can see further than Gwendolen, and guess what is coming, the betrothal scene is like a cold finger laid upon the heart. After Grandcourt has made his polite inquiry, and the word "Yes" has been briefly spoken, this ensues:

With a happy curl of the lips, she said: "Will you not see mamma? I will fetch her."

"Let us wait a little," said Grandcourt, in his favourite attitude, having his left forefinger and thumb in his waistcoat-pocket, and with his right caressing his whisker, while he stood near Gwendolen and looked at her—not unlike a gentleman who has had a felicitous introduction at an evening party.

"Have you anything else to say to me?" said Gwendolen, playfully.

"Yes. I know having things said to you is a great bore," said Grandcourt, rather sympathetically.

"Not when they are things I like to hear."

"Will it bother you to be asked how soon we can be married?"

"I think it will, to-day," said Gwendolen, putting up her chin saucily.

"Not to-day, then, but to-morrow. Think of it before I come to-morrow. In a fortnight—or three weeks—as soon as possible."

"Ah, you think you will be tired of my company," said Gwendolen. "I notice when people are married the husband is not so much with his wife as when they were engaged. But perhaps I shall like that better too."

She laughed charmingly.

"You shall have whatever you like," said Grandcourt.

"And nothing that I don't like?—please say that; because I think I dislike what I don't like more than I like what I like," said Gwendolen, finding herself in the woman's paradise where all her nonsense is adorable.

The marriage is loveless and joyless: with such a pair it could hardly have been otherwise. But, because Grandcourt has a mistress still living by whom he is the father of three children, and because Gwendolen knew this before marrying him, it becomes for her, after a time, a matter for remorse as well. Within only a few weeks she has to acknowledge to herself that Grandcourt is master. Her own will "had seemed imperious in its small girlish sway"; but "she had found a will like that of a crab or a boa-constrictor which goes on pinching or crushing without alarm at thunder." Remorse and self-scorn added to bitter personal unhappiness drive her to seek help from Deronda, whose character she instinctively reveres and whose good opinion she passionately desires. She appoints him her mentor and her conscience. She looks to him as to a savior, asking no longer for happiness, but only that she may be helped to expiate her sins, and be the woman he would have her be, and so find peace. At some risk of involving himself in scandal, he gives her what help he can. He accepts, without facing its implications, the fact of her need of him. And finally, having allowed Gwendolen to depend on him for moral succor and spiritual refreshment, and having supported her in the great crisis of her life when she thinks herself guilty of Grandcourt's death by drowning, he marries the young Jewish girl, Mirah Cohen. Gwendolen is left high and dry: chastened, resigned, desolate. Her tragic destiny is fulfilled.

But this final turn of events, so far from purging the reader's soul by pity and terror and inducing a state of somber exultation, merely irritates him. He resents it, not altogether on Gwendolen's account, and not arrogating to himself the right to dictate to George Eliot who among her characters shall marry whom, but because Deronda's choice of Mirah in preference to Gwendolen, who deeply needs him and with whom he has established a deep and loving (though not amorous) intimacy, is the dramatic crystallization of that perverseness in him which his author cannot persuade us to admire. It is at once a symptom and a symbol of his enthusiasm for Mordecai and Mordecai's vision of Judah which, natural and unexceptionable as it might be in a man born *and. bred* as a Jew, we find difficult to sympathize with in Deronda, who discovers his racial origin at the age of thirty or so. Not because she is English, but because she is a living and suffering and potentially noble human being, Gwendolen engages our sympathy. Not because he is Jewish, but because he is a doctrinaire and exists only to illustrate a theory, Deronda does not.

I have said that in his colloquies with Gwendolen Deronda often comes to life. But if one looked more closely I fancy one might discover that the sense of his reality at those moments is derived rather from his companion than from him: which is to say that Gwendolen, from the abundance of her own humanity, is able to conjure him into momentary existence for us.

## Chapter Eight

## *MIDDLEMARCH*

### I

ON DECEMBER 2, 1870, she wrote in her Journal: "I am experimenting in a story ('Miss Brooke') which I began without any very serious intention of carrying it out lengthily. It is a subject which has been recorded among my possible themes ever since I began to write fiction, but will probably take new shapes in the development." The entry for the last day of that year tells us that the story of Miss Brooke was begun "about the opening of November" and has reached the hundreth page. In order to write it she seems to have turned aside from the Vincy-Featherstone-Lydgate story, with no notion then that the two were destined to be incorporated in one book, *Middlemarch*. It is at their point of junction, the eleventh chapter in the book as we now have it, that the intimate study of Dorothea Brooke gives place not merely to the companion story but to the introduction of the general *Middlemarch* theme, which is the diversity of provincial manners and the significance of ordinary lives.

Both in range and quality, conception and treatment, *Middlemarch* is by any reckoning George Eliot's greatest work. It has, indeed, some claim to be regarded as the greatest English novel of its time. And if in a work so amply designed and masterfully executed it is legitimate to distinguish between one part and another, it is to the first part, conceived and written separately from the story she first proposed to herself, that the palm must be awarded. These first ten chapters, entitled "Miss Brooke" and published as the first of eight monthly parts, were immediately acclaimed a masterpiece. Such contemporary judgments are not always confirmed by posterity; but here we recognize a true verdict. In these ten chapters, which carry the story of Miss Brooke to the point of her marriage with Casaubon, George Eliot excelled herself, as never, in the same degree, again.

That she excelled herself is the exact truth; for here we have not only the authentic George Eliot, her own searching vision of human character, but something that we have too often felt the lack of in her work hitherto: an ease of manner, a lightness of touch by no means inconsistent with profundity, an all but effortless mastery of her material: in a word, self-forgetfulness. Whether this new grace is the effect of her having no "very serious intention" of writing the story lengthily, one can only conjecture; but the difference in tone, both from that of other books and from much that follows in the same book, is unmistakable. While still remaining distinctively herself, George Eliot, she brings to these chapters a neatness, a precision, a dry irony, which recall, once again, Jane Austen. The essence of that difference is perhaps in the distance—neither too much nor too little—at which she, the creator, stands from her creatures: the nice balance she sustains between self-identifying sympathy and emotional aloofness. And it is precisely this most difficult business, the relationship between author and subject, which Jane Austen managed to perfection: though perhaps "difficult" is the wrong word, since success in such adjustments must come rather by grace than by effort.

It will be obvious to a reader of George Eliot's life that in Dorothea Brooke she was portraying at least some part of her former self. But to leave that statement unqualified would be seriously misleading. There is no humor in Dorothea: there is exquisite humor in her portrayal. And while there is humor and irony in her portrayal there is no malice: there is nothing to detract from sympathy and admiration. Dorothea is beautiful, ardent, idealistic. She is also a sad prig. At the age of twenty she is opinionated, innocent, saintly; and her author sees to it that we are equally conscious both of her beauty (of person and spirit) and of her absurdity. Yet—and here surely is a triumph of art—our sympathy is so intimately engaged that we share for the time being, even though we are afraid of what must follow, her preposterous desire that she shall marry the elderly Mr. Casaubon, the dried-up pedant in whom she sees, poor girl, the fulfillment of her passion to be made use of for high ends. In the opinion of the local young men "Miss Brooke's large eyes seemed, like her religion, too unusual and striking." Yet those who approached her found that she had a charm "unaccountably reconcilable" with the alarming rumors of her piety.

Most men thought her bewitching when she was on horseback. She loved the fresh air and the various aspects of the country, and when her eyes and cheeks glowed with mingled pleasure she looked very little like a devotee. Riding was an indulgence which she allowed herself in spite of conscientious qualms; she felt that she enjoyed it in a pagan sensuous way, and always looked forward to renouncing it.

There we have Dorothea, a young girl "enamored of intensity and greatness, and rash in embracing whatever seemed to her to have those aspects"; and, as a foil to her, and a wholesome corrective, we have her pretty and sensible sister Celia. In the first chapter of all, one of the most engaging first chapters in all fiction, there is a scene between the sisters in which each is intimately, effortlessly, revealed to us. Celia proposes that their dead mother's jewels, which six months ago had been placed in Dorothea's keeping by Mr. Brooke, their uncle and guardian, should be brought out and divided between them. Being somewhat in awe of her serious-minded elder sister, she is relieved to find that she takes the proposal in good part:

"What a wonderful little almanac you are, Celia! Is it six calendar or six lunar months?"

"It is the last day of September now, and it was the first of April when uncle gave them to you. You know, he said he had forgotten them till then. I believe you have never thought of them since you locked them up in the cabinet here."

"Well, dear, we should never wear them, you know." Dorothea spoke in a full cordial tone, half caressing, half explanatory. She had her pencil in her hand, and was making tiny side-plans on a margin.

Celia coloured, and looked very grave. "I think, dear, we are wanting in respect to mamma's memory, to put them by and take no notice of them. And," she added, after hesitating a little, with a rising sob of mortification, "necklaces are quite usual now; and Madame Poinçon, who was stricter in some things even than you are, used to wear ornaments. And Christians generally—surely there are women in heaven now who wore jewels." Celia was conscious of some mental strength when she really applied herself to argument.

"You would like to wear them?" exclaimed Dorothea, an air of astonished discovery animating her whole person with a dramatic action which she had caught from that very Madame Poinçon who wore the ornaments. "Of course, then, let us have them out. Why did you not tell me before? But the keys, the keys!" She pressed her hands against the sides of her head and seemed to despair of her memory.

"They are here," said Celia . . .

So the jewels are displayed, and a little argument ensues in which Celia tries in vain to persuade Dorothea to take a share of them. Then Dorothea's eye is caught by the flash of emeralds and diamonds in a ring. It is strange, she remarks, "how deeply colours seem to penetrate one, like scent. I suppose that is the reason why gems are used as spiritual emblems in the Revelation of St. John. They look like fragments of heaven." All the time, says her author, her thought was trying to justify her delight in the colors by merging them in her mystic joy. Inconsistently, as Celia thinks, she decides to keep for herself one ring and one bracelet. "Shall you wear them in company?" Celia asks:

Dorothea glanced quickly at her sister. Across all her imaginative adornment of those whom she loved, there darted now and then a keen discernment, which was not without a scorching quality. If Miss Brooke ever attained perfect meekness, it would not be for lack of inward fire.

"Perhaps," she said, rather haughtily. "I cannot tell to what level I may sink."

What maturity of art is here displayed, compared with that which portrayed for us, all too partially, that earlier saint, Dinah Morris!

Slighter studies though they are, the same dramatic economy, the same quick understanding, the same blend of sympathy and irony, may be seen in the characterization of Mr. Brooke, of Mrs. Cadwallader and her husband, of Sir James Chettam, and of Casaubon. Mr. Brooke is that unusual thing, a comic character whose human reality is not diminished by the element of caricature in the way he is presented. He is a jellyfish of a man, well meaning, resolutely irresolute, his mind full of undigested fragments, his conversation aimless and repetitive and inconclusive. Through willful ignorance and indolence, not ill nature, he is a bad landlord, unaware of the squalor in which some of his tenants live. With all this he is excellent company, in a book. So too are his neighbors. The sensible, managing Mrs. Cadwallader, when Chettam says that Casaubon has no good red blood in his body, caps the remark by saying: "No. Somebody put a drop under a magnifying-glass, and it was all semi-colons and parentheses." Her husband the Rector, when taunted by her with tolerating Casaubon because he owns a trout stream, says genially: "There is something in that. It is a very good quality in a man to have a trout-stream." And Celia, having told Dorothea that Chettam is in love with her (Dorothea), achieves another of her author's lightning strokes of portraiture when she adds: "You always see what nobody else sees; it is impossible to satisfy you; yet you never see what is quite plain. That's your way, Dodo."

II

Some critics have remarked on the "loose construction" of *Middlemarch*. The phrase may pass, if it means only that there is no very precise dovetailing of episodes, and that the connection between the various life stories is here and there comparatively slight. It will *not* pass if it is intended as an adverse criticism, because the total effect of the book on the reader, the imaginative experience it offers him, owes at least as much to its abundance as to its moments of dramatic tension. Nor is he troubled by any sense of disproportion or discontinuity. The tension could no doubt have been increased by pruning away all that is not strictly relevant to the two main themes, the Dorothea theme and the Lydgate theme. Fred Vincy's story, the gathering of the vultures round Peter Featherstone's deathbed, Mr. Farebrother's domestic situation and his love for Mary Garth, Mr. Brooke's incursion into politics, and the unmasking of the evangelical Mr. Bulstrode (this last a crudely conceived and mechanically contrived sequence), these have no very direct bearing on those main issues, and could have been either omitted or greatly condensed. But to purchase dramatic concentration at such a cost would have been a very bad artistic bargain; and George Eliot was right when she insisted, in answer to her publisher's misgiving about the length, that nothing could be left out. Moreover we perhaps beg an important question when we speak of Dorothea and Lydgate as the main themes; for they are themselves contributory to a still larger theme, that of human life itself. Copiousness and diversity, both of incident and character, were of the essence of her intention; and it is the sustained energy with which she combines copiousness with imaginative penetration, breadth with depth, that makes *Middlemarch* the masterpiece it is, gives it an amplitude and a delicacy of draftsmanship which are almost Tolstoyan.

Fred Vincy is Rosamond's brother. He has some of his sister's faults: indolence, self-regard, and a blithe confidence that the universe exists to serve him. But he is at heart a good fellow, saved by a pinch of humility in his composition and by his capacity for affection. His egoism has not the implacable, rapacious quality of Rosamond's. He lives on his expectation of something turning up that will make effort on his part unnecessary, and when he is left stranded by old Featherstone's post-mortem malice, he looks round for other means of support. But he is redeemable, and is in fact redeemed, by Mary Garth. At his worst he is nothing worse than a moral weakling, whereas Rosamond at her best and loveliest is a monster of self-love, in whose softness and sweetness lies concealed an utterly ruthless resolve to have her own way in everything.

There are few scenes in fiction more painful than the scene between Lydgate and Rosamond in which he tells her of his financial difficulties and gets from her nothing but reproaches and self-pitying tears:

"My dear Rosamond, it is not a question of choice. We have begun too expensively. Peacock, you know, lived in a much smaller house than this. It is my fault: I ought to have known better, and I deserve a thrashing—if there were anybody who had a right to give it me—for bringing you into the necessity of living in a poorer way than you have been used to. But we married because we loved each other, I suppose. And that may help us to pull along till things get better. Come, dear, put down that work and come to me."

He was really in chill gloom about her at that moment, but he dreaded the future without affection, and was determined to resist the oncoming of division between them. Rosamond obeyed him, and he took her on his knee, but in her secret soul she was utterly aloof from him. The poor thing saw only that the world was not ordered to her liking, and Lydgate was part of that world. But he held her waist with one hand and laid the other gently on both of hers; for this rather abrupt man had much tenderness in his manners towards women, seeming to have always present in his imagination the weakness of their frames and the delicate poise of their health both in body and mind. And he began again to speak persuasively.

"I find, now I look into things a little, Rosy, that it is wonderful what an amount of money slips away in our housekeeping. I suppose the servants are careless, and we have had a great many people coming. But there must be many in our rank who manage with much less: they must do with commoner things, I suppose, and look after the scraps. It seems, money goes but a little way in these matters, for Wrench has everything as plain as possible, and he has a very large practice."

"Oh, if you think of living as the Wrenches do!" said Rosamond, with a little turn of her neck. "But I have heard you express your disgust at that way of living."

"Yes, they have bad taste in everything—they make economy look ugly. We needn't do that. I only meant that they avoid expenses, although Wrench has a capital practice."

But Lydgate might have saved his breath, for he was talking to a creature incapable of considering anything but her own comfort and convenience. Lydgate lacked the kind of shrewdness and the kind of luck that would have enabled him to get enough money to keep afloat on while pursuing his disinterested aims. And this scene is the beginning of the breakup of all that was good in his marriage. His will was not lacking in masculine forcefulness, but in tactics he was no match for Rosamond; and *her* will, which nothing could break or bend, was the more effective for being hidden under a show of feminine weakness, manifesting itself in tricks, evasions, deceptions, and willful misunderstanding. In George Eliot's view, "poor Rosamond" is a victim no less than he, the victim of her own temperament; and this charity of outlook, so far from detracting from its force, lends a touch of tragedy and spiritual terror to her portrait of a human vampire. You cannot relieve your feelings by a ranting denunciation of Rosamond: her author requires that you shall understand her, as she does, and forgive her what she is.

The brother is won from egoism by a woman's love; the sister's egoism takes love into itself and with spiderish voracity squeezes the spiritual life out of her lover. Except for this significant contrast in their destinies there is no reason, a stickler for economy might contend, why we should be asked to follow Fred's fortunes in any detail, or concern ourselves with the protracted dying of Peter Featherstone, from whom Fred had good reason to expect a handsome legacy. Yet what reader would willingly forfeit the grim comedy of the situation that shows us Peter Featherstone, the wealthy old skinflint whose sole surviving joy in life is the exercise of power and the delight of disappointing his brothers and sisters, being invaded during his last illness by poor relations hungry for legacies?

Old Featherstone no sooner caught sight of these funereal figures appearing in spite of his orders than rage came to strengthen him more successfully than the cordial. He was propped up on a bed-rest, and always had his gold-headed stick lying by him. He seized it now and swept it backwards and forwards in as large an area as he could apparently to ban these ugly spectres, crying in a hoarse sort of screech—

"Back, back, Mrs. Waule! Back, Solomon!"

"Oh, brother Peter," Mrs. Waule began—but Solomon put his hand before her repressingly. He was a large-cheeked man, nearly seventy, with small furtive eyes, and was not only of much blander temper but thought himself much deeper than his brother Peter; indeed not likely to be deceived in any of his fellow-men, inasmuch as they could not well be more greedy and deceitful than he suspected them of being. Even the invisible powers, he thought, were likely to be soothed by a bland parenthesis here and there—coming from a man of property, who might have been as impious as others.

"Brother Peter," he said, in a wheedling yet gravely official tone, "it's nothing but right I should speak to you about the Three Crofts and the Manganese. The Almighty knows what I've got on my mind . . ."

"Then He knows more than I want to know," said Peter, laying down his stick with a show of truce which had a threat in it too, for he reversed the stick so as to make the gold handle a club in case of closer fighting, and looked hard at Solomon's bald head.

"There's things you might repent of, Brother, for want of speaking to me," said Solomon, not advancing, however. "I could sit up with you to-night, and Jane with me willingly, and you might take your own time to speak, or let me speak."

"Yes, I shall take my own time—you needn't offer me yours," said Peter.

"But you can't take your own time to die in, Brother," began Mrs. Waule, with her usual woolly tone. "And when you lie speechless you may be tired of having strangers about you, and you may think of me and my children"—but here her voice broke under the touching thought which she was attributing to her speechless brother; the mention of ourselves being naturally affecting.

"No, I shan't," said old Featherstone, contradictiously. "I shan't think of any of you. I've made my will, I tell you, I've made my will." Here he turned his head towards Mrs. Vincy, and swallowed some more of his cordial. . . .

Their exit was hastened by their seeing old Mr. Featherstone pull his wig on each side and shut his eyes with his mouth-widening grimace, as if he were determined to be deaf and blind.

What reader would wish to forego, for the sake of dramatic economy, such a scene as that? And what reader, for that matter, would care to miss making the acquaintance of even so minor a character as Mr. Trumbull the auctioneer? Mr. Trumbull, in whom, we are told, there was no odious cupidity, nothing more than a sincere sense of his own merit, is favored with a sight of the dying man. When he emerges from the sickroom Featherstone's brother Solomon sets about him:

"Might anybody ask what their brother has been saying?" said Solomon, in a tone of soft humility, in which he had a sense of luxurious cunning, he being a rich man and not in need of it.

"Oh yes, anybody may ask," said Mr. Trumbull, with loud and good-humoured thought cutting sarcasm. "Anybody may interrogate. Any one may give their remarks an interrogative turn," he continued, his sonorousness rising with his style. "This is constantly done by good speakers, even when they anticipate no answer. It is what we call a figure of speech—speech at a high figure, as one may say." The eloquent auctioneer smiled at his own ingenuity.

"I shouldn't be sorry to hear he'd remembered *you*, Mr. Trumbull," said Solomon. "I never was against the deserving. It's the undeserving I'm against."

"Ah, there it is, you see, there it is," said Mr. Trumbull, significantly. "It can't be denied that undeserving people have been legatees, and even residuary legatees. It is so, with testamentary dispositions."

After some more verbal exchanges Mr. Trumbull decides to refresh himself with a little food:

"I shall take a mere mouthful of ham and a glass of ale," he said, reassuringly. "As a man with public business, I take a snack when I can. I will back this ham," he added, after swallowing some morsels with alarming haste, "against any ham in the three kingdoms. In my opinion it is better than the hams at Freshitt Hall—and I think I am a tolerable judge."

"Some don't like so much sugar in their hams," said Mrs. Waule. "But my poor brother would always have sugar."

"If any person demands better, he is at liberty to do so; but, God bless me, what an aroma! I should be glad to buy-in that quality, I know. There is some gratification to a gentleman"—here Mr. Trumbull's voice conveyed an emotional remonstrance—"in having this kind of ham set on his table."

He pushed aside his plate, poured out his glass of ale and drew his chair a little forward, profiting by the occasion to look at the inner side of his legs, which he stroked approvingly—Mr. Trumbull having all those less frivolous airs and gestures which distinguish the predominant races of the north.

The talk presently turns upon marriage and Mr. Trumbull delivers himself in characteristic style:

"A man whose life is of any value should think of his wife as a nurse: that is what I should do, if I married; and I believe I have lived single long enough not to make a mistake in that line. Some men must marry to elevate themselves a little, but when I am in need of that, I hope some one will tell me so—I hope some individual will apprise me of the fact. I wish you good morning, Mrs. Waule. Good morning, Mr. Solomon. I trust we shall meet under less melancholy auspices."

This, indeed the whole chapter, is comedy in the manner of Dickens: a writer with whom George Eliot is not often compared.

### III

That Dorothea's marriage to Casaubon would bring disillusionment was eminently foreseeable, but it loses nothing of interest on that account. The maxim our grandfathers used to write in their school copybooks, *experientia docet*, is the implied theme of every maturely conceived human story; and it is abundantly illustrated in George Eliot's work. With all her pride of intellect she knew that there are things one cannot know except by experience, and that often such knowledge is bought dearly and too late. In *Middlemarch* her vision is as broad as it is deep; she uses a large canvas but fills every inch of it and paints with a fine brush; and the way the several life stories are related to each other and to the pattern of the whole constitutes a triumph of artistic tact. The richness and variety of color, the warm undertones of meaning, the mingling of comedy and tragedy and dramatic irony, the abundance of invention, the densely populated provincial background, the author's imaginative saturation in her theme: these combine to make *Middlemarch* the most satisfying of all her novels, the one in which, with far less pointing and nudging from her than elsewhere, the universals of human life are apprehended in the particulars.

Mr. Shaw has declared that the characters in this novel have no more volition than billiard balls: they are moved, he says, only by circumstances and heredity. But that is not strictly true even of the part to which it seems most to apply, the story of Lydgate and Rosamond Vincy. Lydgate is a man of ideas and ideals, with a noble zeal for his profession, an ardent desire to reform its practice, and a passion for scientific discovery. As we have seen, his wife, who lives like a mole in the prison of her little ego, circumvents his high ambitions at every turn; and it gradually becomes clear that by marrying her he has encompassed his own ruin. But there is no lack of volition here. Rosamond herself is the chief of the circumstances that determine Lydgate's downfall, and Rosamond has not too little volition but too much. She is the embodiment of self-will, not the less but the more effective (for evil) by reason of her indolence, her seeming weakness, her sensual luxuriance. In the conflict of wills between them, hers is predominant; and it is difficult to see on what grounds of art or philosophy that can be objected to, unless we are to hold that it is a novelist's duty always to represent goodness as triumphant, which would be only a refined form of the demand for "a happy ending."

The end of the Lydgate story is dreary in the extreme. Not so Dorothea's, or Fred Vincy's, or Caleb Garth's. Mr. Shaw tells us that there is "not a ray of hope" in this novel. But Dorothea Brooke is herself the sufficient answer to that. It is a tribute to her quality that the reader, falling in love with her beauty and manifest goodness, which not all her primness can disguise, remains deeply dissatisfied with the destiny George Eliot provides for her: her marriage, after Casaubon's death, to a young man who though pleasant enough is palpably not worthy of her. Of all the men in the book only one could have even begun to be worthy of a creature so fine, so fascinating, so innocent and ardent and angelic. Marriage between Dorothea and Lydgate, one cannot help reflecting, would have been a glorious thing both for themselves and for the world: he with his disinterested humanitarian zeal, and she with her radiant religious sense and her noble capacity for service in high causes. But this is not a criticism of the book: it is only a tribute to what Lydgate might have been and to what Dorothea was. The defeat of his plans, the disintegration of a character that seemed destined for greatness, is indeed a dismal tragedy. But the light that must continue to shine in Dorothea, notwithstanding the comparative triviality of her destiny, is the light of human goodness: which is, after all, not merely "a ray of hope," but the only hope of the world.

# APPENDICES

# I

## DAVID FRIEDRICH STRAUSS: 1808–74

[THE ENGLISH translation by Marian Evans of Strauss's vast work appeared in 1846. The original, nine years earlier, had created a great stir in theological circles. The crucial problem in any such study is provided by the miraculous element in the Gospel stories, and here Strauss fell foul of both parties. He rejected the "explaining away" naturalistic theories put forward by one side, no less than the supernaturalism defended by the other: both in his view are wrong, because both assume the existence of a substantial basis of historical fact. Strauss sees the miracles as, not impostures, not inventions, nor yet mere distortions of actual events, but as (in the main) poetic symbols, significant myths, naïve dramatizations of more or less profound religious ideas. His bias is toward metaphysics and away from history, where Feuerbach's (see below) is predominantly humanist. Strauss is difficult to anthologize, because his argument is elaborate and close knit; but the following passage will give some idea of his manner and method.]

### THE DEATH AND RESURRECTION OF JESUS

The proposition: a dead man has returned to life, is composed of two such contradictory elements, that whenever it is attempted to maintain the one, the other threatens to disappear. If he has really returned to life, it is natural to conclude that he was not wholly dead; if he was really dead, it is difficult to believe that he has really become living.

When we form a correct opinion of the relation between soul and body, not abstractly separating the two, but conceiving them at once in their identity, the soul as the interior of the body, the body as the exterior of the soul, we know now how to imagine, to say nothing of comprehending, the revivification of a dead person. What we call the soul is the governing centre which holds in combination the powers and operations of the body; its function, or rather the soul itself, consists in keeping all other processes of which the body is susceptible in uninterrupted subjection to the superior unity of the process of organic life, which in man is the basis of his spiritual nature: so soon as this regulating power ceases to act, the supremacy in the various parts of the body is assumed by these other, inferior principles, whose work in its prosecution is corruption. When once these have acceded to the dominion, they will not be inclined to render it back to their former monarch the soul; or rather this is impossible, because, quite apart from the question of the immortality of the human spirit (*Geist*), the soul (*Seele*) as such ceases in the same moment with its dominion and activity, which constitute its existence; consequently, in a re-vivification, even if resort be had to a miracle, this must consist in the direct creation of a new soul.

Only in the dualism which has become popular on the subject of the relation between body and soul is there anything to favour the opinion of the possibility of a revivification properly so called. In this system, the soul in its relation to the body is represented as like a bird, which, though it may for a time have flown out of the cage, can yet be once more caught and replaced in its former abode; and it is to such figures that an imaginative species of thought cleaves, in order to preserve the notion of revivification. But even in this dualistic view, the inconceivability of such an event is rather concealed than really diminished. For in the most abstract separation, the coexistence of the body and soul cannot be held as indifferent and lifeless as that of a box and its contents; on the contrary, the presence of the soul in the body produces effects which again are the conditions whereby that presence is rendered possible. Thus so soon as the soul has forsaken the body, there is a cessation in the latter of those activities which according to the dualistic idea were the immediate expressions of the influence of the soul; at the same time, the organs of these activities—brain, blood, etc., begin to stagnate; a change which is coincident with the moment of death. Thus if it could occur to the departed soul, or be imposed on it by another, to re-enter its former dwelling-place: it would find this dwelling, even after the first moments, uninhabitable in its noblest parts, and unfit for use. To restore, in the same way as an infirm member, the most immediate organs of its activity, is an impossibility to the soul, since in order to effect anything in the body it has need of the service of these very organs: thus the soul, although remanded into the body, must suffer it to decay, from inability to exercise any influence over it; or there must be added to the miracle of its reconveyance into the body, the second miracle of a restoration of the lifeless bodily organs: an immediate interposition of God in the regular course of nature, irreconcilable with enlightened ideas of the relation of God to the world.

Hence the cultivated intellect of the present day has very decidedly stated the following dilemma: either Jesus was not wholly dead, or he did not really rise again.

*The Life of Jesus* (tr. George Eliot)

# II

## LUDWIG FEUERBACH: 1804–72

[PUBLISHED by John Chapman in 1854, Marian Evans' translation of Feuerbach is the only work which carries her real name on the title page. Feuerbach's conception of religion, expounded with typical German thoroughness (in which, however, he is crushingly excelled by Strauss, *q.v.*), can perhaps best be described as mystical humanism. Though not less destructive of orthodox assumptions it was evidently far more congenial to the translator's mind and temperament than was the attitude of "leathery Strauss," as she once called him. Our first extract is from Feuerbach's appendix to his book, in which he explains and amplifies what he has said in the main text.]

### A. MAN AND GOD

*Man has his highest being, his God, in himself;* not in himself as an individual, but in his essential nature, his species. No individual is an adequate representation of his species, but only the human individual is conscious of the distinction between the species and the individual; in the sense of this distinction lies the root of religion. The yearning of man after something above himself is nothing else than the longing after the perfect type of his nature, the yearning to be free from himself, *i.e.*, from the limits and defects of his individuality. Individuality is the self-conditionating, the self-limitation of the species. Thus man has congnisance of nothing above himself, of nothing beyond the nature of humanity; but to the individual man this nature presents itself under the form of an individual man. Thus, for example, the child sees the nature of man *above itself* in the form of its parents, the pupil in the form of his tutor. But all feelings which man experiences towards a superior man, nay, in general, all moral feelings which man has towards man, are of a religious nature. *Man feels nothing towards God which he does not also feel towards man. Homo homini deus est.*

*The Essence of Christianity*

## B. God Is Love

God is the Love that satisfies our wishes, our emotional wants; he is himself the realized wish of the heart, the wish exalted to the certainty of its fulfilment, of its reality, to that undoubting certainty before which no contradiction of the understanding, no difficulty of experience or of the external world maintains its ground. Certainty is the highest power for man; that which is certain to him is the essential, the divine. "God is love": this, the supreme dictum of Christianity, only expresses the certainty which human feeling has of itself, as the alone essential, *i.e.*, absolute divine power, the certainty that the inmost wishes of the heart have objective validity and reality, that there are no limits, no positive obstacles to human feeling, that the whole world, with all its pomp and glory, is nothing weighed against human feeling. God is love: that is, feeling is the God of man, nay, God absolutely, the Absolute Being. God is the nature of human feeling, unlimited, pure feeling, made objective. God is the optative of the human heart transformed into the *tempus finitum*, the certain, blissful "is,"—the unrestricted omnipotence of feeling prayer hearing itself, feeling perceiving itself, the echo of our cry of anguish. Pain must give itself utterance; involuntarily the artist seizes the lute, that he may breathe out his sufferings in its tones. He soothes his sorrow by making it audible to himself, by making it objective; he lightens the burden which weighs upon his heart, by communicating it to the air, by making his sorrow a general existence. But nature listens not to the plaints of man; it is callous to his sorrows. Hence man turns away from Nature, from all visible objects. He turns within, that here sheltered and hidden from the inexorable powers, he may find audience for his griefs. Here he utters his oppressive secrets; here he gives vent to his stifled sighs. This open-air of the heart, this outspoken secret, this uttered sorrow of the soul, is God. God is a tear of love, shed in the deepest concealment, over human misery. "God is an unutterable sigh, lying in the depths of the heart"; this saying is the most remarkable, the profoundest, truest expression of Christian mysticism . . .

In prayer, man addresses God with the word of intimate affection—*Thou;* he thus declares articulately that God is his *alter ego;* he confesses to God as the being nearest to him, his most secret thoughts, his deepest wishes, which otherwise he shrinks from uttering. But he expresses these wishes in the confidence, in the certainty that they will be fulfilled. How could he apply to a being that had no ear for his complaints? Thus what is prayer but the wish of the heart expressed with confidence in its fulfilment? what else is the being that fulfils these wishes but human affection, the human soul, giving ear to itself, approving itself, unhesitatingly affirming itself? The man who does not exclude from his mind the idea of the world, the idea that everything here must be sought intermediately, that every effect has its natural cause, that a wish is only to be attained when it is made an end and the corresponding means are put into operation—such a man does not pray: he only works; he transforms his attainable wishes into objects of real activity; other wishes which he recognises as purely subjective, he denies, or regards as simply subjective, pious aspirations. In other words, he limits, he conditionates his being by the world, as a member of which he conceives himself; he bounds his wishes by the idea of necessity. In prayer, on the contrary, man excludes from his mind the world, and with it all thoughts of intermediateness and dependence; he makes his wishes—the concerns of his heart, objects of the independent, omnipotent, absolute being, *i.e.*, he affirms them without limitation. God is the affirmation of human feeling; prayer is the unconditional confidence of human feeling in the absolute identity of the subjective and objective, the certainty that the power of the heart is greater than the power of Nature, that the heart's need is absolute necessity, the Fate of the world. Prayer alters the course of Nature; it determines God to bring forth an effect in contradiction with the laws of Nature. Prayer is the absolute relation of the human heart to itself, to its own nature; in prayer, man forgets that there exists a limit to his wishes, and is happy in this forgetfulness.

Prayer is the self-division of man into two beings,—a dialogue of man with himself, with his heart. It is essential to the effectiveness of prayer that it be audibly, intelligibly, energetically expressed. Involuntarily prayer wells forth in sound; the struggling heart bursts the barrier of the closed lips. But audible prayer is only prayer revealing its nature; prayer is virtually, if not actually, speech,—the Latin word *oratio* signifies both; in prayer, man speaks undisguisedly of that which weighs upon him, which affects him closely; he makes his heart objective;—hence the moral power of prayer. Concentration, it is said, is the condition of prayer: but it is more than a condition; prayer is itself concentration,—the dismissal of all distracting ideas, of all disturbing influences from without, retirement within oneself, in order to have relation only with one's own being. Only a trusting, open, hearty, fervent prayer is said to help; but this help lies in the prayer itself. As everywhere in religion, the subjective, the secondary, the conditionating, is the *prima causa*, the objective fact; so here, these subjective qualities are the objective nature of prayer itself . . .

The omnipotence to which man turns in prayer is nothing but the Omnipotence of Goodness, which, for the sake of the salvation of man, makes the impossible possible;—is, in truth, nothing else than the omnipotence of the heart, of feeling, which breaks through all the limits of the understanding, which soars above all the boundaries of Nature, which wills that there be nothing else than feeling, nothing that contradicts the heart. Faith in omnipotence is faith in the unreality of the external world, of objectivity,—faith in the absolute reality of man's emotional nature: the essence of omnipotence is simply the essence of feeling. Omnipotence is the power before which no law, no external condition, avails or subsists; but this power is the emotional nature, which feels every determination, every law, to be a limit, a restraint, and for that reason dismisses it. Omnipotence does nothing more than accomplish the will of the feelings. In prayer man turns to the Omnipotence of Goodness;—which simply means, that in prayer man adores his own heart, regards his own feelings as absolute.

*Ibid.*

# III

## GEORGE HENRY LEWES: 1817–78

[Lewes' *Life of Goethe* is too well known to need quoting from. The following extracts from his less accessible works will give some idea of his literary manners and the range of his interests.]

### A. Edmund Kean

The greatest artist is he who is greatest in the highest reaches of his art, even although he may lack the qualities necessary for the adequate execution of some minor details. It is not by his faults, but by his excellences, that we measure a great man. The strength of a beam is measured by its weakest part, of a man by his strongest. Thus estimated, Edmund Kean was incomparably the greatest actor I have seen, although even warm admirers must admit that he had many and serious defects. His was not a flexible genius. He was a very imperfect mime—or more correctly speaking, his miming power, though admirable within a certain range, was singularly limited in its range. He was tricky and flashy in style. But he was an actor of such splendid endowments in the highest departments of the art, that no one in our day can be named of equal rank, unless it be Rachel, who was as a woman what he was as a man. The irregular splendour of his power was felicitously characterized in the saying of Coleridge, that "seeing Kean act was reading Shakespeare by flashes of lightning," so brilliant and so startling were the sudden illuminations, and so murky the dull intervals. Critics who had formed their ideal on the Kemble school were shocked at Kean's want of dignity, and at his fitful elocution, sometimes thrillingly effective, at other times deporably tame and careless; in their angry protests they went so far as to declare him "a mere mountebank." Not so thought the pit; not so thought less biassed critics. He stirred the general heart with such a rush of mighty power, impressed himself so vividly by accent, look, and gesture, that it was as vain to protest against his defects as it was for French critics to insist upon Shakespeare's want of *bienséance* and *bon goût*. Could audiences have remained unmoved, they might have lent a willing ear to remonstrances, and laughed at or hissed some grave offences against taste and sense. But no audience could be unmoved; all defects were overlooked or disregarded, because it was impossible to watch Kean as Othello, Shylock, Richard, or Sir Giles Overreach without being strangely shaken by the terror, and the pathos, and the passion of a stormy spirit uttering itself in tones of irresistible power. His imitators have been mostly ridiculous, simply because they reproduced the manner and the mannerism, but could not reproduce the power which made these endurable. It is a fact little understood by imitators that the spots on the sun in nowise warm the world, and that a deficiency in light and heat cannot be replaced by a prodigality of spots . . .

He [Kean] had tenderness, wrath, agony, and sarcasm at command. But he could not be calmly dignified; nor could he represent the intellectual side of heroism. He was nothing if not passionate. I never saw his Hamlet, which, however, was never considered one of his successes, though parts were intensely admired. He must have been puzzled what to do with many of the long speeches and the quiet scenes, and could have had no sympathy with the character. Yet Hamlet is the easiest of all Shakespeare's great parts for an actor of moderate ability. Othello, which is the most trying of all Shakespeare's parts, was Kean's masterpiece. His Shylock was freer from fault, and indeed was a marvellous performance. From the first moment that he appeared and leant upon his stick to listen gravely while moneys are requested of him, he impressed the audience, as Douglas Jerrold used to say, "like a chapter of Genesis." The overpowering remonstrant sarcasm of his address to Antonio, and the sardonic mirth of his proposition about the "merry bond," were fine preparations for the anguish and rage at the elopement of his daughter, and for the gloating anticipations of revenge on the Christians. Anything more impressive than the passionate recrimination and wild justice of argument in his "Hath not a Jew eyes?" has never been seen on our stage.

*On Actors and the Art of Acting*

## B. AUGUSTE COMTE

The first point upon which our attention must be fixed, in M. Comte's work, is that important law of mental evolution which he has not only discovered, but applied historically. It forms the keystone of the arch. His object is to construct a positive philosophy,—that is, a doctrine capable of embracing all the sciences, and with them all the problems of social life,—to which no other doctrine *now* aspires; for metaphysics have, since the time of Bacon, been separated from physics, and have lost all power over them. If, therefore, we are to have a new Philosophy which is to supply the present deficiencies, we must have one capable of embracing both the *positive* and *social* sciences. The conception of a social science is due to M. Comte. No one before him ever dreamed of treating social problems otherwise than upon theological or metaphysical methods. He first showed how possible—nay, how imperative—it was that social questions should be treated on the same footing with all other scientific questions. This being his object, he was forced to detect the law of mental evolution before he could advance. This law is the law of historical progression. "The state of the speculative faculties, the character of the propositions assented to, essentially determines the moral and political state of the community, as we have already seen that it determines the physical. Every considerable change historically known to us in the condition of any portion of mankind, has been preceded by a change of proportional extent in the state of their knowledge or in their prevalent beliefs."

M. Comte's law may be thus stated:—Every branch of knowledge passes successively through three stages: 1st, the *supernatural,* or fictitious; 2nd, the *metaphysical,* or abstract; 3rd, the *positive* or scientific. The first is the necessary point of departure taken by human intelligence; the second is merely a stage of transition from the supernatural to the positive; and the third is the fixed and definite condition in which knowledge is alone capable of progressive development.

In the *supernatural* stage, the mind seeks after *causes;* aspires to know the *essences* of things and their modes of operation. It regards all effects as the productions of supernatural agents, whose intervention is the *cause* of all the apparent anomalies and irregularities. Nature is animated by supernatural beings. Every unusual phenomenon is a sign of the pleasure or displeasure of some being adored and propitiated as a God. The lowest condition of this stage is that of the savages, viz., Fetichism. The highest condition is when one being is substituted for many, as the cause of all phenomena.

In the *metaphysical* stage, which is only a modification of the former, but which is important as a transitional stage, the supernatural agents give place to abstract forces (personified abstractions) suppose to inhere in the various substances, and capable themselves of engendering phenomena. The highest condition of this stage is when all these forces are brought under one general force named Nature.

In the *positive* stage, the mind, convinced of the futility of all inquiry into causes and essences, applies itself to the observation and classification of *laws* which regulate effects; that is to say, the invariable relations of succession and similitude which all things bear to each other. The highest condition of this stage would be, to be able to represent all phenomena as the various particulars of one general view.

*A Biographical History of Philosophy*

## C. What Is an Animal?

Since the British mind was all alive and trembling with that zoological fervour excited by the appearance of the hippopotamus in Regent's Park, no animal has touched it to such fine issues and such exuberant enthusiasm as the lovely Sea Anemone, now the ornament of countless drawing-rooms, studies, and back parlours, as well as the delight of unnumbered amateurs. In glass tanks and elegant vases of various device, in finger-glasses and common tumblers, the lovely creature may be seen expanding its coronal of tentacles, on mimic rocks, amid mimic forests of algæ, in mimic oceans —of pump water and certain mixtures of chlorides and car-bonates, regulated by a "specific gravity test." Fairy fingers minister to its wants, removing dirt and slime from its body, feeding it with bits of limpet or raw beef; fingers, *not* of fairies, pull it about with the remorseless curiosity of science, and experiment on it, according to the suggestion of the moment . . .

It must be assumed at starting that the reader knows what a Sea Anemone is, in aspect at least. No description will avail, in default of direct observation; even pictures only give an approximate idea; while to those who have seen neither pic-ture nor animal it will be of little use to declare that the "Actinia is a fleshy cylinder, attached by one extremity to a rock, while the free end is surmounted by numerous tentacula arranged in several rows, which, when expanded, give the animal the appearance of a flower." Assuming, then, that you know the general aspect of the Actinia, you may follow my description of the animal's bearing and habits.

*How* do I know that it is an animal, and not a flower, which it so much resembles? No one yet has been able to distinguish, in the face of severe critical precision, between the animal and plant-organization, so as to be able authoritatively to say, "This is exclusively animal." To distinguish a cow from a cucumber requires, indeed, no profound inauguration into biological mysteries; we can "venture fearlessly to assert" (with that utterly uncalled-for temerity exhibited by bad writers in cases when *no* peril whatever is hanging over the assertion) that the cow and cucumber are not allied— no common parentage links them together, even through remote relationship; but to say *what* is an *animal,* presupposes a knowledge of what is essentially and exclusively animal, and this knowledge unhappily has never yet been reached. Much hot, and not wise, discussion has occupied the hours of philosophers in trying to map out the distinct confines of the animal and vegetable kingdoms, when all the while Nature knows of no such demarcating lines. *The Animal does not exist; nor does the Vegetable:* both are abstractions, general terms, such as Virtue, Goodness, Colour, used to designate certain groups of particulars, but having only a mental existence. Who has been forunate enough to see the Animal? We have seen cows, cats, jackasses, and camelopards; but the "rare monster" Animal is visible in no menagerie. If you are tempted to call this metaphysical trifling, I beg you to read the discussions published on the vegetable or animal nature of Diatomaceæ, Volvocinæ, etc., or to attend to what is said in any textbook on the distinctions between animals and vegetables, and you will then see there is something more than metaphysics in the paradox. In the simpler organisms there is *no* mark which can absolutely distinguish the animal from the vegetable; and if in the higher organisms a greater amount of characteristic differences may be traced, so that we may, for purposes of convenience, consider a certain group of indications as entitling the object to be classed under the Animal division, we must never forget that such classifications are purely arbitrary, and as the philosophers say— *subjective.*

Now what are the characteristic marks of the Sea Anemone, which entitle it to be removed from the hands of the botanist, and placed in those of the zoologist? Rymer Jones declares that its animal nature "is soon rendered evident," this evidence being the manifestation of sensibility. "A cloud veiling the sun will cause their tentacles to fold as though apprehensive of danger from the passing shadows." Unhappily, the fact alleged is a pure fiction; and, were it true, would not distinguish the Actiniæ from those plants which close their petals in the dark. A fiction, however, it is, as any one may verify. If Actiniæ have been seen to fold up their tentacles when a cloud has passed before the sun, this has been a coincidence, not a causal relation; so far from light being the necessary condition of their expansion, they are in perfect expansion in the darkness; and if the venturous naturalist will, with the solemn chimes of midnight as accompaniment, take his lantern on the rocks, he will find all the Anemones in full blossom. . . .

But the Anemone must be an animal, you suggest, because it is seen to catch and swallow other animals. This, however, is no proof. Although the Anemone entraps its prey, or anything else that may come in contact with its tentacles, this is no proof of animality; the sensitive plant, known as the Flytrap of Venus (*Dionoea mūscipula*), has a precisely analogous power; any insect, touching the sensitive hairs on the surface of its leaf, instantly causes the leaf to shut up and enclose the insect, as in a trap; nor is this all: a mucilaginous secretion acts like a gastric juice on the captive, digests it, and renders it assimilable by the plant, which thus feeds on the victim, as the Actinia feeds on the Annelid or Crustacean it may entrap. Where, then, is the difference? Neither *seeks* its food: place the food within a line's breadth of the tentacles, or of the sensitive hairs, and so long as actual contact is avoided, the grasping of the food will not take place. But you object, perhaps, that this mode of feeding is normal with the Actinia, exceptional with the Flytrap. The plant, you say, is nourished by the earth and air, the animal depends on what it can secure. Not so. For granting—what, in fact, I sturdily dispute—that the Flytrap is in no way dependent upon such insect food as may fall into its clutch, we shall still observe the Actinia in similar independence. Keep the water free from all visible food, and the Actiniæ continue to flourish and propagate just as if they daily clutched an unhappy worm. The fact is well known, and is currently, but erroneously, adduced as illustration of the animal's power of fasting. But there is no fasting in the matter. In this water free from visible aliment there is abundance of invisible aliment—infusoria, spores, organic particles, etc. which the animal assimilates, much in the same way as plants assimilate the organic material diffused through the soil and atmosphere. Filter the water carefully, and remove from it all growing vegetation, and you will find the animal speedily dying, however freely oxygen may be supplied. It is on this account that when we make artificial sea-water, it is necessary to allow algæ to grow in it for some two or three weeks before putting in the animals; the water becomes charged with organic material.

Mere sensibility and capture of food, therefore, are not the distinguishing marks we seek, since the plant is found to possess them as perfectly as the animal. Is spontaneous locomotion a sufficient mark? No; and for these two reasons: Some animals have *no* such power; some plants, and all spores, *have* it. . . . Again the question recurs, How then do we

know the Anemone to be an animal?—in other words, what
characteristic marks guide zoologists in classing it in that division? I really know of none but purely anatomical marks.

*Seaside Studies*

# IV

## CALENDAR OF EVENTS IN THE LIFE OF GEORGE ELIOT

1819    Mary Ann Evans [George Eliot], born November 22, at Arbury Farm in the parish of Chilvers Coton.

1826    Is sent to a boarding school at Nuneaton, where she becomes much attached to her teacher, Miss Lewis, an ardently evangelical churchwoman.

1832    At the age of twelve she is removed to Miss Franklin's school at Coventry.

1836    Death of her mother.

1837    On the marriage of her sister Christiana she assumes control of the Griff household.

1838    Visits London with her brother Isaac.

1841    Isaac having married, she and her father move to Foleshill Road, Coventry, where she makes friends with the Brays and Hennells. By the end of this year she has lost her belief in Christianity.

1842    A dispute with her father about churchgoing.

1844    Begins work on translating Strauss's *Leben Jesu*.

1846    Her translation of Strauss published by John Chapman.

1849    Death of Robert Evans, May 31. Accompanied by the Brays, she arrives at Geneva in July.

1850    Returns to England from Switzerland.

1851    Becomes assistant editor of John Chapman's *Westminster Review*. Meets George Henry Lewes for the first time. Resides at 142 Strand.

1852    Meets Herbert Spencer.

1854    Goes to Germany with Lewes, July 20. Her translation of Feuerbach's *Wesen des Christenthums* published by Chapman.

1855  She and Lewes return to England and settle at Richmond.

1856  Her first story, "Amos Barton," begun on September 22 and finished on November 5.

1857  *Scenes of Clerical Life* published by Blackwood.

1859  *Adam Bede* published.

1860  *The Mill on the Floss* published. She and Lewes visit Italy.

1861  *Silas Marner* published.

1862–3  *Romola* published.

1863  She and Lewes move into their last home together: The Priory, 21 North Bank, Regent's Park.

1866  *Felix Holt* published.

1867  Visits Spain.

1868  *The Spanish Gypsy* (dramatic poem) published.

1869  Death of Thornton Lewes, October 19. *Brother and Sister* (sonnet sequence) published.

1871–2  *Middlemarch* published.

1876  *Daniel Deronda* published.

1878  Death of George Henry Lewes, November 28.

1879  *Essays of Theophrastus Such* published.

1880  Marries John Walter Cross, May 6. Dies December 22.

# INDEX